# REAL WOMEN ... REAL LIVES ...

## *PHYLLIS*

Always in the shadow of her brilliant brother, Phyllis let her perfectionism and fear of not measuring up stop her from pursuing her acting talents . . . until a life-changing awareness came late in life, but not too late for her to blossom.

## *ROSE*

Rose hoped for a dancing career until an auto accident ended her dreams. Instead she has fiercely pursued her career in nursing and found her creative energy inspiring her to innovate new teaching techniques, face personal challenges, and further test her limits.

## *CATHY*

Art became Cathy's way of overcoming a restrictive upbringing, which made her distrust her own worth. Struggling to claim her aesthetic vision, Cathy remains in conflict between her dreams of creating a large sculpture and the small paintings she sometimes produces—but life without her art is unthinkable.

## *GERRIT*

At first, Gerrit handled the business side of her husband's photography business, then she learned to become a photojournalist. While her marriage did not survive, her enormous talent has brought her public recognition, and her love of challenging the limits of photography in her darkroom makes her "happy beyond description."

please turn the page for praise for *Awakening Minerva*

◆

"This book inspires us all to look from within and face the obstacles to our creativity—to expand our visions and realize our dreams."

> —Helene Lerner-Robbins, president,
> Creative Expansions, Inc.

◆

"AWAKENING MINERVA gradually guides to the exploration and development of the creative energy that lies in me as well as in every woman in the world. Believe it or not, this book will bring out the feminine power in every woman."

> —Mrs. Jin Odero, deputy general manager,
> Lin Jiana Hydro Power Company, Ltd.,
> People's Republic of China

◆

"I agree with Dr. Firestone that it is our ability to utilize our creativity that enables us to change our lives. That's how I changed mine."

> —Janet Cheatham Bell, author of
> *Victory of the Spirit*

◆

# AWAKENING MINERVA

## THE POWER OF CREATIVITY
## IN WOMEN'S LIVES

Linda A. Firestone, Ph.D.

WARNER BOOKS

A Time Warner Company

Warner Books, Inc., 1271 Avenue of the Americas, New York, NY 10020
Visit our Web site at http://pathfinder.com/twep

 A Time Warner Company

Printed in the United States of America
First Printing: July 1997
10  9  8  7  6  5  4  3  2  1

**Library of Congress Cataloging-in-Publication Data**
Firestone, Linda.
    Awakening Minerva : the power of creativity in women's lives /
Linda Firestone.
        p.  cm.
    ISBN 0-446-67045-6
    1. Creative ability. 2. Women—Psychology. 3. Minerva (Roman deity) 4. Mother goddesses. 5. Feminist psychology. I. Title.
BF411.F48 1997
153.3'5'082—dc20                                                96-32456
                                                                      CIP

*Cover design and illustration by John Martinez*
*Book design and compostion by Nancy Singer*

**ATTENTION: SCHOOLS AND CORPORATIONS**
WARNER books are available at quantity discounts with bulk purchase for educational, business, or sales promotional use. For information, please write to: SPECIAL SALES DEPARTMENT, WARNER BOOKS, 1271 AVENUE OF THE AMERICAS, NEW YORK, N.Y. 10020

for
ben, lily, and tom

# ACKNOWLEDGMENTS

I acknowledge Professor Morris I. Stein for allowing me to adapt and use his background questionnaire. I am indebted to Professor Lowell Swortzell for his insight and support throughout the research and writing of this book. I thank Colleen Kapklein, my editor, and Malaga Baldi, my agent, for their support and assistance. I am deeply grateful to my family, friends, my husband, Tom, and all the women who supported my work with their freely given enthusiasm and interest.

Lastly, I acknowledge the power of the ideas embedded in the beings of the Goddesses. The images that came to me were a continued source of inspiration. In myriad ways I feel my strength and recognize the possibilities for the future in those brief encounters with places, events, and people that touch my life and shape me. To that part of the universe and of us, which makes creative behavior possible, I give thanks.

# TABLE OF CONTENTS

❧

# AWAKENING MINERVA

# VOICES REMEMBERED

I yearned to find an image that would represent to women and men the nature of a creative woman. So I turned to the past, as I so often do. The quality and strength of the role model I was seeking would be found in antiquity. Strong modern models do exist, but I needed an image that existed outside of the society we know, outside of the political and cultural references we presently hold. I wanted an image grander than any living man or woman.

Over the years, I have found understanding, strength, and hope about myself in the real and mythical women of the distant past. The past offers me clues to the present. I see my personal and cultural history and understand the roots of my perceptions, both positive and negative. But what kind of image would serve this book and its readers? I knew in my heart that it must be a woman, a woman who could speak to people of diverse cultures and political backgrounds. In my anxious state of seeking, I finally found the name of Minerva.

The embodiment of wisdom, strength, beauty, and love, she waited to be called upon after centuries of silence. I was exhilarated. Minerva represented all the potential creativity within a woman. Minerva would be my guide and inspiration through this work. In Minerva I saw the materiality of possibility. She was a strong female figure whose powers transverse a range of activities: she was known for her wisdom and physical strength. She excelled as a warrior, a teacher, and a handler of horses. She ruled the marketplace and the arts. Craftsmen prayed to her for their work. Minerva was Goddess to all: men and women, rich and poor. She was worshiped far and wide for many centuries and gained a large following. Minerva's growth as a Goddess encapsulated for me the growth of a woman expressing her creativity. I had found a complete image in Minerva.

Then my editor suggested that I find other female deities. I agreed, but not without some hesitation and skepticism. While I could relate Minerva to this work, I could not quite understand how any other Goddess would work as well. Instead, I found a variety of female deities who were as potent as Minerva, whose images could speak to and inspire different women. The symbolic image of a Goddess who could address different parts of us might also encourage action.

The image of the Goddess can provide a woman with a path to renew herself after trauma. The image of the Goddess can lead a woman to a new understanding or provide the impetus for her to alter the course of her life. The flow of creativity is embedded in a woman's private journey. The expression of a woman's life, in all its aspects—work, play, interpersonal relationships, whether positive or negative—uses some degree of creativity. It does not matter if that expression is small or large. Its essence remains the same.

The powers embodied in the images of the Goddesses came to them through recognition and validation. In time, the powers of the Goddesses grew, and their reach broadened. The potential power contained within a woman's essential creative nature is the same as that of the Goddesses. It flows within her body. Her essential creative nature is part of her life force. If she nurtures her essential creative nature and validates it, a woman will grow in strength and personal expression.

## INSIGNIFICANCE REBUFFED

The most potent of all the Goddesses was "the Goddess," or "Mother Earth," as some refer to her. Symbolically she is the essence of creativity; she is the creator of all things. In the *Book of the Goddess*, Carol Olson, the editor, writes, "[T]he Goddess is associated with life-giving powers, renewal, rebirth, transformation and the mystery of death." All these qualities are present in the creative act and the creative life. I had an inkling that my editor was on to something. Perhaps the Goddess represents more than the traditional symbol of fertility, as it relates to childbearing. Role models like the Goddess can stimulate the imagination and offer a woman a way to interpret her life. These images can help women to make sense out of the changing rhythms of their lives. We all need role models to help shape our lives and our visions.

The Earth Mother is an extraordinarily old figure, far older than I could have imagined and far more potent than I would have thought. One can reasonably argue that our lives as women were inextricably altered so many centuries ago when Goddesses, like the Mother Goddess and Minerva, began to lose their power. Their place was supplanted by male gods who were given their stories and powers. Not only were the stories of the Goddesses rewritten and retold glorifying the male deities, but the female deities were reduced in significance. Many of them were given sinister natures or completely eradicated. Under the new stories, the natural order of life, the ebb and flow of change, which included life and death, began to acquire inherent qualities of good and evil. This introduction of good and evil intruded upon the continuity of all life experiences.

Joseph Campbell once stated that the Goddess and her influence can be placed in history only as far back as five thousand years ago. "She was a very potent figure in Hellenistic times in the Mediterranean, and she came back with the Virgin in the Roman Catholic tradition. . . ." Researchers over the last twenty years have found evidence that indicates otherwise. The Mother Goddess was worshiped far more than five thousand years ago. I have read dates and descriptions of Goddess worship as far back as fifteen to twenty thousand years ago on every continent of the globe. This diminishment of the Goddess, and Goddesses like Minerva (who is a reincarnation of the Mother Goddess), by a prominent male figure like Campbell signifies the trivialization of women's influence in the past. It perpetuates the diminishment of women's accomplishments in the development of culture then and now.

The serious lack of role models and mentorship available to women of all ages has had far-ranging ramifications for women seeking to fulfill their potential. Who can a woman turn to for inspiration? The use of mythology offers a woman a way to fill the gap created long ago. Powerful female images provide a woman with intellectual, emotional, and spiritual support. This kind of support is needed to inspire the woman pursuing her essential creative nature and personal expression. Unlike Minerva, who was birthed from the head of Jupiter fully formed and clothed in armor, a woman is not born fully developed. Her development, if she is lucky, lasts a lifetime. But the images of the Goddesses provide a woman with a context for her place and potential in the universe. Being honored is the history of the Goddesses, which paints a path a woman can follow to recognize her own power, substance, and ability to endure. A woman grows big with creative potential when she validates her own and other women's expression. In *Women Who Run with the Wolves*, Clarissa Pinkola Estés writes, "[I]n archetypal lore there is the idea that if one prepares a special psychic place, the being, the creative force, the soul source, will hear of it, sense its way to it and inhabit that place. . . ." That path inward can be guided by the image and meaning of the Goddesses.

What does mythology have to do with a book on creativity? *Awakening Minerva* seeks to reveal creativity in all its expressions, not by weighty academic discussion, but by example. The stories of mythological women and real-life women offer you the opportunity to experience intellectually, intuitively, emotionally, and imaginatively what it means to be a woman and to be creative. The mythological women mentioned in this book have a history and a life of their own; their powers and cultural origins differ, but their creative gifts are clear. I call upon the reader to engage in a creative act, to open herself to the possibilities symbolized by the Goddesses. The potential for creating, for life-giving, for symbolic death and rebirth not only defines the path of a woman's life but the path of the creative experience. This is not a book about finding a new religion or new religious symbols. This is not a book about the Goddess in her varying forms. Women call upon the images of the past to understand their own potential for creating themselves anew in the present. With the Goddesses, women have the potential of latching on and journeying to places within themselves they may not have dared to journey to before. By awakening the image of the Goddess within, by acknowledging and utilizing the potential within herself, a woman becomes one who lives a potent, powerfully creative life.

# WHAT IS CREATIVITY?

The older I get, the more sensitive I become to being a woman. This sensitivity brings a fundamental awareness to my life. It is emotional but not negative; I am not easily hurt by my femaleness. What I see in the world, how I see right from wrong, how I construct a thought, experience my children, or express myself is influenced by the fact that I am a woman. This awareness is not new to me, nor is it, I suspect, to most of my readers. This knowledge has slowly grown strong within me over the last twenty years. But the depth of my sensitivity has been more recent. Perhaps it is that I finished my schooling at thirty-nine, perhaps it is this book about women (my first, written in my forties), or perhaps it is because I have had my children so late in life. My sense of myself is continually growing, changing, becoming clearer. All life experiences become part of my being. My life is in process; my creative expression is in process. My response to my creative expression reflects the development within my being, and part of that expression is conditioned by my femaleness.

This fundamental awareness led me to write this book. I had been in the library scanning the literature on women and creativity for another project. I found material on "creativity," but not on women and creativity. It was puzzling. I kept looking, only to be disappointed. My disappointment led to frustration and then to anger. I knew how to research a topic—I had done enough of it to write my dissertation—but I was at a loss. I asked for help several times, but the response was always the same: "Women and creativity, that's too broad a topic; there is so much written." That answer was based upon an assumption that was not grounded in the available literature. Works dedicated to exploring any aspect of women and creativity were difficult to find. I became singularly focused on this topic. Something was amiss; it did not make sense to me. Since my search began, a few books have appeared on the bookstore shelves about women. These books are about creativity in love, work, and addiction. Given the demographics of the female population, one would think that "women's books" on any topic would be easily accessible. Yet the women's section in any bookstore remains relatively small and the topics limited. Historically, most research, regardless of the topic, has focused on men. The results of the research have generally been viewed as universal to both men and women.

The literature on creativity available to the general public, from which I exclude most of the research literature in the specialized journals, can be categorized into several areas: (1) analysis of works done by artists, (2) increasing creative potential through the arts, e.g., drawing to exercise the left brain/right brain combination or journal-keeping, (3) business books on creative problem-solving, and (4) creativity and mental illness. Scholarly research usually focuses on (1) creativity in children labeled "gifted," (2) the creative process, (3) creative environments, (4) creative thinking, (5) testing creative behavior, and (6) identifying characteristics of creative individuals.

Creativity research as a discipline began in earnest in the early 1950s when the president of the American Psychological Association expressed concern over the lack of attention paid to creativity. While it still remains a small discipline, interesting and enlightening results have been obtained over the last forty years. Unfortunately, but not surprisingly, research concerning women—how, what, and why they create—has begun to appear only over the last fifteen years. A few significant studies were conducted during the 1940s, 1950s, and 1960s, but there was little follow-up and no sense of urgency about adding to the literature. Female scholars generally conduct the studies on women, but a number of male scholars have recently called for more research to be conducted on the subject of women and creativity. In the early 1980s, Frank Barron and David M. Harrington wrote, in their article "Creativity, Intelligence, and Personality," about a study conducted on women. "[T]he study . . . called the field's attention to the critical role which social context, expectation, and pressure play in determining whether creative talent is fostered and if so, how it is directed." How these issues are manifested in women's creative lives is at the heart of *Awakening Minerva*.

The way we speak about creativity, and the way we have learned to view creative behavior, has been based upon research and philosophical assumptions that are fundamentally biased, sexist, racist, and exclusionary. The paradigm traditionally used to define creativity has been beset with the same problems. Having now stated my political objections on a basic level, I admit that the research that has been done, despite its exclusion of women, cannot be summarily disregarded. It only highlights the deficiencies inherent in evaluating creativity and creative behavior from a traditional stance. Rowena Helson, a researcher of creativity, wrote, "[O]ne might think that it would be easy to move from the idea of woman as creator of children to the idea of woman as creator of ideas, but this does not seem to be an easy transfer. One reason for this is that scientists, including psychologists, usually think of creativity in terms of a phallocentric male model, such as the problem-solving paradigm. . . . The emphasis is on such traits as forcefulness, achievement, orientation, [and] speed of reaction in which men tend to excel."

Since the 1950s, as a society we have rethought and energetically debated gender and gender roles. Now it is time to rethink our concept of creativity. How do women manifest their creativity? To honestly seek the answer, one must seriously and respectfully look to women themselves. Therefore, the sole focus of this book is women. The subject is a complex one. To clear the path and avoid confusion, I will introduce the key topics of concern that influence our concept of creativity. These topics reach deep into our beings. They are not so easily analyzed by simply stating, "So and so is a painter; she is creative," or "I like her work," or even worse, "I could never do that . . . , she is so creative. . . ." People (men and women) may be born with an aptitude in or heightened sensitivity to some discipline, but that in and of itself does not guarantee growth as a creative person. Creativity needs to be nurtured and validated. It needs to be stimulated and shaped; otherwise it remains unused potential. This unshaped potential does not lay dormant. In many serious cases, unused creative energy becomes a powerfully destructive force within a woman's life.

How can you determine what it means to be creative, to engage in a creative act, or to lead a creative life? When people talk about creativity, they do so by unconsciously placing value judgments on the product, the process, or the person. These value judgments, based upon specific belief systems, are how people interpret their lives. These value judgments color the interactions people have with other people, places, and things. If one seeks to alter or broaden a concept, one must begin by clearly articulating that concept—and then finding the weaknesses, the limitations, or the erroneous underpinnings contained within the concept.

The individual concepts of creativity contained within this book are expressed by women who are typical of the general population. These concepts are not the thoughts of academics removed from the general population of women. Sometimes the women maintain concepts that are rigid and narrow, limiting the scope of their potential. Sometimes their concepts are expansive, uplifting, and inspirational. The definitions and the rationales behind these concepts offer you an opportunity to see negativism and positivism at work in the daily lives of women. The opinions expressed within this book allow you a context within which to question your own value system. Does it serve you and promote the desire and energy to express yourself creatively? Does it hinder you, and stop you from exploring the possibilities? Does your definition and value system for determining creativity make it impossible for you to consider yourself a creative person, a creative woman? Are you creative? The answers may not be readily available to you. Women often do not think of themselves in such terms, even while others do. By limiting your potential, you limit your creativity, thereby limiting what you can offer yourself and the world.

Many women limit themselves because they believe that (1) to be creative one must be a genius, a man or woman of extraordinary gifts, (2) real creativity is expressed only through the arts, and (3) creativity means bringing something new and meaningful into the world that must be recognized by the world as such. Imposing the criteria of "new and meaningful for the world" on a product relegates almost all behavior noncreative. Think of all the women you know. Most are not in the public sphere and so will not produce something "new and meaningful for the world." Does that mean what I do, what you do, what your daughter does, as a teacher, an executive, a nurse, a housewife, a communications consultant, an engineer, or a volunteer is insignificant and uncreative? Frank Barron and David Harrington believe that "commonly used definitions for creativity vary in several ways. First of all, some definitions require socially valuable products if the act or person is to be called creative, while others see creativity itself as being intrinsically valuable, so that nothing of demonstrable social value need be produced. . . ."

Before you can begin to consider "value," you first must confront the issue of public and private expression. Does anything that I produce or anything you create need to be recognized by an established institution before it can be labeled creative? This is a multilayered problem. Women are still not fully included in many areas that are considered public. Their pattern of gaining and keeping positions within these public areas remains uncertain. In an article in *Gender and Society*, Jerry A. Stanford has written that in nontraditional careers recently opened to women, an equal number of women leave the profession as enter it. There are a variety of reasons: raising a family, sexual harassment, lack of upward mobility within the organization, and just plain discrimination.

Where then do most women perform or exhibit their creative behavior and expression? In the private sphere. Many women in the world are not part of the public sphere, are not in positions of power. As a consequence, their actions must occur within the private sphere. It is absurd to think that creativity can be relegated to only one context or to one realm of being. Creativity can and does happen in small private acts everyday. What constitutes the difference between a public creative act and a private creative act? Public acts receive recognition or "critical acclaim" from established institutions. Private acts occur within the everyday realm of living and may or may not receive "critical acclaim." There is another way of defining public and private. William J. J. Gordon believes that there are two ways of being creative: (1) to allow yourself to let go of one image that is replaced by a new one—making the familiar strange, and (2) by associating the strange with the familiar to make a connection intellectually. If the discovery is given to the world, it is public; if it is used to make knowledge accessible to ourselves (as a personal learning process), it is private. If you do not know how you judge value in relation to public and private actions, you cannot reasonably understand how you define creativity.

Researchers grudgingly acknowledge that creativity does exist outside of monumental acts. Monumental acts can fall into many categories, but the impact upon society is always widely felt. For example, Joan of Arc's vision placed her at the forefront of the French military. This uneducated peasant girl assumed leadership of the French troops in the war against the British. Had she not been betrayed by the leaders of the warring factions of her own people, she would have succeeded in her effort. Harriet Tubman's behavior revealed how creativity could be used to help save lives from the torment of slavery. She became a guide for the underground railroad, leading runaway slaves to freedom. She appeared in support of the young but growing women's suffrage movement. Her activities earned her the nickname Grandma Moses. The profound impact that the life of Marie Curie had upon the scientific community cannot be overestimated. She was the first woman to win a Nobel Prize (in fact, she won two). Because of her courage and vision she was the first scientist whose work on radioactive elements led to an understanding of the nature of the atom. She also studied uranium and radiation, and founded the Curie Institute in Paris. Such contributions to the world are indeed monumental. But most of us are not destined to be written about in the history books. That does not mean that we do not engage in creative behavior or that our behavior does not have a profound impact on the lives of those around us. Researchers tell us that creativity exists on two levels—eminent creativity and everyday creativity ("big C" and "little c" creativity). This distinction has been made to try and differentiate between people who produce grand products, like in the sciences or arts, and those who do not. Whether or not the distinction of eminent and everyday is significant will be further explored through the lives of the women in this book. You can be the judge.

To further understand the problem of addressing creativity in the traditional manner, let us explore a few examples. You have a friend who is a woman, a mother, a wife, an artist. Her primary personal creative expression is painting. However, at this stage of her life, she has chosen to focus her energy and attention on her children; she is now a mother full-time. She has retained her studio and works there when her children are in school. She enters judged art shows sporadically. She sometimes shows at street fairs, or in banks and libraries, but rarely. She does not have an agent, nor does she seek to sell her paintings or earn an income from her work as an artist. Her work, while it is shown occasionally, does not go through the traditional "critical dialogue." Staying outside the "critical dialogue" can mean several things. She does not enter into a dialogue about the value of her work with other artists who comprise her community. She does not seek legitimacy through art institutions like museums or established galleries. She is not reviewed by the art critics, nor is her work analyzed in a historical context. Does this mean she is not creative? Does her isolated approach to her artwork reflect upon her craftsmanship or her ability to paint her vision? Institutions, such as museums and major galleries, confer status upon an artist and make money as a result of that official action. You cannot fairly talk about the legitimacy of an artist, about professionalism, without also discussing how difficult it is for a woman of any caliber to be taken seriously by these very institutions. The politics of this issue helps to shape the public and private debate. You concede, for argument's sake, that she may still be considered creative.

We turn now to another example. The woman is the same, the family structure is the same, and her choices to raise her children and maintain her studio are the same. This woman paints periodically. She does not show her work to the general public in any context. She does not share her work in any of the nontraditional ways women find to share their work. Instead, this woman engages in a "critical dialogue" with one or two other women friends she has known since art school. She paints primarily for herself, completely outside the public realm. Is she creative? There are qualitative differences between the motivation and drive of these two women which can directly affect their creativity. An in-depth discussion of the problem will be addressed later in the book.

Perhaps you think these two examples are limited since they look only to women in the arts, though these scenarios are not uncommon among female artists. The problem of understanding public and private spheres always leads one to gender roles, societal expectations, and a woman's own perceptions of appropriate behavior. All women with careers and families are forced to make choices. Whatever their creative expression, it is altered by the time and emotional demands of family and children. A woman must continually choose between her personal needs and her family's needs. These choices are framed within the struggles that follow and are shaped by a woman's belief system. A working woman continually struggles with priorities: family or career? How does a woman understand her role as a woman, wife, or mother, and how does that affect her self-image? How do the physical, emotional, and intellectual constraints placed upon her through these issues affect her productivity? The influences that affect self-fulfillment directly impact upon creative self-expression. This book does not offer you simplistic solutions. Instead, by example, I offer the paths other women have taken to negotiate life and creative self-expression.

Regardless of how you frame the question or state the problem, the issue of public and private remains constant. By contrast to the two women artists described above and to further delineate the issues facing women and their creativity, here are two other examples. One woman is an artist, a talented artist. She has gone to good art schools, has had a mentor, and has received some public recognition in the form of grants and gallery showings. Yet she is tentative about her ability, about sharing her work publicly and benefiting from it financially. She is tentative about the quality and vision of her work. She fights against her own creative expression. As a result, long periods of time go by when she does not "make art"; she is frustrated and can become depressed. A second woman is a "stay-at-home mom." She enjoys being with her children. She joyfully creates games and projects for them. She provides a safe, loving, supportive, stimulating environment that fosters exploration. This mom is not troubled by the path she has chosen. She is not tentative about herself or her creative expression. She understands that she has something wonderful to offer her children.

Though it may be an unfair comparison, I ask you, as a means of defining the problem of creativity, which woman is leading the creative life? Which woman is producing something tangible and of value in the world? Some people might answer the artist. I disagree. I would say the "stay-at-home mom." Yet within the context of public and private, and of the traditional criteria used to define creativity, the "stay-at-home mom" will not receive the recognition that is rightly hers. There may be lip service paid to her role as mother. Indeed, there is an expectation that exists that a woman will perform this role happily, lovingly, and creatively. But society at large does not value or honor her work or her ability. For some, this lack of recognition and value has a devastating effect. Talented women who choose to become full-time mothers can suffer from depression and low self-esteem. This often leads to self-doubt and a tentative approach to life. Tentativeness is a killer of creativity, and both their perceived abilities to be parents and creatively express themselves (which includes mothering) are negatively affected.

Women in traditional female roles (mother, teacher, secretary, nurse, volunteer) participate in the world. They bring something to the world, if they do it well, but they function mostly in the private sphere. The irony is that within these roles women express their creativity in nontraditional ways. Nontraditional paths in creativity are outside the public sphere, outside the arts and sciences. These nontraditional paths, however, can lead to extraordinary everyday occurrences. Because everyday occurrences have a profound effect upon us as individuals, they cannot be considered ordinary at all. The fact that their activities occur within the private sphere does not diminish the creativeness behind these women's expressions.

We have trained ourselves intellectually, emotionally, and spiritually to "see" and comprehend creativity narrowly. We have limited and weakened the potential within each of us. Loosening the blinders around our eyes makes the possibilities for creative expression seemingly limitless. Creative expressions are not bound by the legitimacy game played out in the arts. They are not bound by issues of professional and nonprofessional, public and private, or income-producing and volunteer. I am not arguing for making the ordinary and the mundane creative. I am not proposing that everything we do as women is creative. However, "big C" and "little c" creativity both have value. Perhaps only a special few can exhibit "big C" creativity. What matters most for women in their daily lives is the knowledge and trust that they have something personally creative to share with the world, even if that world is their family, friends, and the PTA.

This brings us to another aspect of the relationship between gender, society, and creativity. The issue is androgyny. Generally, when people refer to creativity, they do so as though it were an androgynous act. Since the 1970s many studies have been conducted with an underlying assumption that creativity is androgynous. But can you say with certainty that creative expression is grounded in androgynous behavior? Researchers analyzing how people create are confronted with aspects of personality, intellectual capacity, educational background, social position, professional status, gender perspectives, economic class, religious or spiritual beliefs, political beliefs, personal relationships, and manner of communicating: in essence, everything that combines to make a person respond to life in a uniquely personal way. Some of these, if not all, are linked to gender perceptions, whether conscious or unconscious. All of these areas influence creative expression. Are the experiences that arise from these perceptions, that shape creative behavior, androgynous in nature?

No one completely understands creativity or the creative process. Women and men are different, so it stands to reason that they express their creativity differently. The question is, where do the similarities and differences lie? The majority of creative people studied over the last forty years have been men. The findings have been universally applied to both men and women. But I am uncomfortable with the concept of androgyny. I cannot completely understand how males or females create, think, or perform, and ignore gender. Whether biological or cultural in origin, creative behavior is shaped by the personal perceptions and experiences we have of the world.

Some social scientists believe that we all see the world and express ourselves through different intelligences. That is why one person paints, another uses words, and a third sees mathematics as the source of creative expression. According to Howard Gardner, these intelligences can be broken down into seven categories: linguistic, logical-mathematical, spatial, musical, bodily-kinesthetic, interpersonal, and intrapersonal. These are all alternative ways of conceptualizing how the human mind finds expression and learns. It seems to me, then, that creative expression, regardless of the mode of intelligence, must be influenced to some degree by one's gender. To personalize the problem, say one person is a social worker, another is an organizational wizard, a third is a dancer. Within each person's approach, whether conscious or unconscious, an element of gender influence exerts some pressure upon that person's perception and creative expression. Androgyny, while theoretically possible, is highly improbable in the world as we live in it.

In the last twenty years, a growing number of scientists have championed the need for and rationale behind a holistic approach to creativity research. Holistic in this context means examining all aspects of a person's life. I have written this book using a holistic approach to understand a woman's creative expression. To maintain this perspective, and to respect the different intelligences or ways of perceiving and acting, I explored family and educational backgrounds, religious training, economic class (both past and present), marriage, biological changes, trauma and crisis, and children and issues related to child-rearing and work, career choices, private time, mentorship, work environment and work process, personally held definitions of creativity and guiding images, leisure-time activities, and gender perceptions. I believe that the women in this book are like the women you have met and known throughout your life, and offer the reader inspiration as well as insight into different forms of creative expression.

This project was not conceived by a social scientist. Nor were the lives of the women in this study analyzed from the scientific perspective of a psychiatrist. As you might suspect, the majority of people conducting research in this field are from the sciences. I come to creativity research from the arts, and though I have relied upon psycho-social approaches in interpreting the data, I do not interpret what I see or hear quite the same way as a scientist would. I was not concerned with statistics in understanding the differences between women and their creative expressions. My approach merely serves to illustrate the point of this book. A psychologist working in the field of creativity research brings a different sensitivity to interpreting the data than I do. One is not better than the other. Rather, the interpretations are different. The interpretations stem from different intelligences, different modes of seeing and understanding the world.

*Awakening Minerva* explores the similarities and differences among women working toward eminent creativity and those working in everyday creativity. The following questions frame the context of the women's stories: What do women think about creativity, and how do they define creativity? What kind of global perceptions support creative output and lead to a creative life? Are there differences in behavior and philosophical approaches to creativity between women who work in the arts and women who do not? Do women artists manifest creativity in the other facets of their lives? Do women who are not artists see themselves as creative? What perceptions hinder or promote creative expression? What kind of external pressures stop creativity from developing or being expressed? What influences the choice to share creative products in the public or private sphere?

The focus of this book is three-fold: (1) how researchers understand creative behavior, (2) the manner by which creativity is understood, defined, and incorporated into women's daily lives, and (3) how women can use other women, mythological or actual, as role models and symbols for creative behavior.

According to Albert Rothenberg in *The Creativity Question*, "[C]reativity consists of the capacity for or state of bringing something into being. And bringing something into being involves at least three separable components: an agent, a process and a product." I chose not to look at product to try to understand women's daily creative expressions. Product is the end result of many steps; it is the result of a process. Product does not necessarily inform me or you about women's responses to the world, or about their process. The women, and those experiences that have shaped their lives, thoughts, feelings, and creative expressions, are of far more significance to me, and I hope to you, than any product they may produce. The women's stories are the link to understanding their creativity, not their products.

The women who participated in this study did so voluntarily. I am deeply grateful to them for sharing their lives with me. The women ranged in age from their early twenties to their late eighties. They were from different socioeconomic classes, races, religions, family structures, educational backgrounds, and political and sexual persuasions. They varied in life experiences: loss of a parent at an early age, loss of a child, loss of a partner, single mothers, women in traditional family structures, women in nontraditional relationships, religious women, working women, retired women, unemployed women, women who had been abused as children, who had been abused as adults, women who were in recovery from addiction, women who were being treated with medication for depression, women who had suffered through the darkness of a breakdown, women who were artists but were unable to work, women who were "making their art" but were unable to respond to the opportunities public success offered them, women who were responding to the success in their lives but were not artists, women who had not experienced the pain of major loss or trauma, as well as a host of other life experiences. In several stories, women chose to seek professional counseling to help them move through serious problems.

I believe that counseling is a creative process that can be used to reshape one's life and free one's creative expression. It was, however, not used as a criterion for choosing the stories contained within this book.

The women's individual responses to the variety of experiences in their lives give you an opportunity to see how they utilize their creative powers. You can learn about yourself through another woman's experiences. In the spirit of learning, which is part of creative behavior, the saying "identify, don't compare" seems appropriate. That concept is the basis for taking another woman's experience and translating that knowledge into something useful for yourself. The personal stories offered here allow you a context in which to question, review, and articulate your own processes.

I have changed the names of all the women to guarantee anonymity. Their real names do not inform you about your own creativity, but their stories might. I have made slight grammatical changes in the women's statements to make reading easier. All other details of their lives remain as they were expressed to me.

Lastly, I have included a series of exercises that can be used by anyone wishing to engage their creativity, whether to acquaint yourself with your own creative voice or to deepen ownership of your creative expression.

The power within each woman is revealed through creative actions and creative thinking. There are joys and frustrations that accompany a woman through her pursuit of her personal creative expression. Creativity in all its healthy manifestations is a celebration of self. The more a woman celebrates her creative voice, the more there is to celebrate. If I can value your voice, I can learn to value mine; if I can share my knowledge with someone, my voice grows. Every action I take that challenges me and deepens my creativity also reveals to me what creativity is. Creativity is accessible to anyone who values it, wants it, and seeks it.

CHAPTER ONE

# GENERATING LIFE: A CONTEXT FOR CREATIVITY

❧

Astarte ruled the lands of the Pharaohs. Her shrines date back to Neolithic times and flourished during the Bronze Age. She is also known in the Bible as Asherah. In the Middle Ages, Christian writers reworked her story, making her an evil deity. Prior to Christian writings, she was an all-powerful female Goddess, one of those considered to be the Mother Goddess.

> In the beginning of time there was Astarte. Known as the Lady of Byblos, she was one of the oldest forms of the Great Goddess. No king dared to rule without first paying homage and asking her guidance. She was the "true sovereign of the world," tirelessly creating and destroying, eliminating the old and generating the new. *(The Woman's Encyclopedia of Myths and Secrets)*

> Astarte was viewed as a heaven goddess whose name meant womb. She became associated with "everything that

governed the generation of life." Astarte was the goddess of fertility and sexuality, but some sources reveal that she was goddess of the dead as well. She was also known as the Lady of the Water, and would rule over the voyages at sea. She was the archetype for the cult of the Virgin Mary in the Middle Ages. *(The Myth of the Goddess)*

Women are a combination of lightness and darkness, good and evil, strength and weakness. They are Goddesses of their own creation, both internally, and externally. Their dominion is possessed of potential and hope, as well as rugged emotional terrain. That which is within guides their use of the terrain, from the path they travel internally, to the world they create for themselves externally. Transformation, change, regeneration is the method; creativity is the name of the process. Creativity is self-expression. It is self-esteeming. It is powerful. It is a life force.

The process is rigorous. It demands your full attention to the possibilities of change, to the necessity of being symbolically destroyed, regenerated, and finally rebirthed. It echoes the way of the Heaven Goddess. Astarte's image helps define a creative being whose purpose in generating life includes, but is not limited to, pregnancy and childbirth. In the shadow of her image and the transformative capacity of her power a woman gives birth to herself anew. This newness may be shared by your immediate circle of relations and friends, or it may touch the larger unknown public. As a creative woman, you are always in process, becoming someone different than you were a day ago, a year ago, a decade ago.

Through Astarte, ruler over everything, generator of life, you can see your own actions, large or small, public or private, as endowed with the same life-giving capacities. In its essence, that power expressed by you is experienced by your families, your friends, your community. As a manifestation of creativity, it may be witnessed at any place along the circle of people you touch daily. Unfortunately, as a culture we are stuck in mediocrity. We are not trained to see what is in front of us nor what surrounds us. We do not honor or promote creative behavior, creative thinking, or creative people. We do not value the need to create something different; we do not honor personal style; we do not encourage a different path. We are eager to limit the possibilities by moving straight to the "bottom line," ignoring the need for process. Financial remuneration is the criterion for judging our actions and products. Women are too willing to judge themselves against this criterion. They are not discriminating when they should be and are accepting when they should not be. Are we a creative nation? Are we a creative culture? Are women as a group creative? Are you a creative person? How do you define creativity? By comparing the traditional meaning of creativity with those definitions given by the women in this book, you gain insight into your own concept.

Creativity is a commonly used word, overused in some contexts and underused in others. The word easily elicits a response, though its meaning may vary. People do not often stop to think about the meaning they have assigned to this word. The context for the meaning is then clouded by an aura of nebulous, unarticulated criteria and judgments. Generally creativity is assumed to be the domain of an exceptional few, yet it is haphazardly used in business titles or to describe eccentric behavior. Our culture is eager to identify, quantify, and label.

Little children overtly display creative behavior. Howard Gardner believes that "children are more willing to work in metaphor and suspend rules to achieve a desired effect." Though they do not know it, these same children break the rules, take risks, and as a result develop self-expression and self-esteem. They are acting creatively. You often hear the word "creative" used in discussing children. Indeed, I believe all children, like adults, are creative in one forum or another. The difference is that children willingly and enthusiastically enter the necessary state of anarchy for a brief period. Within this space and time, creativity occurs and change is the result. If there is not a tolerance for this state of confusion and delight, if the child refuses to take the risk and follow an impulse, the ability to follow the metaphor and suspend reality will be buried. The child then grows into adulthood unable to respond to her own essential creative nature. Fortunately, intervention can correct this tragedy, even in adults. It is possible to awaken the creative spirit at any time in one's life.

Children give us insight into acting creatively. Their use of metaphor and disregard for structure or rules contain powerful examples for adults. A child at play will respect parameters when they are needed and disregard them when they are not needed. Through this type of behavior, a child allows herself the right to explore, to go beyond the obvious, to go far afield. At first glance, a child makes connections to seemingly unrelated things. These seemingly unrelated connections can reveal answers not readily available at the surface level. This process is crucial in creative thinking. Young children experience this naturally; most adults do not. Without preparation or concentrated forethought, the child takes the risk to engage her imagination and her desire to create and explore. I am speaking of children up to six years of age. Research indicates that by seven years of age children are no longer responding from that creative, innovative, free place inside. By nine, the dynamic has been severely altered; the rules become significant, doing it the "right way" becomes paramount. What was once instinctive and natural will need to be taught and relearned. A few children are able to withstand the structure imposed upon their imaginations; they are able to retain their desire to explore and a healthy disregard for the rules. These children generally maintain their creative expression.

My son and his friend, both of whom were four years old at the time, were sitting in a restaurant. They had been coloring. The paper had the outline of farm animals. Both children were busily involved with their pictures when my son's friend looked over and stated that his drawing was better than my son's. Acknowledging that their pictures were different, I added that they were both good. He persisted, "No, my drawing is better because I stay inside the lines." They were both coloring the figure of the cow. His cow was one color, and he had stayed within the lines. My son's cow was multicolored, and he had not stayed within the lines. The friend's father joined the conversation: "He is right. The lines are there for a purpose. You should stay inside the lines." His value judgment was given to the boys as a rule. I said to the boys, "When you draw, you can do whatever you wish." It takes only a few unsubstantiated rules, authoritatively pronounced to children, and their concerns will reflect those rules. Their impulses will be reigned in, and their willingness to explore hindered.

There are many environments and conditions that can diminish or kill creativity. Lack of spontaneity and freedom to free-associate will help guarantee that creativity does not flourish, not in a classroom of schoolchildren, not in the home, not on the job, nor in any environment related to adults. Are your concepts ladened with unbending rules and rigid structures? Do you give yourself permission to move through the process of creative behavior and give expression to your essential creative nature? Do you value your creative impulses by exploring them? Do you respond to the world from a spontaneous, joyful posture? In *Symbolization and Creativity*, Susan K. Deri writes, "[C]reativity refers to the innumerable ongoing actions, reactions, decisions, and choices—unconscious, preconscious, and conscious—which give form and texture to an individual life."

Giving form and texture to life through creative behavior is the goal. The majority of the women I spoke to initially struggled to define creativity. Those not involved in the arts had never been asked to articulate their thoughts on the subject. Many women felt, even those in the arts, that creativity was too large and powerful a concept to verbalize. Many of the women artists were painfully tentative about defining the word and about viewing themselves as creative. I was most surprised to find that, in almost all cases, working within the arts was not a criterion for defining and understanding creativity. Only three women offered a definition for creativity that was specifically bound to the arts. However, several women used the arts as examples of their personal creativity, even though it had not been part of their definition.

I explored two contexts through which women could define creativity: a general definition of creativity and a personal definition of creativity. My own bias had led me to believe that most women, especially those not working in the arts, would hesitate to define themselves as creative. Most women were willing to call themselves creative. Contradictions arose, but as each woman was given the opportunity to articulate and expand upon her beliefs, the contradictions disappeared. All the women fell into one of three categories in defining creativity: (1) creativity as a personal expression, (2) creativity as the ability to take risks and an openness to life, (3) creativity as transformation and the making of something new.

Each woman was asked to describe an image or a feeling that had motivated or guided her throughout her life. Then each was asked to place that idea into her general definition of creativity. I wanted to see if the two concepts were compatible or whether they were exclusive. People are full of contradictions and restrictions. Contradictions and restrictions are often based upon blindly accepted rules. These rules may disallow creative behavior. As each woman spoke, the parameters of what was personally creative kept expanding. I believe this is a natural phenomenon. The mere act of articulating beliefs, giving voice to your thoughts, makes them real in the universe.

The act of speaking your thoughts is a powerful experience. You feel it physically; you hear your voice. You engage your intellect, and that gives you something to latch on to. Articulating your thoughts can help you engage your creative process and move into creative behavior. In this chapter, I have chosen two women from each of the three groups delineated above, for a total of six women. Their words and stories will demonstrate how women use these defining concepts in creating their lives.

## CREATIVITY AS PERSONAL EXPRESSION

Giving voice to your thoughts and moving your ideas into the universe makes you master over your thoughts. That act makes your thoughts real. The ideas that are positive gain strength through this kind of acknowledgment. Giving voice to your thoughts can alert you to negative impulses and minimize their disruptive powers. The manner in which you give voice to your thoughts and feelings is a manifestation of your personal style. Some women demonstrated a painful restraint and tentativeness about their ideas, work, mothering, and their creativity. On the other hand, some women represented through their personal style the quality acquired by living a creative life. They were fertile with ideas, breathlessly on the go in their work, emotional lives, relationships, and their abilities as mothers. Their lives were alight with energy, exuberance, and joy. They were as the Goddess, generating life.

Alexandra is an active sixty-two-year-old white woman. She has led a life of service to others. She is a nun. Her path has not been traditional. She has not been married or given birth to children, nor has she been tied to a parish church. At present, she works as a public advocate for children in a large foundation. She negotiates the needs of her community with the foundation, the city, and state agencies. The role she serves is to clarify the needs of those she represents as she moves from one problem to the next. Alexandra's life and her work demonstrate how creativity is called upon daily in her attempt to help the children, educate those in positions to help, write her position papers, acquire funding, and negotiate life in a small convent with other older women. Clearly more than one skill, one form of communication, one discipline is called upon in her efforts. The image of her guiding force and her definition of creativity are echoed in her approach to life and work. Who is Alexandra? What environment helped shape her? How does that manifest itself in her view of creativity?

Alexandra is one of two children. She was raised in a large northeastern city. Her father worked for the transit authority; her mother took care of managing the house and raising the children. Both her parents had an elementary school education. Her grandparents were farmers; one of her grandfathers was a farmer/inventor. She is from a lower-class environment. Her religious training has been Roman Catholic. Those are the obvious facts of her life. The more subtle facts are the ones that Alexandra expressed in our interview, the ones that color her responses to the world. There was never an abundance of money available to her family as she was growing up. Alexandra felt her mother provided a stimulating environment for the children with limited funds. She recalls with warmth and pride that her mother expressed her creativity in her sewing, her cooking, her ability to make people feel comfortable, and the help she gave others.

Creativity, as Alexandra frames it, is a personal expression: "Creativity is that inner ability to do something exciting, challenging, rewarding. It is being helpful to others and to yourself . . . It is the ability to recognize the spirit within yourself, the courage to follow it and to go with the flow." Alexandra has not wavered from her definition and has integrated who she is and how she sees the world into the context of her definition of creativity. Personal expression has been the light that has guided her own unique expression. Accepting the challenge to help people has been a major force moving Alexandra's life. It has given her great excitement and pleasure. The challenge is not always easy, but the rewards have been immeasurable. Her guiding force, in relation to her definition of creativity, is propelled by her faith. "Because I want to help others, I find the needed resources within myself and the outside world. Nothing is too challenging. I am not afraid to help people feel better about themselves, to live better. I find this a very exciting thing to do." This personal way of seeing creativity is not unique to Alexandra because she is a nun. Meeting the challenge to help others and/or to do God's work was expressed by other women outside of the religious community.

Alexandra has no difficulty in speaking of herself in the context of creative behavior. "Most of the time, I think I am creative. But sometimes I feel I am not as creative as I could be. In my reflection of what I have done in the past, I can see I have started many things in my own career. For instance, I started a teachers' center. I am developing this position at the foundation. I am starting with nothing. It is challenging to go to people I know and don't know. As a public advocate, I have to determine what is the best way to attack city hall. I come from a different background. In the convent, I try to get people to see things my way. I am a take-charge person." Always present in speaking of personal creative behavior is a healthy articulation of "I." A woman insecure about her place and value in the world cannot enunciate her creative expression with clarity. She cannot easily manifest creative behavior.

Often women have trouble "owning" their creative actions or believing they have value. Yet there can exist a dichotomy of reality. A woman's perception of herself can be in opposition to the perception of her held by others. As I hoped to understand how this might influence a woman's life, I asked each of these women how they were perceived by others. The difference in perception can be a valuable tool in reassessing how you define yourself and your contribution to the world. Sometimes other people's perceptions lead a woman to reevaluate her creativity and abilities. Others' perceptions allow a woman to see her self-worth positively. I do not promote listening to or validating the destructive images others in your life might offer you. I do not encourage destructive behavior, no matter how creative it might appear. For Alexandra, the perceptions offered by others were positive. She stated without hesitation that she was viewed as creative. Her creativity and ability to build leadership qualities in others has always been openly acknowledged by her superiors. They knew Alexandra was a valuable member of the community. Being able to accept other people's positive perceptions can also be personally rewarding. Morris I. Stein writes, in "Creativity Research at the Crossroads . . ." "A person's self-perceptions, self-evaluations and their underlying psychological characteristics, may well change after manifesting creativity and being regarded by others as creative. The feedback one gets after a creative work can produce changes in one's self-esteem and one's behavior."

Alexandra's personal expression is channeled through her ability to listen to and understand people's needs. It is present in her ability to solve problems, and it is manifested in her spiritual relationship with her God and her religious community. Not everyone has the capacity to do the kind of work Alexandra has been doing. Do not be fooled: it is not solely a learned skill. The style and approach to her work are part of her creative expression. It has been nurtured and shaped over time. The evolution of her path suggests an ongoing creative process. Discipline, commitment, a woman's passion for her essential creative nature, and the manifestation of that nature are the fundamental elements for creative behavior.

Personal expression, evidenced in a diversity of lifestyles, is the wonder of creativity. Cari's path is unlike Alexandra's. It is not so orderly. Orderliness is merely the function of style. Cari differs from Alexandra in all outward manifestations. She frames her thoughts and her actions differently. But Cari, like Alexandra, understands creativity as a personal expression. Cari is an energetic thirty-seven-year-old woman. She was born and raised both in England and India. Her father is Burmese and her mother Finnish. Cari is one of three siblings, a middle child, with an older brother and a younger sister. She looked after her sister when they were young, but Cari felt closer to her brother.

The sense of security and safety felt by Alexandra was not present in Cari's home. Her father was a commercial pilot who, because of his job, was away from home frequently. Despite his demonstrative acts of love toward his children while he was at home, his constant absences were a hardship for all of them. The loss of her father was compounded by the pain of her mother's depression when her dad was away. The pain of her inner life was coupled with the pain she saw in the world around her. As a child, Cari lived in England for several years before her family moved to India. She loved England and felt life was safe there for both people and animals. In contrast, Cari's experiences in India were vivid and difficult. "I saw a lot of death in India. People and animals weren't treated very well. There were dead animals on the side of the road. People were also living on the side of the road." In India, her sister was raped by a man who worked in the house. He also fondled and placed his penis upon Cari's body. Neither Cari nor her sister spoke of this issue until recently. As a result, Cari spent many years feeling responsible for her sister's rape. Her father's absence, the male servant's violations of the young girls, her mother's depression and attempted suicide, the poverty and death that surrounded her—all severely hindered Cari's sense of security and safety. These experiences solidified her feeling that "life was not respected in India."

Often a guiding principle is used as a survival tool. It can change as your life changes. Cari's early experiences in India helped shape her guiding force. "The main thrust has been to respect all forms of life," she says. "For me that has been primary and very motivating. Most of my decisions come out of that." Cari has a strong desire to feel love, respect, and warmth in this world. Presently she is married, and has adopted two children and several animals of various species, to whom she is devoted. She is dedicated to her ideals and committed to providing a loving environment for her children and her animals. Cari and Alexandra have managed to create guiding principles that have served them positively through their lives thus far. Their guiding principles have been the channel through which they maintain their personal expression.

Cari sees her mother as creative. She bakes, knits, reads, and draws. Cari's mother, despite her depression, was crucial in shaping a positive view of the world for her daughter. She described her mother's vision of a world as one in which nature, animals, bugs, and plants are respected and "deserving of kindness." Cari's guiding principle is grounded in her mother's vision of respecting life. In many cases, even though the mother-daughter relationship may have been strained, the daughter adopted what she described as the mother's philosophical approach to the world. This approach becomes part of a woman's personal creative expression. Many events, thoughts, feelings, and observations combine to make creative expression possible.

Generally our lives are lived in connection with a small circle of people. A woman takes care of her home, her family, her career, her relationships. Most women do not travel the world regularly, live in exotic places, or meet famous people. As individuals, women draw upon the knowledge of those around them to help broaden their vision and perception. Cari has developed a talent for identifying needs and solutions for those needs. She has her own business; she publishes specialized books, creates children's programs, and finds ways to help others in need organize the outer structure of their lives during crises. She often gives her talents to people in need without payment. Cari is willing to share herself and her expertise, even her home, if necessary, when someone is in need. In this way, Cari moves between working in the private and public spheres. Her personal style and her need for action place her definition of creativity within a context of her life. She says creativity has "something to do with manifesting action in the physical world. Creativity is expressing who you are in terms of your spirituality and emotionality in the physical world. My mantra is respecting all life. Creativity is those things I do which are life-enhancing. Playing with my animals is creative. Raising my sons is creative. My work is creative when it is life-enhancing. It stops being satisfying, or it becomes dark and lacks creativity when it does not contain that life-enhancing quality." Cari does not judge her creative behavior in relationship to financial considerations. She would like to receive an income from her work projects, but sometimes she does not. She finds this reality satisfactory. Feeling creative is of the utmost importance for Cari. As she explains, "I couldn't exist in any job. It doesn't matter if I have money in my life. Right now I am lucky; my husband has enough money. I can have businesses that do not generate a lot of money. There have been times in my life when I have not had enough money. But this need in myself overpowers the need to pay the rent."

Researchers report that creative people find pleasure and satisfaction in what they do. Satisfaction is the payback for the intense involvement and commitment required for creative behavior. The greater the satisfaction derived from creative behavior, the more motivated a woman is to pursue other similar activities. Both Cari and Alexandra illustrate a level of satisfaction they receive from their commitment to their principles and their pursuit of self-expression. The forward flow of their creative energies is seen in the context of their work paths.

Alexandra's work path can be broken into three phases, each one reflecting her personal creative style. Initially Alexandra taught school. She lived in a convent where the mother superior aggressively urged the nuns to develop themselves as people. Alexandra remembers this mother superior with fondness. Quality leadership provides women with inspiration, broadens their horizons, stimulates and deepens their creative experiences. That path builds self-esteem and self-expression and a solid creative persona. The nuns were encouraged to take music lessons, piano lessons, dancing lessons, driving lessons—whatever—as well as continuing their formal education.

Alexandra was sent to study new math. She was then given the task of teaching new math to other teachers. While working on her master's degree in education, she was sent to another school as principal of religious education. By now Alexandra's path had been clearly defined. She worked only in poor communities. Helping people was central to who she was and how she expressed herself. These communities were in need. Her work was challenging and the problems serious. Creative thinking was fundamental to problem-solving. Again Alexandra was transferred, this time to become head of a convent and director of an experimental school. The program was unique. The school demanded a five-year commitment from everyone, including Alexandra. Toward the end of her assignment, Alexandra felt an intense need for change. She had functioned as a teacher, a principal, and an administrative director in impoverished environments for a number of years. That need for change was the inner urging of her essential creative nature and began the second phase of her path. Sometimes change is immediate and great. At other times, change is evident in small, subtle shifts in focus. Such a shift can lead to an alteration in your perceptions and your responses. The ability to respond to the impulse, the inner urging, enables a woman to create something new. As the image of Astarte reminds us, it generates life. Alexandra had become attuned to her inner source and responded to the shift in her being.

She decided to study the educational system in England. Following her inner urging, without a job, without a place to live, and although her superiors were skeptical, she flew to England. Because Alexandra sees creativity as meeting a personal challenge, it is not surprising that she saw this as exciting. Being resourceful and determined, she quickly found a job as a lay teacher in a poor school (her basic vision had not altered). She found a place to live in a hostel run by a religious community. Alexandra deliberately sought a secular school environment where she could learn and teach. Her year in England was rejuvenating for her. She was navigating unknown waters and fulfilling her personal destiny. Alexandra characterized this year as "the most creative year" in her life. She had unconsciously set things in motion, and change came quickly. Her vitality and her creativeness were sought after. She was asked to return home and become the director of a new education center. The goal of the center was to develop new teacher-training programs. Alexandra decided she needed to finish her experience in England first. Her respect for her personal development and style can be used as a positive role model for other women.

As the year came to a close, Alexandra's superiors wanted her to return to the traditional parochial school environment. But Alexandra knew that a new challenge would best express her creativity. She refused her superiors and articulated her needs. This was a crucial time for her that challenged her to grow. Because of the depth of her need to be an innovator, Alexandra was unwilling to let anyone, even her superiors, force her to step backward. The ability to pursue one's ideas, in the face of opposition, is at the heart of creative behavior. Alexandra's desire was granted. She remained director of the center for seventeen years until the inner urging for change came upon her again. That inner urging began the third and most recent phase. As had happened before, opportunities arose when she opened herself up to change. Simultaneously Alexandra was offered the principalship of a school in another part of the country as well as the opportunity to work as a public advocate for a large foundation. Alexandra met the challenge. She took her expertise in education and administration to the foundation and became a public advocate. Alexandra is a successful public advocate. She is determined, directed, secure, dedicated to helping others, and willing to learn. She welcomes the unknown, faces change optimistically, and meets the challenge. That is her personal style and the expression of her essential creative nature.

Unlike Alexandra, whose path has evolved slowly and steadily, Cari's path can be characterized as having twists and turns. The twists and turns are part of her personal style and approach to the world. Her experiences include acting, casting, producing, and publishing mainly theater-related literature. Cari's creative expression is channeled through more than one outlet. This dynamic causes other people to label Cari as creative. Unlike Alexandra's positive response to her own creativity, Cari is hesitant. She says, "The things I am involved with are considered creative by the world. The fact that I publish books, I do the writing, I run around doing different projects. It becomes a huge expression thing." While Cari will admit she is creative, sometimes she wonders about it. She adds, "People who have a tendency to do a lot of things get called creative. That happens with me." She also develops children's theater programs and awards shows that acknowledge children who have been involved in "life-enhancing activities in school, community, nationally and globally." Her relationship with her children is unequivocally viewed as a creative expression. Like many women, Cari's experience of her self as a creative person was altered when her sons arrived. Before becoming a mother, Cari was endlessly trying to feed her creative energies through work. Her children caused her to experience her creativity differently. Her awareness of herself deepened. But a nagging question about her creativity remains. She describes a day broken up by several different activities. She believes that "people look at a day that looks like that and think that person must be creative because that person is doing more than one thing. People think I'm creative because I have a thousand ideas a day."

There is a difference between having a thousand ideas a day and developing to completion some of those ideas. There is no rule that states that personal creative expression is restricted to one domain. In an article in *The Journal of Creative Behavior*, Donna Y. Ford and J. John Harris III write, "[C]reativity is those attitudes by which we fulfill ourselves. . . . Creativity is the actualizing of our potential. . . . It is the integration of our logical side with our intuitive side. . . . Creativity is more than spontaneity, it is deliberation as well. . . . It not only generates possibilities, but also chooses among them. . . ." People respond both to Cari's free-flowing inventive thinking and to her ability to translate some of those thoughts into reality. They respond to her ability to allow the ideas to "manifest in the physical world." Many women do more than one thing. That style is grossly misunderstood in this society. As a result, women often do not appreciate their abilities and suffer from feelings of inadequacy. Some women flounder. They do not know how to focus or direct their energies. The issue Cari raises is of another kind. Approaching life through an interdisciplinary perspective is qualitatively different than floundering and being undirected. Cari's question about herself needs to be answered; an honest evaluation of her own process will inform her of the inner truth. If it is within her nature to approach the world through interdisciplinary actions, then her style needs to be respected and developed. If it is avoidance, then the avoidance needs to be addressed. Cari's ability to look at the world and quickly see needs and possibilities should be fostered and encouraged.

Seeing a need in the world and having brilliant ideas are not enough. The creative woman must be able to move through the process of thinking, action, and completion or the creative force is wasted. Researchers have found that many uniquely gifted people will never approach their potential. These people are often far more gifted than those who become successful in the public sphere. The difference between the two groups is the ability to put their thoughts into action. Those who make it into the public sphere are not as concerned with "getting it right" or with what other people think. They possess an aggressive protective quality about their need to express themselves. They do express themselves, whether in mathematics or music or another field. It is that simple. They follow through on their ideas despite the fears and uncertainties of life.

CREATIVITY AS RISK-TAKING

The commonality of meaning in the definitions of creativity bind the women in each group together. Personal expression, risk-taking, and transformations cannot be achieved by complacent, lazy, disinterested behavior. Assertiveness and direct involvement with your passion enables these three concepts to become real in your life. Risk-taking and an openness to whatever occurs characterized the women's perceptions in this group. They regularly used words such as "seeing," "no boundaries," "going beyond," and "going further."

Risk-taking can conjure up images of daredevils and rebels; these images do not apply to Rose or her personal style. She is a pleasant-looking, forty-four-year-old African-American woman. She is a dedicated educator. She is divorced and has never had any children. She comes from a large, closely knit family, with seven sisters and brothers. Her birth position is in the middle. (Some researchers believe that birth position affects the development of creative behavior, but I have not found any correlation.) Playing in the basement with her sisters as well as Wednesday night prayer meetings are prominent memories of her childhood. Her sister, who recently died of cancer, was her best friend. "I saw my sister almost every weekend, and we would take the kids [her sister's children] different places." She has taken on "more responsibility" in caring for her nieces since her sister's death.

In her youth, Rose resented her father because of his expectations of her. She explains, "If anything went wrong in the house, I was the one he came to. I was always the person he sought out. As I got older, I was the only one who could get his car." In adulthood she had a good relationship with him. Her father was a postal worker and her mother was a self-employed beautician. Her parents were happily married until her father died of a brain tumor several years ago. He was always an active man. During his illness, he determined that he would not be kept alive with tubes in him. Rose was angered by his decision but learned to accept it. Four years ago, her mother was operated on for cancer; there is now a recurrence. Rose's mother, having recently watched her daughter suffer and die of cancer, has also chosen not to go through surgery again. Rose believes, "I have begun to come to terms with her decision. It is an informed decision. Whatever decision she makes, I support it."

As a result of her sister's death, Rose has been reevaluating her life. She has come to accept her gifts or assets, and has acknowledged her deficits. Learning to take more time for herself and her feelings has become more important. Grieving the loss of her sister and coping with the degenerative nature of her mother's illness have helped Rose identify who she is and what she wants. Astarte's image hovers over this process. With each new experience, Rose deepens her own sense of self and opens herself to the reality and the possibility for creating her life anew. Being responsible for her nieces, respecting and supporting her mother's choices, and growing in her work reflect the changes that have occurred within Rose. Her soul-searching and honest personal evaluation of self rely heavily upon her tolerance to confront, to generate new life, to risk. The result of that process is an openness to what comes. Slow, deliberate, thoughtful evaluation have defined her risk-taking style, but this latest phase is perhaps the most profound. Although slowness and risk-taking may seem contradictory, they are not. Change cannot occur without some dimension of risk. The most intense experience a woman will face is found in reshaping or regenerating her life.

Rose's ability to take a risk at a difficult time reflects a strong sense of self, and a strong drive. Researchers have found that these two qualities are necessary for creative behavior. Rose's history will show that the forward direction in her life is the result of self-evaluation. Every step leads Rose to new territory. Resting long enough to learn about herself and her needs, she willingly moves on. The more any woman attends to her own needs and follows her dreams, the more she can accomplish.

Rose defines creative behavior in simple terms. She says, "Being creative means taking a risk. It is the sense that you are not placing boundaries on anything you are doing. Sometimes being creative does not meet with other people's approval. For example, there is a little game I play with my students. I use it as a teaching strategy. Most students enjoy playing the game, but some people don't. They would rather I adhere to the lecture. That to me is taking a chance, taking a risk. Some people will like it, others will not." Risks can be seen in small acts or large acts. Risks can be private or public. For our purposes, the concept of taking a risk has tremendous significance on a personal level. Research has revealed that there must be a tolerance for risk-taking, for challenge, for the unknown, and a healthy disregard for the opinions of others. While Rose exhibits creativity in her teaching techniques, she is simultaneously teaching her students to engage in learning through a creative process—that is, through play.

Not surprisingly, Rose defined her guiding image in terms of her creativity. She believes in following your dreams regardless of whether you succeed or not. The path of following your dreams affords you the opportunity to learn and grow, even if that means displeasing others. As a result, Rose translates dreams into goals. "I try to categorize my dreams into two different kinds: my real dreams and my not-so-real dreams. Those are: I can sprout wings, fly around, and cure the world. I cannot set about a plan to do that, but that's okay. But then there are those dreams which are more concrete. I can establish plans and work toward them."

Women learn about themselves from listening to other women speak of their struggles, accomplishments, and dreams. Self-evaluation can also be stimulated by the perceptions others present to you. Rose has gained a new awareness of herself as a creative woman because of others' perceptions. She explains, "I think as I began to reflect on my previous experiences, I had difficulty accepting my creativity. Other people saw it. But recently, when I looked back on a number of things that I did, I looked at them and said, I did take a risk! It did take a thought process to come up with these ideas. I feel that I am creative. Now that I have identified that, I feel that I am able to work with my creativity more and explore different things. For example, with my teaching, I have been able to develop a different approach with my teaching staff. I focus not only on content but on building the self-esteem of individuals. I want to make students more active participants in their learning experience, as opposed to me being the major subject of all their attention."

Acknowledging your gifts and talents allows you, as Rose pointed out, to take the risk and develop them. Phyllis also defines creativity as risk-taking, but she has suffered from perfectionism and an inability to acknowledge her achievements and gifts. It has made a good portion of her life painful. I have included Phyllis in this chapter for two reasons: because she reflects the results of unfulfilled creative energy and desires, and because she has in the later years of her life taken risks and reclaimed her personal creative expression. Phyllis is seventy-two years old. She is white, married, the mother of three grown children, and a retired business-school teacher. Her early life, like Cari's, was not joyful or easy. She was born in the midwest to a family of limited means. Her mother immigrated here from Russia; her father was born in northeastern United States. Neither of her parents were educated beyond middle school. Despite their lack of formal education, her parents felt it was important for both Phyllis and her younger brother to be well-educated. Phyllis is a bright, articulate woman. But her life, not unlike many bright women, was compromised by the shadow of her brother and the demands of her father.

Phyllis's relationship with her brother was complex and confusing. While she spoke of him in warm terms, she recalls, "He was a genius. He was good at everything. At nine years old, I wanted to take piano lessons. He was five, and he wanted to take piano in the worst way. One year later I had to give it up, he was so good at it. He played every instrument in band. He was a wonderful human being. He was my mother's shining light." Even at a young age, Phyllis's perfectionism made it impossible for her to pursue her creative expression. She loved music, singing, and dancing, but since she could not play as well as her brother, she would not play at all. Despite her deep affinity for music, she chose to deny herself that which gave her joy, that which was part of her creative expression. This pattern of denial would be repeated throughout her life. Her inability to outshine her brother was covered by yet an even darker shadow. Though her brother was a genius, he suffered, as did her father, from manic depression, and he committed suicide in his early thirties.

Her brother was sensitive and warm, but her father was aggressive and domineering. Her father suffered several nervous breakdowns during Phyllis's youth. In the middle of the night he would be taken to the hospital, and the children would be hurried out of the house to stay with their grandmother. Their grandmother openly expressed her hatred for Phyllis's father, compounding the mix of emotions already felt by the children. Those were confusing, frightening, terrible, shame-filled times in the children's lives. Despite these painful disruptions and her father's verbal abuse of her mother, Phyllis says she dearly loved her father. It was not to remain so simple as time passed. She explains, "He treated me as the woman. I think my mother was jealous of me." Growing up as an independent young woman was made more difficult by her father's demands of loyalty to him. "I thought I loved my father until I wanted to become my own person. Then he turned on me." After her brother's death, her father physically abused her mother and then divorced her. By then, Phyllis was married, with a family of her own. Her father had become aggressive in his attempts to intrude on and control her life. For instance, he wrote her neighbors scathing letters about his daughter in hopes of alienating them from her.

Phyllis's sense of self was formed in this competitive, confused, and hostile environment. She describes her motivating principle thus: "My guiding principle is humanity. I think about the results of what I might do. I was always very active in things that concerned other people." As a result of her guiding principle, Phyllis was active in the PTA, the civil-rights movement, and the Vietnam peace movement. Motivation, stemming from early childhood experiences, often feeds into creative behavior. In Phyllis's case her personal expression, having been repressed in her youth, took on the form of caring for others. In *Creativity: The Magic Synthesis*, Silvano Arieti writes, "[E]arly experiences can play a determining role in stimulating and directing the individual toward a certain kind of activity. The child who grows up in an environment that lacks stability and consistency may become an inventor in the field of mathematics, where he searches for and finds a feeling of certainty for some aspects of the world. The child who feels falsely accused may become a promoter of innovations that guarantee civil liberties."

Phyllis's definition of creativity is not narrow, but the path she created for herself throughout her life has been restrictive. Indeed, her concepts are expansive. Her guiding principle contains a vision for eminent creative behavior. Despite this reality, Phyllis had a great deal of difficulty following her passion. She did not value those activities she engaged in. Phyllis believes that "being creative is doing something that is a little bit different from what other people do, or are able to do. It is making something." She says, "I never thought of myself as creative. I never thought of myself as having talents when I was growing up. But I always loved art and music. I never thought of myself as being creative because I never did anything. I didn't stay with it. But I always had this feeling that there was something in me that wanted to come out." You can sense the negative value judgments that have limited her appreciation for what she has done with her life. Though the arts are not a criterion within her definition of creativity, they seem to be a crucial element for determining personal creative behavior. Conceptually Phyllis refers to the arts first. Perhaps that explains her inability to acknowledge and value the other things she created in her life.

The measurement of self is determined by what you do and produce in the world. It leads you forward, challenges you to go beyond your comfort zone, to explore the limits of your being. In contrast to Phyllis, Rose has always appreciated herself and her dreams. Despite her losses and the illness of her mother, Rose has continued her forward-moving direction. She possesses a strong drive, and is goal-oriented and energetic about her life. She is not tentative or hesitant about herself. She explains that a lesson learned from the loss of her sister is to "now look at the glass, metaphorically speaking, as if half-full, and then deal with whatever comes up. To encourage people, my students, to be more positive in their approach to life is being positive. It is spiritual and has helped me."

Rose offers you the opportunity to examine risk-taking from a different, deliberate, thoughtful place. This pattern began to manifest itself in her adult life soon after she graduated from college. Her quest for knowledge, which drives her, has lead her from discipline to discipline. She began with a two-year degree in nursing. Life was complex, and there were problems with a boyfriend. Rose had always wanted to dance; her essential creative nature was calling out to her, and she needed to respond. She moved to another state, went back to school for a B.S. in physical education and started dancing. While she was away at school, she had an automobile accident. She was badly hurt and could no longer pursue her dream of dancing. Circumstances forced her to reevaluate the direction of her life.

She finished her degree and returned home. Dancing was no longer an option, so she decided to get another degree in nursing. While working as a nurse, she decided to teach nursing. That decision meant more schooling, commitment, and discipline. First she had to get a B.A., and then she went on to receive a master's degree in education. Just within these few years, Rose altered the direction of her life several times. With each transition, Rose committed herself to the process of change. While she earned her master's degree, she worked first as a nurse and then as a clinical care instructor. In a short time, she was promoted to director of education for nurses and staff at a large hospital. There was still more to be learned. As a director, she was not in constant contact with patients. She wanted to keep her nursing skills fresh, so in her spare time she became a community health-care worker. Time passed, and Rose began to feel an inner urging. She left the hospital in order to give herself time to think about her life. For eight months Rose worked full-time as an independent community health-care worker. Finally she knew what had to be done. She needed to return to school for her doctorate. Rose felt an advanced degree in nursing would be limiting; instead she chose to get a degree in higher and adult education. This would allow her to "interface with other disciplines," which in turn would allow her to address the needs of her students better. During this phase, she went back to teaching nurses. She completed her degree and was promoted to director of the registered nurses program. Her promotion came right before her sister's death.

Work is not the only way Rose faces personal challenges and changes. She expresses her creative nature outside the context of her work. The flow of her life is rooted in Astarte's image as a generator of life. Because she is busy shaping the content of her life, she is in contact with a variety of experiences. She helps develop children's programs with various organizations, is involved with community work, cooks, gardens, does home improvement projects, explores the possibilities of her computer, designs programs for students, and caters parties. It is her hope to open her own catering business when she retires. The flow of creative energy is in constant motion. It moves you from one experience to another. With each experience Rose has given herself a challenge: do it differently and do it by herself. Rose is compelled to test her limits. She is not frightened by results, nor is she cowed by the thought of potential failure. Rose values the experience of trying. Neither fear of failure nor perfectionism stops her. For example, Rose decided to do certain home improvement projects by herself. These recently included tiling a bathroom and designing the landscaping for her yard. She speaks with pride of her experience. She has been rigorously involved in the process of generating new life, not only for herself and her nieces but also for her students.

Rose's ability to avoid the trap of perfectionism is a requisite quality for creative behavior. That is the philosophical basis for the leap into active participation and growth. The demand of perfectionism diminishes one's ability to take risks, to move into the unknown, to grow, to be creative. Perfectionism often kills the creative impulse, and it can rarely be achieved. The lesson and value is in the process, not the product. Phyllis describes herself as a perfectionist, so it is not surprising that she was unhappy in her life. She entered college when most women did not attend school and she did well. But her heart's desire was to be a performer. "I didn't want to do what I did. But my father was a very domineering man. He insisted when I went to college that I take something practical. I wanted to take elocution lessons for performing. I was always singing. I loved to sing and dance. It was in my body. I never did anything with it." Feeling unable to overtly defy her father, she moved east to live with her aunt after graduation. If

Phyllis did not value her own intellectual talents, a professor from college did. He helped her get a job with the federal government. She wrote articles that were published nationally. While in Washington, Phyllis met and married her husband. They moved north, and Phyllis got another job writing articles about municipal funding with a federal agency; these articles were published in the newspapers weekly. Her blooming career was short-lived. She had her children in quick succession and did not return to work.

Phyllis was painfully confronted by her perfectionism after the birth of her first child. Her son had physical problems, which caused Phyllis to seek counseling. She was helped in her relationship with her son; she accepted his imperfections, but she was unable to judge herself less harshly. Perfectionism still held the reins of her creative expression. As a result, her mothering was not experienced as creative; her political activism during the sixties and seventies was not creative; her work on the PTA was not creative; her teaching was not creative; not even her brief but successful stint as a writer for the federal government was creative. I cannot help but wonder, if Phyllis had fully accepted her choices—to be a mother, to be politically involved, to be a teacher—how thoroughly creative she might have been in any one of these areas.

Phyllis's frustrations and anger grew. She felt restrained. She states that it "never occurred to me to work outside my home. It wasn't done then." Phyllis grew large from overeating. "I kept eating when the children were young. I had a very unsatisfactory life. I did not find being a mother and housekeeper creative. I should have been a businesswoman. I should have had help in the house." When her children were grown she decided to go back to school for a master's degree in secondary education. She taught at a business school for fifteen years until a physical ailment forced her to retire. She loved her teaching and thought she was a good teacher. She explains, "I did not just teach my students about business, I taught them about life."

Phyllis has managed, late in life, to give herself to her early passion. In retirement Phyllis has been studying art and has been taking acting classes. Her abilities now are acknowledged by her classmates, as well as her teacher, and now she can hear that and accept it. Phyllis believes too that she is good at what she does and loves her involvement with the arts. Also in retirement, Phyllis and her husband travel when they can and take classes at Elderhostels, a continuing education program for senior citizens at various universities around the world. Phyllis's transition from living an unsatisfied life and eating herself into sickness to feeling content has its own creative framework and risk-taking process. It began when she returned to school, when she responded to her essential creative nature and her desire to express herself. That step made it possible for her to pursue her passion in retirement. She could have chosen to live the last part of her life in pain, disgruntled and angry. Instead, she has been actively reinventing herself. It is an exciting prospect at any point in one's life.

Phyllis's early story demonstrates what happens to bright, talented, creative women who do not know how to channel their creativity, and who cannot value the choices they do make. An article in *Gifted Child Quarterly* presents an overview of studies conducted on women in the 1970s. Those studies revealed that of two groups—gifted single women and gifted married women with children and with no career—the gifted married women with children and with no career scored lowest on self-esteem and sense of personal competence, including child-care and social skills. A study conducted in the early 1990s, also published in *Gifted Child Quarterly*, found that gifted women still suffer from depression, low self-esteem, and underachievement. Mentors for young women could help ease their path, regardless of their choices, whether they have children and a career, or no children and no marriage. I will examine these and other issues related to gender, role, and creativity in a later chapter.

## CREATIVITY AS TRANSFORMATION

The four women we have met thus far illustrate how creative behavior exerts enormous pressure upon one's life. To maintain or engage creative behavior, a woman must be able to overcome fear, keep perfectionism in check, and take time for self-reflection and rejuvenation. This entails plunging into the unknown and allowing change to occur. That effort may produce a new career, a new approach to a discipline, or the impetus for a new specialized book. When researchers speak of the qualities inherent in "creativity," they almost always speak of it in relationship to a need that must be addressed or a problem that must be solved. The last two women understand creativity as transformation and/or as making something new. The awareness that a problem needs to be handled differently reflects the motivation behind transformations.

Mary's life is alight with possibilities. Painting has always been part of her life, but now Mary feels the need to explore other avenues for her creative expression. Her children have helped to bring about this transformation. Mary is a thirty-nine-year-old white woman, married with two children. She was raised in a lower-middle-class family; her mother managed the household, and her father worked as a washing-machine mechanic. Mary received a great deal of love from her mother. The love given to her by her father was compromised by his aggressive physical contact with her, which included kissing. Throughout her life, Mary felt this aspect of their relationship was inappropriate. She did not categorize it as incest, but she felt it had an unhealthy impact upon her. Mary is one of three sisters. Her relationship with her sisters varied greatly. The closeness she felt with her younger sister did not protect her from the sting of jealousy she felt from her older sister. Mary chose the path of least resistance, as many women do. She worked hard to be the "good girl." Despite her diligent efforts to avoid trouble with her parents and her older sister, she failed to please them. While desperately trying to please others, Mary lost part of herself. This family dissonance carried over into a verbally abusive marriage. Her fragile ego could not withstand the verbal assault. She sank into a deep depression. Therapy and medication are now helping to alter this. Mary is learning what it means to own her voice. She is beginning to express herself and her needs in her significant relationships. She told me that her husband has also been taking medication, which has been "life-altering." For Mary, the medication has lifted the bottom of her depression. Her marriage has greatly improved, and the abuse has stopped. Socially she is a charming, warm, approachable woman.

Mary's inability to articulate her physical and emotional needs found an outlet in painting. However, this manifestation of creative behavior did not just burst forth upon the scene. It needed to be stimulated and supported. Research shows that being born talented is not an indicator of future creative behavior. Talent must be stimulated, cultivated, and shaped through training and practice, and finally, it must be used. Mary is a landscape painter. She has a passion for nature, beauty, and music. These passions were sparked by her mother. In some capacity, Mary's mother provided a stimulating environment and helped lay the groundwork for Mary's passion, making art.

Underlying Mary's drive is her guiding force. "It is funny, because there are two things I think of, and they are antithetical. One is to be able to get away, to escape, and the other is to merge with something. The first one is getting away from my father, from my parents. The second one is merging with the forms of nature and visual reality. There is a conflict between wanting to merge with my parents or another human being, as in going back to the womb, and the opposite, moving freely through life without being smothered."

Both these images, merging with and escaping from, are inherent in the idea of transformation. The underlying psychological motivation for merging varies from person to person, from experience to experience. In Mary's case, her ability to merge is expressed in a healthy, self-affirming action—her painting. Mary's creativity, expressed through her "making art," has its roots in her early survival needs. Mary has always honored this form of personal creative expression. She welcomed it into her life as a child and has developed as a professional artist. Her definition of creativity is simple and traditional. The thought that first comes to mind, she says, "is to make something from nothing. It is not exactly nothing. It is making something from randomness. I guess I really never defined creativity for myself. Creativity is making something out of possibilities." Despite the crucial role painting has held in her life, despite the awards and the grants she has received for her work, Mary does not identify her art as a demonstrative example of her personal creativity. She says, "Sometimes I feel about my painting or drawing that people think of it as a creative thing. I do not think of it like that. For me, it is almost unconscious. It is so separate from what I do." A different understanding of personal creativity has begun to emerge for her. Now she feels she is more creative with her children and her friendships. She believes her sense of humor is a creative expression as well. She says, "In some ways these more conscious activities demand more creativity, because I have my 'schtick' down with my painting. When you are resolving a problem with your children, or making some game up, it is very active. You have to really be there and make something new from nothing."

Personal transformation may lead a woman to approach a range of creative and expressive behavior she dared not consider before. This type of transformation does not usually occur with one big action. The transformation may be the culmination of little steps, small risks, with life-altering changes. There may be times of great emotional and financial upheaval. Approaching life through a vision of transformation characterizes Hazel's path. She views change as an opportunity to regroup her energies, reevaluate her life, and gain strength in the process.

Hazel came to this country from the Philippines in the late 1970s. She is forty-seven years old. The hardships she has endured have forced her to use her innate creativity to survive. She has learned a way to integrate the joys and opportunities for growth that she has been given. She was raised in the mountains of Nueva Vizcaya province. Her family was considered financially well off and well-educated. Both her mother and father owned and operated a store. Her mother has a college degree in elementary education, and her father has a degree in business. During World War II, Hazel's father was a prisoner of war in a Japanese prison camp. He was one of one hundred thousand to be taken on the famous Bataan Death March through the mountains. Her father, who is physically small, never completely recovered from the ordeal, either emotionally or physically. It was a grueling march in bad weather, with little to wear and almost nothing to eat. The majority of those forced into the march did not survive. In her father's case, negotiating his ordeal and surviving reflect a monumental act of creativity. It cannot be placed within the same category as creating artwork. Such acts of survival must be acknowledged as significant and creative because he is alive today.

Hazel is like her father, physically small, with a deep inner drive to survive. She says, "Sometimes I think I create situations just to overcome them." While this tendency may have gotten

Hazel into difficult situations, it has also been the key to her ability to move forward in her life. This concept was cemented in her psyche at a young age. While some of the need to overcome can be attributed to her father's experience, her own childhood experiences helped perpetuate this guiding image. Life in Hazel's family was at times tense and confusing. She is one of five sisters and brothers. Hazel's mother almost died in childbirth. When Hazel was two years old, she was sent away to live with her aunt; she was told it was because her aunt had no children. Throughout her early years and her teen years, she shifted between her mother's house and her aunt's house. She refers to her aunt as "her second mother." Hazel characterized her aunt as a well-educated, well-spoken, well-read woman. Her aunt was strong-minded and imparted to Hazel the importance of doing her best, and the responsibility of making something of her life. Her aunt never hesitated to tell Hazel of her expectations. She wanted Hazel to become something special.

Transformations occur when a woman respects the impulses deep within her. They emanate from a place through which creativity flows. Hazel believes that "you change with change. You can reinvent yourself." She defines creativity in that way. Like Alexandra and Rose, Hazel's ability to respond to and productively use change in her life illustrates her personal style of creativity. She sees her life as creative because of her ability to survive. "I come from another culture and to be able to interweave yourself into the mainstream of another culture, to be able to find your own niche in another culture, you have to be creative." She adds, "I would like to see myself doing more things that are not totally connected with making money. I always wanted to write and paint. I have always done well with flower arrangements." Hazel sees parenting as a profound creative act; she told me that her biggest success has been in becoming a mother. She reflects on that comment, adding, "I am a good parent, and my relationship with my son is the most precious thing in my life." She gains strength and inspiration from her son's free-flowing energy. She learns from watching his youthful spontaneity. Her own desire for creative behavior is stimulated by their relationship.

Not unlike Phyllis's desire to be a performer, Hazel had aspirations to be a painter. Everyone told her she was creative. "My teachers, my mother. I could draw. In college, I wanted to major in fine arts, but I was stopped. My mother said I could not support myself as a painter. She told me to do it as a hobby." Sadly, the realities of Hazel's life leave her with little time to paint or do flower arrangement. Working to support herself and her son has left her with little spare time or energy. Unlike Phyllis, who was frustrated by her unused creative energies, Hazel sees herself as using them to parent. But Hazel had to learn to commit herself to her creativity. She learned to commit herself after her son was born and emotional paralysis threatened to consume her life. Her struggle to gain control of her life reflects the power of transformation and the release of creative energy.

Transformation is moving from one reality to another. Some women have described the transformative experience as spiritual. They felt they occupied a spiritual place or a spiritual stance in the process. The creativity that occurs during this transformative phase enables a woman to understand, see, and imagine herself and the world differently than she did before. The most commonly described feeling of this spiritual place was that of being a vessel. In its essence, and to use Mary's words, it is the act of merging with something outside yourself. Part of merging requires the suspension of self for a period of time. For Mary, merging allows her vision to be expressed in the act of painting. Her vision then becomes real in the world. For Hazel, it allows her to negotiate difficult times and respond to ideas for new business concepts.

The idea of merging as a process to create something is echoed in Mary's description of her working process. "When I am painting or drawing, I am completely alone. My mind is empty of things in my life. It is almost like a trance. My work is representational. When I work from nature it feels as if what I am looking at enters me. I am a vehicle for whatever I am looking to express. The spirit or nature of the thing comes through me and out my hands. If I am sitting in a field and painting trees, there is the feeling of merging with them. Sometimes I feel their spirit is expressed in their gesture. Trees are connected to the earth; you can read their history in their form. How they dealt with the forces of nature, with being blown. That comes through me, and I do the portrait of them."

Mary was formally trained as a painter and now works exclusively as a landscape artist. She uses the time her children are in school to paint. She is one of many talented women artists who have been publicly acknowledged for their work, who juggle "doing" their art and attending to their family obligations and commitments. Mary is not unhappy with her choice. Her understanding of creativity has shifted; it is becoming more private and less public. Does that diminish her creativity? I think not. The changes in Mary's personal life have been monumental, even if they occur in the private sphere. Her relationship with her children, her sense of humor, her relationship with her friends are all, as Mary sees it, creative expressions of herself. They are vital, inventive, engaging, self-affirming, and always in process. The significance Mary now places on these other facets of her life represents a broadening of her creative expression. For the first time, she explains, "I am starting to become more creative and adventurous about decorating. One of the wonderful things about getting older is accepting myself. My need to get away was reflected in my environment. I did nothing with my environment because I didn't want to feel I had to stay there. Now with my children, especially lately, I have been doing things in the house and I think I could be good at decorating." Underlying this attitude has been her ability to confront those issues that have plagued her throughout her life. She has taken the creative energy used in repressing her inner voice and has found the courage to release it. Her depression demonstrates how powerful repression of self can be. Her feelings about creativity are explained by the sensation of light and joy she now feels. These feelings are the result of a personal creative transformation. It is a new form of personal expression, one that looks and feels different than her artwork. The excitement of living her life more openly and freely, of valuing herself and her place, has expanded her vision of creativity and broadened and deepened her experience of it. Such creative experiences cannot be judged publicly through status or financial success.

The more a woman works to understand and express her creativity, the deeper her connection to her essential creative nature becomes. Hazel values her abilities and respects her creative impulses. She was working in the Philippines as an urban planner, but she saw an opportunity to come to the United States and start an import basket business. It was a big risk: a new country, a new culture, a business she had never done before. Hazel is not easily daunted, especially when her instincts tell her something is worthwhile. That is a common quality among "creative" people. They believe in what they are doing and are not easily dissuaded by momentary setbacks or other people's opinions. Her vision was difficult to translate into a reality here. But even when her new business began to fail, she respected her instincts and her vision. She flew back to the Philippines and convinced her brother to quit his job and run the business. It is now a successful international business. Hazel works as a consultant for the business, conferring with her brother on product designs.

While Hazel struggled to save her business here, she gave birth to a son out of wedlock. The father abdicated responsibility for the child completely. Hazel was overcome by depression. It was an emotional and physical struggle to stay at home, take care of her child, and make the basket business work. Trying to negotiate a number of traumatic experiences at one time debilitated Hazel for a number of years. Whenever she could she slept—that was her way of coping. She went on welfare and moved in with one of her business partners. She could no longer support herself or her son. Her relationship with her business partner was fraught with hostility, anger, and resentment, but there she stayed until her son was old enough to go to nursery school. Hazel then became active on the school board and thus began her path out of depression and toward her essential creative nature.

Hazel understood her special ability to speak to people and to sell a product. She found a job with a major bank as a product representative. After several years at the bank, she moved into the government sector and worked in community preservation and then in energy conservation. She also moved into her own apartment. Several years later, funding for her job was phased out, and she was left unemployed. She decided to gamble and start her own business as an energy conservation consultant. Hazel indicated that she always liked being in charge of her own business. Financial circumstances demanded that she take the father of her child to court after eleven years of no communication. That action began a second transformation. It forced her to address years of buried anger and resentment. It was hostile. Hazel explains, "When I was in court, I wrote a poem about turning around my pain, about where I have been and where I am now." Writing the poem released the negative energy she had carried inside her all these years. Acceptance made it possible to channel this energy productively into her present life. Hazel has begun dating since writing that poem and has gone into therapy to face other personal problems. The power of a creative act in response to crisis can be a lifeline. It can be, as it was for Hazel, a doorway to a brighter, more fulfilling future.

Hazel is goal-oriented, directed, and principled. She is dedicated to ethical business practices. Her business inclinations are rooted in a sense of responsibility to the larger group. Her desire to bring work to the peasants in the mountains helped shape her basket business. She writes in her questionnaire that if she had it all to do over, she would enter a profession "that would service third-world countries, the underprivileged (specifically women and children), because there is so much poverty in the third world and the bigger, advanced nations take advantage of them." As her business has grown, Hazel has taken a risk and is acting as the general contractor and is overseeing the jobs herself. To get bigger jobs she needed to be bonded. She had not been in business long enough to meet all the time and financial requirements. Trusting in her ability to communicate, she applied and got the necessary bonding anyway. She is currently the only woman in her industry in her city doing this kind of consulting. Hazel writes that one of her goals has been to be the first woman at something. In Hazel's life, transformations were the result of making new emotional and intellectual connections to meet urgent needs. These are manifested in building new businesses, creating new designs for the basket business, making ethics an integral part of doing business, and parenting.

The ability to "change with change," as Hazel describes it, comes from a creative stance, and it manifests itself in basic fundamental ways. How a woman describes it, whether as a personal expression, risk-taking, or transformation, is of no significance. The thread that joins these three sets of women is their ability to utilize their creativity to change their lives. The commonality for all of these women is a learned ability to accept their gifts, respond to their impulses, and make new connections. Astarte reveals to women that which is possible in the ever-changing structure of their lives. A woman can generate enormous creative powers by responding to her essential creative nature. The women you have met thus far are vital and productive. In their process toward owning their essential creative natures, they demonstrate the power of the Goddess within: the power of generating life as a context for creativity.

## DEFINING CREATIVITY FOR YOURSELF

All you need for this exercise is paper, pen, and time for reflection. Sitting in a secure quiet place, where you will not be interrupted, ask yourself, "How do I define creativity? What are the criteria I apply when I say someone or something is creative?" Your answer can be a few sentences or a series of phrases that reflect your thoughts. Make sure you allow your mind to go wherever it wishes. This is *your* definition. If you have taken word association as your path, is there something common in the words you have written down? Are they action words? Do they reflect a certain kind of behavior or thinking? Try then to place that idea into a sentence about creativity. Now ask yourself what in your life has been your motivating force, your guiding principle. Perhaps it has held negative connotations for you and has caused you to struggle emotionally. Whatever it is, identifying it is significant. How does your guiding force fit into your definition of creativity? Are they compatible or are they at odds?

Last, and most important, make a list of all your positive attributes. Then add to the list all that you think you do well. Do you define these activities as creative? What do other people say about you and your behavior? If you have been told by others that you are creative, in what context has it come up? Write only key words like "problem-solving," "cooking," "arts and crafts," "mothering," etc. Look at your two lists. Do they reflect the same qualities?

To help think of things you do well and identify anything creative about yourself, ask someone who is *supportive and positive* about you. Write down their responses and compare them to your own. Are you limiting yourself, diminishing yourself? You will use this information in a later exercise. If you have done this properly, you have taken an honest inventory of your attributes and gifts.

## CHAPTER TWO

# THE VISUAL REALM:
## CREATIVE PERSONALITIES AND WOMEN ARTISTS

The Mother Goddesses Tohu Bohu, Themis, and Tiamat, all of the Middle East, were possessed with powers of creation and destruction. They could create, destroy, and re-create the elements to fit their image. The term used to describe the imposition of order that they placed upon the elements was *diakosmos*.

> The Mother Goddess imposed order "on the elements in Primal Chaos, to bring about the creation of the world. . . . The philosophers' idea was that the Goddess created manifest forms for her own adornment, giving rise to all the material world. . . . Her true spirit moved within and behind these things, unseen. Through the life of the universe she constantly arranged and rearranged the outward manifestations of her 'order' to make infinite numbers of different living forms. At doomsday she destroyed them all, to begin over with the next creation." *(The Women's Encyclopedia of Myths and Secrets)*

It is an unrelenting reality, brutal in its insistence: order must be formed out of chaos, and chaos must be created to find order. The universe exists and is understood through these ever-changing states—chaos and order. Shifting states bring about change and challenge; they bring about a redefinition of form and context. The Goddess seeks meaning through *diakosmos*. In the destruction and reordering of things a deeper meaning is revealed. Her search and her expression are essential to her nature; neither can be stopped. Through the flow of change and re-creation, the Goddess seeks to secure her vision. Destruction and creation, ongoing and constant, color her reality daily. The manifestation of the flow is present in physical qualities she brings to the world. It is within this visual realm that her inner vision is birthed. Does she seek beauty? Does she seek to right that which is wrong through the visual realm? The impetus for the destruction and for self-expression can be understood in this context. Self-expression drives the Goddess forward, thrusting her time and again into chaos, to be rescued by a momentarily created order.

Women who are compelled to give visual form to their inner vision can understand that need through the concept of *diakosmos*. But the Goddess, compelled by *diakosmos*, also offers all women a context to understand the drive behind their own creative nature. Women are driven by their essential creative natures. They must give homage to that inner calling. Women artists see and understand the world and its truths through the visual realm. Form, texture, color, and physical relationships shape their experience. To understand their passion it helps to examine the qualities that help or hinder their ability to express their creativity.

Researchers have tried over the years to pinpoint qualities or "personality traits" of creative people—that is, traditionally speaking, people who function in the public sphere. The traits attributed to these people, in and of themselves, are not unique to this group. However, certain combinations of traits do seem to be present in people who are public about their creativity. It is simplistic to believe that one can understand creativity by identifying and listing personality traits of "creative people." In *Growing Up Creative*, Teresa M. Amabile writes, "Creativity does not describe a person; it describes ideas, behaviors, and products that are appropriately novel. Any normal human being is capable of producing creative work in some area, at some time." Adults who produce through creative behavior are dedicated and disciplined in their endeavors. They take risks, tolerate unclear situations, and possess the power of perseverance. They maintain an appropriate attitude of nonconformity to society's stereotypes. They are self-motivated and have the ability to wait for rewards. Amabile makes a distinction between appropriately novel behavior that is creative and anti-social behavior which may be different but is not creative.

Silvano Arieti, in *Creativity: The Magic Synthesis*, writes that many characteristics attributed to creative behavior can be detrimental to creativity "if not accompanied by other traits. For instance, intelligence . . . may actually handicap creativity if not accompanied by originality and if used for a too-strict self criticism. . . . [O]n the other hand originality may lead us astray if not corrected by self-criticism. . . . Divergent thinking may even bring us to psychosis, if it is not matched by logical processes. . . . Rather than a single trait, then, it is a special combination of several traits—in a special family environment, in some socio-historical situations, occurring at a given time and place—that produces the synthesis we call creativity." This last statement provides you with both the problem of understanding and defining creativity as well as a context for the differences in how and why people create.

Creative behavior is the need to produce something new in the world. It is always grounded in a personal response to the world. A woman's presentation of self is predicated upon many influences. Early childhood experiences, primary relationships, and exposure to a variety of stimuli help shape her particular perspective and approach to life. Fortunately for us as women, if these responses are negative and inhibiting, they can be altered and their impact diminished with an honest and thorough effort. A woman's approach to life can be broadened, opening her path to her creative spirit and her essential creative nature.

Creative behavior thrives when a woman possesses a passion for her creative form of expression. She must also derive pleasure from engaging the creative process. She must be curious, possess a willingness to learn in depth that which she needs to express and the method by which her inner vision can be expressed. These traits and the ability to express one's passion are not formed within a woman at birth. She must learn them. The knowledge needed can be learned in a formal classroom setting or it can be self-taught. A woman's inner vision can be clarified, and the skills required to express that vision acquired, through teachers, friends, role models, mentors, and life experiences.

Risk-taking includes a tolerance for uncertainty, a willingness to move through chaos, and the search for a new order. Facing disappointment, frustration, and the feelings associated with those painful experiences are also bound to risk-taking. In the image of the Goddess, the woman who displays creative behavior embraces the challenge to create anew. Undaunted by the challenge before her, she reworks her ideas or even the context of her creative expression. Her strong inner sense and her vision push her through risk-taking and its results. The emotional stakes in creative behavior are high.

Commitment, availability of materials, production of product, and finally the sharing of the product—these separate one woman and her creative capacities from another. Negative traits that hinder creativity and stop the impulse to produce a creative product further separate women and delineate their creative capacities. Are you someone who has great ideas but cannot begin them? Are you someone who can begin a project with great enthusiasm and gusto but cannot finish it? Do you struggle against reworking or rebirthing the project to improve it? Do you settle for something less because of resistance to the process and then, feeling disappointed, choose not to share it? Are you a woman who produces something and cannot share it with the world no matter what the quality may be?

In a 1973 issue of *Perceptual and Motor Skills*, Louise Bachtold and Emmy Werner wrote of a study that examined the differences between women artists, writers, and women in the general population. They found that while women artists and writers were "more assertive, self-assured and independent minded, they were also more easily emotional, changeable, lower in frustration level for unsatisfactory conditions, and may have a tendency to evade necessary reality demands. . . . [They were also] more wrapped up in inner urgencies." In *The nature of Creativity: Contemporary psychological perspectives*, E. P. Torrance, who has studied creativity and creative children for many years, writes, "[S]ince I reached the conclusion that the essence of the creative person is being in love with what one is doing, I have had a growing awareness that this characteristic makes possible all the other personality characteristics of the creative person. . . . To maintain an intense love for something and survive . . . [the] pressures, one has to develop courage, independence, perseverance and the like."

Because the creative process can be long and arduous, traits like perseverance, patience, and tolerance for the unknown are necessary. Time, thought, and feeling also contribute to the creation of something long before it reaches a clearly articulated stage. In their article "Inching our way up Mount Olympus," Howard E. Gruber and Sara N. Davis write, "[T]he creative person must . . . have some approach to managing the work so that . . . inconclusive moves become fruitful and enriching, and . . . a sense of direction is maintained. Without such a sense of direction, the would-be creator may produce a number of fine strokes, but they will not accumulate toward a great work."

The women you are about to meet work only in the visual arts. Their stories reflect personality traits that both help and hinder their ability to pursue their essential creative natures. As you read about these women's creative abilities, life perspectives, feelings about making art, and responses to events in their lives, keep in mind the personality traits discussed thus far. If their struggles appear familiar, it is because we all wrestle with the same issues at some point in our lives. Artists are not exempt from the struggle for self-expression and self-worth. The six women chosen for this chapter range in age from their thirties to their eighties. They are representative of all the artists interviewed for this book. The diversity of their life experiences does not diminish their need to express themselves through the arts. The criteria for determining those classified as "women artists" are training, dedication to expressing their vision through the arts, and identification of that expression as professional versus an avocation. You will meet women elsewhere in this book who work privately in the arts but by their own determination do not consider themselves "artists."

Almost half the women interviewed for this book worked within the arts (including music, theater, writing, editing, dance, and the fine arts). These women can be placed into three groups, which break down not by definition, as was the case in the last chapter, but rather by emotional state, the ability to produce art in the world, and the ability to share it publicly. I found these delineations most intriguing. Despite being professionally trained and in several cases publicly acknowledged, several of the women artists had difficulty accepting their talent, pursuing their passion by producing a tangible product in the world. The intensity of their struggle was directly related to a combination of personality traits described earlier. Negative perceptions shared by all three groups of women artists were a sense of isolation, feelings of not being heard and valued, rejection, and feeling different as a child. These feelings may be the key to their drive for personal expression. In each case, these feelings were the impetus for the women to "make art." You learned, in the previous chapter, that as a means of controlling her environment, both physically and emotionally, a woman makes life choices and career choices that inform her definition of creativity. She either acts upon her essential creative nature or she rejects it. There is nothing in between. Prominent in all three groups of women artists was the lack of "voice" and an inability to escape their physical reality. Even those women whose childhood homes could be considered "normal" possessed a sense of separateness, a longing to be heard, and the desire to be different. These women created an acceptable environment for themselves early in their lives through the arts.

The first two women artists are in their thirties. They are the most emotionally troubled and the most tentative of the three sets of women profiled in this chapter. They hesitate to accept their creative ability and pursue their passion. When a woman engages in such psychological struggles, work becomes difficult to confront. These first two women artists also appear to be the most privileged. They maintain studios outside of their homes without regularly producing anything or frequenting their studios. They do not share their work in any public context. The second two women are in their fifties. These women were and are actively part of the feminist movement, especially as it related to the art world. They are semi-productive in making their art and struggle to regularly share their work in public. They are not as tentative as the first two, and are engaged to some extent with a community of artists. Their main problem revolves around the business of assertively selling and showing their art. The last two women you will meet are the most prolific and the most public. They are the oldest, in their late seventies and eighties. Their ability to produce has been consistent throughout their lives. They possess a clarity about their talent, their work, and their vision and a simplicity through which they approach their lives.

## COMPELLED TO GIVE FORM

Clarity about her talent, her vision, and her worth seem to elude Cathy. She is a thirty-nine-year-old woman. She grew up in a cross-cultural environment, born to an American father and a French mother. She was raised in the suburbs of a large northeastern city. Cathy believes that several members of her family express creative behavior. Her father worked in television as an art director while her mother managed the home. Both her grandfathers were considered creative by family and friends. One made significant contributions in the treatment of eye ailments, and the other was a farmer/inventor. He invented mechanical machines for the farm, though he never had them patented. Her grandmothers were at ease in their social setting. They physically manifested a concern for an aesthetic in their attire as well as their home decor. Cathy also considers her mother's aesthetic sense strong and its expression creative. People concerned with aesthetic values have always touched Cathy's life. Indeed, a strong bold aesthetic has become of great significance for her. She believes that creativity and aesthetics are inseparable. She tries her best to express this learned aesthetic sensitivity in her attire, her children's attire, and, like her grandmothers, the decor of her home. Cathy's husband also sees the world through a keenly developed visual aesthetic. He is a dealer in black-and-white photography.

Her childhood home was lively, energized, and influenced by people who were exciting. But she also describes a home that was steeped in strong Methodist underpinnings. Her father, while loving, was extremely strict. Cathy felt unable to express her thoughts or to oppose him. Her teenage years were characterized by submission. Her inability to find power and validation in her words and thoughts resulted in deep-seated tentativeness and distrust of herself. By necessity, Cathy followed her brother's lead to respond to the world. But she did not integrate his response patterns as her own. Needing her father's approval and relying upon her brother to negotiate the world, Cathy slowed her exploration of herself and undermined her ability to trust herself and her voice.

Art became an outlet in this personally uncomfortable atmosphere. She liked to make art; it was her means of coping with the stress. She described a young girl who moved through adolescence as a recluse, doing her artwork. In adulthood, Cathy still struggles to negotiate her world, to express her thoughts and overcome her desire to be reclusive. Making decisions is difficult for her. Her timidity is in direct conflict with her image of herself as a woman artist who has a developed aesthetic sense and vision. Cathy chose sculpting large pieces as her art medium. Yet she does not make her sculptures because the process takes a lot out of her. There is no escaping the presence of a large sculpture, nor the fact that Cathy is unabashedly present in these large works. Sadly, if she "makes art," she makes small drawings or paintings. The artist side of Cathy needs and wants to make her art, but her resistance to her voice and her desire to hide push her away from her inner strength and vision. Because she does not often make her art, she is compelled to channel her creative aesthetic vision through the same forum used by her mother and her grandmothers. Unfortunately, that does not satisfy her.

The need for *diakosmos*, the Goddess's need to reorder the old, is seen in Cathy's behavior even though she denies herself the full expression of her essential creative nature. This situation, as you can imagine, is extremely painful for Cathy. Her comments about her need and desire to make her art reveal this painful, lonely reality. While Cathy represses fulfillment of her essential creative nature, the need and inner urge continue to control her. The inner anguish experienced by Cathy can be altered by attending to that which gives her life its personal perspective. Nothing further would be mentioned concerning the pain of not making her art, if Cathy felt content to express her creative vision through her attire and home decor. Instead a deep undercurrent of dissatisfaction pervades Cathy's life. I will address that in more detail momentarily.

In her conflicted state, insecure and isolated from herself, Cathy searches to define creativity. She seeks to relate her criteria of creativity to herself and the life she has made. She relies upon outside relationships. This pattern of using others to define oneself can be placed within the framework of "codependency." When a woman has little or no concept of herself and she is dependent upon others for framing who and what she is, that woman is always at risk emotionally. Cathy has difficulty speaking of herself. She has trouble articulating her thoughts and feelings. Her ideas tend to be connected to her father, her children, and her role as mother and wife. She struggles to accept her talent. She reluctantly offers this description of herself: "I am shy and reclusive. . . . It can be a great attribute, to be alone and to be reclusive, if you are an artist. You can go very far to create. In the situation I am in, being reclusive can be a defect. I am shy, but I am working on it. I tend to blow up easily and I have mood swings. I can get depressed." When I asked her to state her assets, Cathy was able to say only that she was "gentle and loyal. Too loyal." In one context, Cathy is right. Making art is a solitary activity. However, an artist's life must be filled with the experiences of the universe or she has nothing to draw upon for inspiration and impetus. Cathy's view of the artist as recluse is difficult to reconcile with the artist who is sensitive to the world around her and who has an urgency to express her vision. What shapes her vision if not the experiences and her responses to life? Cathy does, despite her hesitancy, possess a clear understanding of how she defines creativity. Haltingly, she says, "I do not know how I am going to define creativity. An openness? An ability to . . . God, this is hard. Creativity is an ability to translate . . . something from the interior to the outside. It is something you bring from yourself to the world, the outside. . . . It is a translation."

Her father believes Cathy has great talent as an artist. Her husband and her friends agree that her approach to life and her strong aesthetic sensitivity reflect the depth and breadth of her creative behavior. However, Cathy does not accept their perspective or experience of her. She is a prime example of a woman who maintains an image of self that conflicts with one held by those close to her. For Cathy, creativity means the expression of something personal, and while she does not believe that creative behavior is found only in the arts, she judges her creativity by the production of artwork. She explains, "I have not made art in so long it is hard to talk about creativity." She goes on to contradict herself by stating, "I think dealing with an aesthetic creatively is what I do. I'm always interested in making something beautiful, I think of it through everything. It has to be beautiful in my eyes; I don't think it has to be beautiful to the rest of the world." Cathy speaks of this ruling aesthetic sensitivity but does not value it as a real expression of her essential creative nature.

She vacillates. "I have questions about whether I really am creative. I go back and forth. Maybe it was my father's dream that I be an artist. Maybe it is not true. But everybody around me thinks that I am creative. A lot of time I think that I am not." In her youth, her father was a big supporter of her artwork and a believer that she possessed great talent. She leans upon her father as her guiding image. She states, "My father has been a guide, because he really believed that I was a great artist. He wanted me to pursue art. But I think it is something in me. I just have to do it." This self-doubting does not help to motivate Cathy to go to her studio. It does not help her to make her art or to translate that which is within her to the out-side. Resisting the emotional and physical commitment need-ed to produce a large sculpture extracts a greater price on Cathy's psyche than moving through her process and doing her work. Continually she fights her creative nature. Her actions defy the call of the Goddess within to make her art. She represses her inner vision and resists any move toward her creative expression. She leaves herself in a state of chaos, doubting her talent, her vision, and her ability to produce. Floundering in the chaos, the potential new order dies a slow death within her. Cathy's essential creative nature cries out for expression, but remains only untapped potential.

Cathy is not alone in her suffering from anxiety and ambivalence about making art. Lucy tries to negotiate the ambivalence in a more convoluted manner. She goes more reg-ularly to her studio but does not show her work. Time given to other aspects of her life trouble her deeply. Lucy has spent a good deal of her time shut off from her emotional life and shut off from the world. Both Cathy and Lucy know the powerful feelings contained within creative behavior and both know the commitment it requires. Both women know the rewards asso-ciated with producing and the pain involved in its avoidance. Why then does Lucy struggle at all to obtain authority over her creative nature while simultaneously fighting against it? What compels Lucy to want to make her art?

She was born and raised in a major metropolitan city in the heart of the South. She is a thirty-eight-year-old woman, the second oldest of four sisters. Her parents both hold grad-uate degrees. Her mother is a social worker, and her father is a lawyer. Lucy wrote in her questionnaire that her mother is a highly creative thinker. She characterizes her father as creative and honorable. Her grandfather, also a lawyer, loved poetry and limericks. She felt her imagination was stimulated by the people and places early in her life, especially her grandfather. Her grandmother, Lucy says, "was active and popular in the community, painted beautiful watercolors, embroidered, and later practiced bookbinding." Lucy felt honestly supported in her ambition to be an artist by her grandmother.

Outwardly, life for Lucy was not difficult. She came from an upper-middle-class family where money and possessions were not an issue. Something was missing, however. Lucy says her parents lavished love on her, but she grew up mistrusting their love and support. She felt smothered by their constant attention. She complains, "Mother was too there. If she had been a little more distant we would have had to fend for ourselves." Yet her desire to have had to struggle for something seems incongruous with the reality of her childhood as she described it. Her struggle, which began in her early teens, has centered around finding, accepting, and valuing her own voice.

Researchers tell us that an *excessive* amount of unwarranted and unjustified praise can have the same impact upon a child as criticism. It can diminish their creative impulses and sense of value. Beth A. Hennessey and Teresa M. Amabile, in their article "The conditions of creativity," address the issues relating to intrinsic motivation and the effect of rewards upon children and creative behavior. Rewards and/or the promise of future rewards can have a detrimental impact upon children and act as a constraint.

Despite Lucy's "easygoing" childhood, she states, "I was raised in such a way that I did not take myself seriously. I feel like I was not encouraged to do something that could be a serious endeavor." Life became more difficult for Lucy as a teenager. She felt inadequate and different as though she did not look right. To add to her inner turmoil, Lucy found herself ostracized for being Jewish. Her manner of coping with her anxiety and dealing with these difficult feelings was to "bury them." She would repeat this coping mechanism some years later when she was raped in college. The reasons for creative expression were planted early in Lucy's life. The need to order the chaos around her was evident.

Lucy's desire has always been to be an artist. At an early age, she was given encouragement and praise about her drawing, primarily by her grandmother. "I love making art. I think that I always felt that I had something of my own to contribute to the arts," she further explains. Fundamental to creative behavior is the belief that you have something to say. Lucy believes that creative behavior is self-expression. "Creativity is bringing to an experience a way of thinking that is your own. It does not rely on other people or the perceptions of other people. It is letting your own perceptions come through. It is how you use them." She has spent most of her life making her art and considers herself creative. She describes herself as having "an unusual vision. I try to make things that other people have not made. I look inside myself and let my own natural way of making an object guide me." Lucy does not feel free to make her art, nor has she felt able to share her art with the world in many years.

Lucy and Cathy deeply felt their inner vision and their desire to express that vision through the arts at an early age. It is not surprising that they both decided to pursue formal training as artists. Cathy told me how important art school was to her. It was a goal she sought to fulfill, and indeed she was trained as an artist at a prestigious art school. Upon graduating, Cathy moved to a large city. There she briefly made her art. Unable to support herself through her art, she took a job as a receptionist for a television production house. Her aesthetic sense was utilized when she became a clothes stylist for commercials. Cathy has worked as a free-lance stylist for ten years.

During the past ten years she has not actively made her art. With her creative expression repressed, Cathy has fallen into the jaws of depression. Her doubting comments affirm her concern that she is merely a creation of her father's fantasy.

She maintains her studio but infrequently goes there. The strong feelings that making art elicits from Cathy are too painful. Research indicates that creative behavior is conditioned upon a tolerance for strong emotions and uncertainty. It is so because those are the conditions of the creative process. In her present state, Cathy's passion will remain the source of great pain and depression for her. Despite her inability to approach making her art, she declares that self-expression is channeled through her art. "But," she adds, "it is not convenient. I would like to go back to making art. I feel I really need it. I would like to make a children's book. Those are my real passions." Her conflict must be resolved to release her essential creative nature.

People are successful in their creative expression because they actively pursue that expression. It is as simple as that. They do not wallow in self-doubt. In "Creatively Counseling the Unemployed, Undercreative and under the weather," Michael F. Shaughnessy describes behavioral qualities that inhibit creative behavior. Problems with motivation, impulse control, perseverance, misusing abilities, translating thought into action, completing tasks, failure to initiate, fear of failure, procrastination, excessive self-pity, excessive dependency, wallowing in personal difficulties, and distractibility all contribute to hindering a gifted and talented person from performing well.

From her comments, you can sense that social and familial commitments are a burden for Cathy. She believes her obligations take time from making her art. Cathy senses herself being pulled. This experience is shared by other women. Time constraints and familial pressures exact their toll on women artists whose discipline requires time, quiet, isolation, and strong self-motivation. These pressures can hinder a woman's commitment to her own work. Livia Pohlman writes in her study "Creativity, Gender and the Family: A Study of Creative Writers" that ". . . [W]omen confronted a peculiar dilemma. Their identities were often divided three ways—as a wife, a mother, and a writer—with their sense of self as a writer being in conflict with the gender expectations of being a good wife and mother. . . ." But Cathy never aggressively pursued her passion. Passion has not been enough to move her into her studio. It has not motivated her to confront her creative process or her fears about her artistic abilities. She admits that her depression is directly related to the amount of time spent away from her studio. She confesses, "I need to do my art in order not to be depressed."

Lucy, like Cathy, honored her commitment to her art when she chose formal training, first receiving a B.S. and then an M.F.A. in art. After completing her master's degree, Lucy moved to a large metropolitan city. She found work in an art gallery, a photo gallery, and a sculpture gallery part-time. She remained in these jobs for three years while making her art. But it took Lucy several years to settle her living situation. Finally she obtained a loft and rented out part of it. This enabled her to meagerly support herself, make her art, and quit her jobs. She sporadically accepted temporary part-time jobs offered by friends, but it was a lean existence. She characterizes her existence as "hand to mouth."

The shadowy side of Lucy's emotions began to manifest during these years. As Lucy described these years, I was struck by the deprivation and depression that colored this period of time. Was it a romantic image of a starving artist that drove her, or were those feelings of her youth and her rape motivating her alienation and deprivation? These bleak conditions did not serve Lucy or her art. She grew despondent about her work and about her abilities. She says, "I felt out of touch with the art world. I did not feel like I was a real conceptual person. For about five years, I suffered through this struggle with my work." One year she did manage to sell some of her work. Though she continued to work in her studio, she was unable to show her work. "I felt like throwing everything away," she recalls. The darkness of this time was self-imposed. But she managed to form a relationship with a man, her "first love relationship." When their friendship ended, she was unable to cope with the loss and drank herself to sleep every night. She was spiraling downward. The idea of the artist committed body and soul to her art, isolated in her studio, may sound wonderful to some, but the stark reality of that existence hurt Lucy. Not long after the disappointment of her failed love relationship, Lucy met her husband. In a short time they married, and three years later they had a child.

Her daughter and her husband present problems for Lucy. Early in her development as an artist, an ideal about making art emerged. She explains, "I try to make my art as pure as possible. I do not let myself be cluttered by day-to-day chores and pressures. I try to keep things easy so I can work with my creativity." Lucy, like Cathy, compartmentalizes her life. Sometimes clutter exists that can be removed. But living life on a daily basis means negotiating life on many levels. Are the daily experiences of life only clutter? Experiences for these two women are not understood in the context of a whole life. Cathy and Lucy are mistaken in their effort to isolate their art from their lives. Their error is proved by the fact that they have not been successful in their approach. Their essential creative natures have not been nourished by their perceptions.

While Lucy seems to have attempted to stay with the process of making her art more regularly than Cathy, both are plagued with questioning and insecurity. Their belief that they have something special to offer the world through their art is not given the attention that it demands. Unfortunately, both Cathy and Lucy are fond of a way of life that is reclusive and solitary. This approach and style of living neither feeds their creative spirits nor enables them to share their work in some public context. Their anguish is easily heard in conversation with them.

What were the sources of their resistance? Why do they not share their vision? Why would they continue on a path that was self-punishing? What stopped Cathy from going to her studio? What stopped her from doing her work? Cathy answers, "I think it is time and procrastination. I think it is a big deal to go to my studio and let it all out. It is a big process; it is very draining. In the life that I have, that a lot of people have, making art takes a big chunk out of you. It takes a lot of time. Other people's ideas stop me. I think, maybe my work will not be interesting." Managing her time can be worked out, especially since Cathy has a babysitter. But she gets closer to the problem when she declares that "fear of failure is a big issue for me. It has to be perfect in every way." Fear of failure stops her; perfectionism stops her; fear of rejection stops her. This combination induces her to abandon her process and to deny herself her personal expression. One can visualize the struggle she engages to physically move herself into her studio and make her art. Getting there, however, is only the first step. Once there, she must battle with perfectionism. Can anything reach a state of perfection? Is anyone best served by abandoning a project before some resolution has been reached? Should a project be destroyed, abandoned, or placed aside for a time? Should you avoid your creative expression entirely because you cannot reach perfection? Imperfect work still offers a woman the opportunity to learn and improve. Nothing is gained, lessons are not learned without expending the energy and time producing something. Even the worst work is more engaging than no work.

Cathy's strength ultimately lies in her making her art, in releasing her creative expression. Integrating her experiences as a mother, a social being, and a wife within the context of her art will free her art and feed her vision. The flavor of her life can shape her sculptures. Studies indicate that Cathy's depression will not lift until she takes responsibility for her life. In this case, responsibility for her life means doing that which she needs to do for herself: make art.

Like Cathy, Lucy sees facets of her life as intrusions. Unlike Cathy, Lucy regularly goes to her studio, though the level of her productivity is not clear. In fact, she went back to her studio to make her art four to six weeks after giving birth to her child. Though she is committed to her daughter, she expressed the importance of having her "own life." She believes she is a good mother but is concerned with spending too much time with her daughter. She says, "I do not want a clingy type of relationship with her. I want her to be independent." Lucy left her daughter to return to her studio because she felt she needed her own life back. She wanted her own identity and her own work. Since the mid-1980s, Lucy has shown her work only a few times. She acknowledges this as a problem. Because Lucy still does not take herself seriously, she struggles to produce her work and engage in a critical dialogue with others. Lucy has declared herself a professional artist. She must show her work.

The problems that hinder creativity, listed earlier, are present in Lucy's attitude and behavior. At times she seems overcome by "a life anxiety." There is anxiety and confusion about defining her role as a mother and wife. Her husband's expectations of a mother and a wife compound the problem. Her fear, self-doubt, and lack of self-worth have stopped Lucy from having a public career based upon her art. She has sought help to try to expose her feelings and clarify her roles. Being private is not to be confused with deliberately withholding yourself as a defense against the world, against your fears, against failed expectations. Such a defense leaves a woman unable to produce the quality or quantity of product that is within her. A woman avoiding her own voice becomes afraid of her voice and her vision. Lucy's vision must be shared, primarily because the withholding of it is too painful for Lucy. Donald W. MacKinnon wrote in "The Study of Creative Persons" that "self-image and ego-ideal are of crucial importance in determining the level of creativeness with which a person lives his life and practices his profession. . . ." Isolation imprisons Cathy and Lucy in their fears and cuts them off from themselves. In sharing who and what you are, risky as that may be, you grow and develop inner strength and feed the center of your creative spirit.

## RESPECTING THE CALL OF *DIAKOSMOS*

In contrast to Cathy and Lucy, the tenor of the struggles in Jossey's life have been different. Now in her fifties, Jossey, unlike our two younger artists, does not question her talent or her creative expression. She makes her art because she wants to. She believes making art is her primary creative expression and that the act of making art gives her joy. Jossey's struggle centers around allowing herself to benefit publicly from her art. She was born to a lower-middle-class family in the midwest. She is the oldest child and has one brother and two sisters. Her mother was a French teacher. Her father was educated but was "unfocused" and had no chosen profession. In response to her grandfather, who was a lawyer, her father was rebellious and declared himself to be a socialist. She described her father as very popular with the children in the neighborhood. Jossey's grandmother was a concert pianist until she married, when she stopped playing the piano, abandoning her creative expression. That choice left her grandmother nursing bitterness throughout her life. But Jossey also remembers her grandmother as child-like, as having a creative imagination. Her grandmother loved to "create stories about everything."

Jossey characterized her family situation as one of devastation. Her early years were filled with anxious times and negative influences. Jossey's grandfather died when Jossey's mother was five years old. Ironically, Jossey's father was killed in an automobile accident when Jossey was six years old. His death was to change the course of her life. It confirmed the family curse: men do not live long in her family. Jossey lost her sense of place, physically and emotionally, when her father died. Her mother moved the children to Florida to live with her grandmother and another female relative. Jossey was raised in a household of adult women who were trying desperately to cope with the "family curse." They decided that Jossey should attend an all-girls school. Jossey accepted early in her life that the curse promised to envelop her; there was no escape. When her grandmother died several years later, Jossey's loss was compounded by the added responsibility of caring for her brother and sisters. She told me she had to learn to deal with other people's responses to her "brother's retardation." As a child she used to daydream a good deal to cope with her outer reality, and so she floundered. It would be years before Jossey would be able to take herself seriously, see herself as worthy, and understand the profound controlling influence "the family curse" had upon her life.

Jossey describes herself as a creative person. She sees her creativity reflected not only in her art but in having an "inventive mind and having led an inventive life." For Jossey, playfulness and inventiveness are the "substrata of creativity." She believes that "creativity is keeping the route of access open. Creativity is having a willingness to accept what comes up." In her adult life, Jossey has had to learn how to live a creative life. Now in her middle years, she approaches her life with honesty, simplicity, and a kind of spirituality connected to that approach. Staying open to possibilities is critical for creative behavior of all kinds. Jossey sees creativity expressed in the life around her. She believes that "everyone has the possibility for inventiveness. But most people are not prepared to do the work to approach life from an open stance."

As with the Goddess's need for *diakosmos*, Jossey has been compelled to invent and reinvent her life. Circumstances have demanded that she reshape her life. In the process, she has taken these opportunities to learn about herself and her art. Jossey has found her strengths, her weaknesses, and the gifts she has to offer to the world. This knowledge has altered her guiding image, which was once based in the "family curse." Now her guiding image is grounded in love. Her love reaches out beyond the limits of her physical body. "I have always believed in love. It has been the center of my occupation. It has been the thing that has been a force. It has been the magnet that pulls me and holds me together." Love as a guiding force was shaped, in part, by watching her ex-husband battle unsuccessfully against cancer. She has one regret about her life, walking away from her marriage, from a good man. Because of the "family curse" Jossey feels she did not have children, and because of the "family curse" she feels that her ex-husband died of cancer at the age of thirty-six. The "curse" was so strong that even in "divorce he could not escape it" she says. During her ex-husband's six-month illness, and despite his relationship with another woman, Jossey helped to nurse him. She fought hard to keep him alive, knowing it was a losing battle. Jossey says battling death was monumental, sad, and painful. It became a life-transforming and life-informing experience for her.

She reaches out from that place of love to share herself as a teacher. In its ideal form, teaching is a loving, creative act, comprising two levels. First, sharing one's knowledge and understanding reveals a personal love for the subject. Second, a supportive interaction between student and teacher is an expression of respect for oneself and for the students. Other people have told Jossey that she is creative, especially as a teacher. Jossey adds, "I get experiences of feeling creative from students, particularly female students. I became shocked to realize that I am somewhat of a model and that's when I begin to sense that my creativity, as transmitted to someone else, may be real."

Jossey is not alone in her desire to share her love of art. A significant part of Ellen's adult life has centered around teaching art. Her understanding of herself and her art are positively challenged in the student/teacher exchange. That challenge is one that stimulates Ellen's mind and spirit and fuels her creative impulses. It helps place painting in a context of her whole life. She explains, "Relationships are important to me. Painting is, of course, but it is only a part. I think there are two issues: painting and people. Painting is a major part of my life, but I don't think everything about my life gets expressed in my paintings or drawings or prints. Product is product. Process is more interesting. It is all about paying attention, being, feeling, and responding to a situation. I am an excellent teacher. I like to teach because it keeps me thinking. It keeps me honest, and it's a big responsibility."

Ellen was born and raised in a lower-middle-class family in the northeast. Her parents both immigrated here from Russia. They brought with them the pain and hardship of their lives in Eastern Europe. Ellen's grandmother died during childbirth. This marked Ellen's mother for life. Ellen's paternal grandfather disappeared when Ellen's father was very young. Though her paternal grandmother remarried, her second husband was hardly ever around. The struggle to overcome a host of negative feelings and fears experienced by her parents, especially her mother, was inherited by Ellen at an early age. When Ellen was eight years old, her favorite aunt died, further clouding the atmosphere of her youth. Ellen wrote that her Aunt Mary showered her with a great deal of love. She deeply missed her aunt's lust for life and the freely given love. That same *joie de vivre* was never expressed by Ellen's mother. The balance between her mother's fear and her aunt's optimism was lost. Ellen's father died when she was in her early twenties. His place in her life was not as clearly articulated as her mother's.

Life at home was trying. Both Ellen's parents worked. Her father was a sheet-metal worker, and her mother was a secretary. Extreme differences existed in her parents' educational backgrounds: her father received a formal education through the first two years of college; her mother received only an elementary school education. Despite this difference, Ellen felt that her mother and father had a happy marriage. But the responsibilities placed upon Ellen to care for her brother and sister, as well as the negativity that hung over the household, made Ellen's youth painful. Her role, not unusual in families then or now, impinged on Ellen's ability to take care of herself first. Ellen did not learn as a child how to state her feelings and needs directly. She never felt entitled to express her needs. Making herself and her life a priority became problematic. Not being entitled has meant she has not rigorously pursued her career. Now in her fifties, Ellen is working through this problem, she is learning how to express herself directly and to go after what she needs.

Many young women possess a fragile sense of self during their teenage years. In the last chapter, you read how Mary, the painter and mother of two children, suffered the loss of self because of a jealous sister and a physically inappropriate father. Earlier in this chapter, you learned how Lucy's sense of self was diminished when she was not taken seriously at home, when she was ostracized at school for being Jewish, and when she was raped. Cathy's ability to express herself was thwarted by her father's strict and unbending manner and her need to constantly seek outside approval. Jossey became a prisoner in her own life, ruled by a "family curse." You can easily sense how these experiences might hinder a young girl's sense of herself and her courage to seek her inner urging for creative expression.

Like other teenage girls, Ellen was susceptible to the need to feel acceptance. Instead she felt alienation and rejection. One reason, she states, was her family's inability to afford new clothes. Ellen's mother bought the children clothes from the Salvation Army. Ellen writes, "I remember walking with my brother to school, and feeling ostracized when students found out my clothes were from the Salvation Army." Feeling as though she had less than others, inheriting her mother's unspecified life fears and anxieties, and taking care of her brother and sister collectively produced a fragile teenage ego. That is when making art became important to Ellen.

Connections remain a crucial element in defining Ellen's life and work, despite experiences early in her life. Ellen understands the value of connections in her life through images of work. Connections are the fundamental image for her guiding force. She says, "The first thing that comes to my mind is how I think about making work. It has to do with the issue of making connections. They are not always conscious connections. Sometimes you see something one place; then you see it some other place. Suddenly you see it all over. It becomes the impetus to think about something. Connections have to do with visions. For me, the whole issue of creativity has to do with making connections."

Since Ellen's philosophical approach to her life and her work is related to connections, she rejected the manner in which I questioned her about vision. She argues, "I don't like that word personal particularly. I do not think we are all so unique; that it is only my vision, because vision addresses a larger community. In my community of artists, if you make things you are communicating. If you make objects, then you make them to communicate. It is not masturbatory, otherwise I wouldn't want to show them." For Ellen, this idea of communicating and making connections has been translated into areas outside of making art. She left her first marriage because the quality and kind of connection she wanted was lacking. Ellen remarried and had one child. Her husband, an architect, fully supports her passion. Her son has been influenced by both his parents' visual perceptions of the world and has pursued the arts as a teenager. He takes great pride in his mother's artwork.

Ellen's connections to her husband and son are in contrast to members of her birth family. She characterized her relationship with her mother and brother as steeped in anger, resentment, and hostility. She was confronted by that reality when her brother died an untimely death at forty years of age. Despite the harsh sentiments she expressed about her brother, the pain of his loss overtook her. She was unable to paint for a long time after his death. Ultimately, connections to her life and to her painting held her together and pulled her through the crisis. The urge to paint came back to her and the fog that had surrounded her after her brother's death lifted.

Outside her art community and her teaching, Ellen's commitment to connections is just as strong. She was a founder of a large soup kitchen in her area, and has always been active in women's rights organizations. Recently, after teaching for twenty-five years, Ellen has taken a sabbatical. In keeping with her nature, she has chosen to work in a not-for-profit social service agency. Her sabbatical from teaching has not stopped her from painting, and she is preparing to show a new body of work. Connections, as Ellen states, feed her painting.

The need to make connections through "two-dimensional objects, paintings, prints, books, drawings" is experienced as a "real physical need" in Ellen. This need must be responded to or as Ellen puts it "I get crazy. That need comes out of a desire to explore specific issues about vision." Ellen believes this need is partially responsible for her creativity. She frames her definition of creativity in similar terms: "I think most people are talented; they have some level of high sensitivity. The question is how that sensitivity gets focused or honed. I have always thought about it as making connections. Anyone in my field can learn how to render; not everyone can learn how to draw. The difference has to do with the projection of one's self, intellectually, emotionally, physically, into a drawing. That has to do with being able to make connections. It has to do with vision. It has to do with being able to connect an emotional state with a physical state. It is how one perceives the world in a nonsequential, progressive way."

The intuitive knowing that these women feel about their art started at an early age. Unlike Ellen, who experienced her commitment to and love of art in her teen years, Jossey grew into her commitment. In her teen years, Jossey met a boy and wanted to get married. Her mother had other ideas. It was her mother and not Jossey who filed an application for art school. Jossey was accepted and went. She found separation from her family very difficult and took a leave of absence to return home. She finished her college education, earning a B.F.A. in painting. Shortly after graduating, Jossey took an exam to become a social worker and passed. She worked in a challenging neighborhood and excelled at her job. Her agency wanted to send her to school to get her master's degree in social work, but Jossey felt it was the wrong choice. Nevertheless, that was a rich and rewarding time for her. During that nine-month period, she did not make her art. Deciding against a career in social work, she left her job and worked as a waitress two days a week. She earned enough money to support herself and dedicated the rest of the week to making her art. Having set the wheels in motion, she was slowly working her way to her art.

Jossey then met the man she was to marry a year later. She recalls, "My husband was a very good artist with a lot of standing. Through him, through his connections, I began my showing career. He was the first person who truly believed in me and made it possible." Her husband was responsible for Jossey making her art. He "insisted on the discipline" she would have to develop. That discipline involved dedicating herself to her intention as an artist. For the first time, she began to take herself seriously. She went to her studio to work seven full hours a day, regardless of the output. When Jossey was not waitressing, she was to be found in her studio. Jossey learned a great deal more about herself as a woman artist when her husband became the assistant to a famous artist and they traveled to Europe. She recalls, "I was still not taking myself seriously as an artist. It occurred to me, after traveling around, that I had seen what men did and I really wanted to do something that women did. This was before the women's movement."

Jossey and her husband returned to the states and moved east. With that transition began the dissolution of her marriage. In that first year, her husband supported her; this had a devastating effect upon her self-esteem. To maintain her independence, she accepted visiting artist jobs at universities around the country. Travel and long periods of time away from home placed a strain upon her marriage. Jossey feels the "family curse" directly contributed to the ultimate destruction of her marriage. This man taught Jossey through his life, his work, and his death about inventing her life and making her work. Her husband forced her to confront her life as an artist as well as her beliefs. He was the instrument by which she would learn to reinvent herself. She believed everything in her life was doomed until she experienced her ex-husband's death.

A woman cannot fulfill her essential creative nature unless she believes she has value. If a woman is lucky she learns that lesson early in life. But many women must first move through adulthood before they discover their voice and their value. Ellen always took her art seriously. Her passion began in earnest when she was fifteen years old and became serious when she reached eighteen years of age. She went to college and received a degree in art history. She continued her training and received two more degrees: an M.A. in art history and an M.F.A. in painting. Her immediate family did not support her decision to pursue her art. Her father, who loved making things, seems to have influenced her decision. But he died when Ellen's pursuit of her art was just beginning. She married and received love, support, and guidance from her former mother-in-law. She used her former mother-in-law as a role model. "Within certain circles" Ellen says her former mother-in-law is a well-known artist. As a role model, her former mother-in-law demonstrated how a woman can paint and have a life (family, friends, and children). This loving, supportive, influential relationship continues today.

After graduate school, Ellen worked as a curator in a museum and used a room in her apartment as a studio. She has always had simultaneous interests in art history and painting; since the mid-1960s, she has worked professionally in both areas. After working at several museums, she decided to shift her focus from full-time curatorial work to free-lance work. She explains, "I was a museum professional. I quit my everyday job to make my work." In the late 1970s, she started showing her work. "I was also teaching art criticism, art history, or studio art simultaneously with everything else. Now I teach and do my work. I felt I was not getting any younger. I had to focus on doing it in a more concentrated way."

The shift in attitude that was happening to Ellen was also happening to Jossey. Jossey felt time passing. The manner in which she led her life no longer felt satisfying. She decided to change the way she shaped her experiences. She had to settle down and take herself more seriously. Instead of traveling from university to university, Jossey accepted two teaching positions, both within well-respected universities. She now splits her year between these two schools. Jossey is dedicated to her students, especially her young female students. She recounted a recent incident in which a few of her talented, attractive, female students were the only ones *not* to submit their work for a scholarship. Jossey perceived the talent within these young women, but they did not take themselves or their art seriously. Their choices, their lack of faith in themselves, and their willingness to sell themselves short deeply disturbed Jossey. She shared her perceptions, her disappointment, and her anger with them. One of the young women sent her a thank-you note. Perhaps that young woman will be spared a lifetime of pain and depression. Cathy and Lucy are examples of the painful reality that accompanies a repressed creative spirit.

Jossey, like Cathy and Lucy, has fought against an internal current to own herself and her creative expression. But it was a battle worth fighting. She has had to overcome inertia and take responsibility for success in her life. Jossey declares there are "areas of myself which are deeply damaged. I have had a horrible time managing my career. There is no excuse for me not showing, and I haven't shown in a couple of years." Nevertheless, Jossey has maintained her discipline through her teaching and her painting. She has recently entered a new phase in her work. It is a significant shift in the form of her expression. Now, instead of abstraction, Jossey is exploring the use of real images, and it thrills her. She believes that her age and her maturation as a woman have helped to bring about this change. As she approaches her mid-fifties and in keeping with her definition of creativity, Jossey remains open to exploring the possibilities in this new stage of her life with enthusiasm.

Two major shifts have occurred in both Jossey's and Ellen's lives. The first shift related to self-examination, which spurred the sense that they needed to take themselves seriously as women and as artists. The second shift is the one they are in now. Approaching life with an openness coincides with middle age and menopause. Like Jossey, Ellen's work is evolving. She speaks of the change in the context of her working process. "Now I am trying to just let it happen and not think about it so much. It is part of the business of turning fifty. I was always afraid of my work. I was afraid it would not be smart. So I would think about it all the time. If I am smart, my work is smart. Now I believe the most interesting part is the time when I'm not thinking about it. I am just making my art. When I am totally there, it's separate from any other kind of activity." Ellen is describing stepping aside and letting go. This state of being is crucial in the creative process. It comes with an awareness and trust in yourself and your process.

Ellen attributes her struggle to more regularly show her work publicly to "internal art politics, my personality, and my inability to push myself." I asked her if she knew well-known women artists who successfully negotiate the art world. Why are those women able to play the political game of the art world? Ellen says that those women "are totally convinced that what they are doing is brilliant. But I also think because they are women, they are not as well known as they could be. Women are not afforded the same respect as men. Historically girls were sent to art school as a finishing school. There was no intention that they do anything other than be cultured for their husbands. All of art history, music history, literary history, film history, video history is male."

Perseverance, risk-taking, and a strong sense of self reflected in a woman's ability to make and show her work are qualities that separate women who publicly pursue their passion and those who are unable to pursue their passion or share it. The positive presentation of self in the world is tied to feeling deserving of good things. A woman who believes she is deserving of good things accepts success in her life and translates disappointment productively. The inability to process from that core place of being deserving can affect your commitment to your creative expression. Teaching has helped to keep the passion alive for Jossey and Ellen. It has demanded that they challenge themselves in this world. Teaching has maintained the connection to their work when they were unable to publicly share their work. It has defended them against isolation. Jossey and Ellen have not shut themselves off from their essential creative natures or the life around them. Sharing their vision through teaching is an outward expression of creativity. By contrast, Lucy's and Cathy's approach to their art is inward, private, and exclusionary. Perhaps that is why they question their creative abilities and worth so relentlessly: they keep themselves isolated from that which helps define their vision and feed their creative expression.

## THE STRENGTH GAINED BY MOVING THROUGH *DIAKOSMOS*

The last two women included in this chapter offer insight into the attitude, perceptions, and personality traits of productive women artists. Their place within the realm of creative behavior sets them apart from the other women artists you have read about thus far. These two elderly women have been professionally successful all their lives; they have always earned a livelihood from their work. Victoria is seventy-seven years old and Gerrit is eighty-seven years old. Both women are opinionated yet open, warm, approachable, and assertive about their need to do their work. I was intrigued by the differences in the structure of their personalities and those of their younger counterparts. Their drive, sense of self, sense of place, clarity about work, and simplicity about approaching work—all helped define their internal structure.

Victoria was born to a lower-class family. She was one of four children, the second oldest and emotionally the "strongest" of two sisters and two brothers. She described her mother and father as both very creative. Her mother loved art and demonstrated a talent for it in high school. An art teacher who believed in her mother's ability suggested that her mother go to art school. Victoria's grandparents were horrified. They believed "bad girls go to art school." Succumbing to her parents' view, Victoria's mother became a bookkeeper in her brother's business. Victoria's mother found expression for her creative abilities by making her daughters' clothing and accessories, as well as beautiful embroideries. Victoria describes her father as a "personality person. He wanted to be an actor; he could sing; he could tell jokes; he had a wonderful sense of humor. Everybody loved him. He did not belong in the practical world, and there he was." Lack of money pervaded the family experience in Victoria's youth. There were difficult times when her father was out of work. Once, for a period of two years, her father was unemployed; the family situation was grave. She recalls, "The neighbors took up a collection. My mother was very proud; she went crazy. I was the strongest, so I was elected to return the money."

Though Victoria was fond of both her mother and father, she decided she wanted more in her life. Victoria says this was not a rejection of her parents as much as it was a rejection of the life they led. The guiding image moving her life has always been grounded in exploring. She explains, "I did not like my parents' lives. It was a narrow life, so I read a lot of books. I wanted to escape things. I was not going to grow up and lead the life they led. The world is very big. There is so much to see and do and learn. I just could not live like other people."

Victoria has been driven to live her life by experiencing as much as possible and by making her art. When she was a young girl, she read *Little Women*. Victoria explains one of the young girls in the book wanted to study art in Europe. That character was very appealing to Victoria and had a profound influence upon her vision. Victoria still possesses that copy of the book. She explains, "I liked to draw. It was something I liked to do. Nobody told me to do it. I could make things. It was my entertainment. I read and I drew." These two needs are powerful motivation for Victoria, even today. Drawing and reading became a means of coping with the stress she felt. They became a stable, solid form of self-expression in her early years that has remained steadfast throughout her life. She knew what she wanted at an early age and never wavered in her commitment to live her life fully.

Victoria has lived her life and defined what is important with simplicity, clarity, and honesty. Like Ellen and Jossey, teaching has been an important expression for her. Encouraging people and painting have been fulfilling life experiences. Behind Victoria's commitment to painting and teaching is an inner respect for herself. There were never doubts. Respect for herself and her commitment are the core of her definition of creativity. She believes "that the word 'creative' is so misused. It should mean inventive. It is making something, thinking something, putting together the odds and ends of knowledge that you have acquired over the years. If you ask me what art is, I do not know. I do not know what creativity is, either. When people say he is a creative person because he draws well, that is not necessarily creative. Painting is creative because I am creating something on a piece of paper. It may not be earth-shaking, but it is personal. Even if it is a portrait, which I specialize in, nobody does it like I do. No one does it like anyone else. You put your mark on a piece of paper; in that sense it is creative. My teaching is creative because I am getting all these people to do all these wonderful things."

Teaching became a significant part of Victoria's life when her children were young. Victoria humbly compares herself to some of the people she has taught and their level of inventiveness. Because she does not view herself as inventive, she cannot identify herself as particularly creative. Yet she has been stimulated and inspired by the children's free and easy expression of self. She says, "Some of the ideas, especially on the junior high school level, were mind-blowing. I never felt superior. I always encouraged. I never told the students how to do it, unless it was something technical. I never made demonstrations." In describing her technique as a teacher, Victoria says, "My ideas come; it is not a pre-planned creativity. When I see what the students are doing, something in me can think of what they should do to move along. They think I am great, but I really do not. I think mostly it is the supportive thing. I think everyone can do something."

While Ellen, Jossey, and Victoria have always found inspiration in teaching, Gerrit has never taught. Her friends are always suggesting that she teach; she has a lifetime of experience and vision to share. Gerrit insists that she does not know enough. Gerrit's craft was learned on the street, in the doing. She did not formally train as a photographer, and I believe her sense of "not knowing enough" comes from that reality. Touched by the cruelty and the brilliance of others, life had lessons to offer Gerrit that would shape her vision before she learned her trade. Death, war, abandonment, and self-awareness were the physical and emotional realities that would give texture and content to Gerrit's vision. Unlike the other women artists, she did not express her creativity at an early age. Gerrit's career as a photojournalist was instigated by circumstances in adulthood.

Gerrit experienced a warm, loving childhood environment for a few years, but those cherished times were taken from her when she was still very young. She was born in Posen, a province of Germany, before World War I, to an upper-middle-class Jewish family. She was third youngest of five children, four girls and one boy. Her memories are at best sketchy. Any sense of love and security she received ended with her mother's terminal illness. Gerrit was eight years old when her mother was sent to a sanatorium. Two years later, suffering from tuberculosis, her mother died away from home. One year after her mother's death, her father remarried. He chose a woman twenty-five years younger than him to be his wife. That ill-fated marriage lasted nine years. Gerrit's older sisters were hostile to their young stepmother. They resented her taking their mother's place. Gerrit did not have strong feelings about this woman but followed her sisters lead and treated her badly. Her father's absences did not ease this transition. Her father was often away on business, but even when in town, he was never at home. He was a gambler. Gerrit felt that men were not to be trusted, that they would abandon her. Being her father's favorite child did not lessen the sense of abandonment that was to stay with her throughout her life. The loss of Gerrit's mother was devastating for her, but death had not finished clawing away at her. The isolation and abandonment she would experience with her mother's death and her father's absence was to be twice compounded. Six years after her mother's death, one of her sisters also died of tuberculosis. This was followed by the horror of Nazi soldiers ending her elder sister's life at Auschwitz, a Nazi concentration camp, during World War II. Though her younger brother and sister lived through the Nazi occupation, Gerrit did not have a close relationship with them.

At the end of World War I, all those living in Posen were ordered to either move to German lands or declare themselves Poles. Her family moved to Germany. At nine years of age, after her mother's death, Gerrit began to raise herself. She was not noticed in the emotional chaos that controlled the household. She spoke with no one, shared her feelings and thoughts with no one. Gerrit joined the *Vanderfogel,* a semi-political German organization. This organization, though German, had strong Zionist underpinnings. It was like the youth group she had belonged to in Posen. She reflects, "I think this gave me direction in my life. This was my way of discovering the world. These groups were very idealistic. I developed a powerful sense about justice. I still have this view of the world. I see how imperfect the world is and how much could be done. I am a fighter and I get very hostile." The direction and philosophical perspective she developed while in the youth movement was to become Gerrit's guiding force later in her life. Expressing that vision would be part of learning to be a photographer. She muses, "When I think back on my childhood, I do not remember anything. As a teenager I think I lived like a vegetable. I lived pretty unaware except for that idealistic thing which was implanted in me." Gerrit does not believe that her childhood experiences or her idealism have influenced her photographs. Could it be that the experiences that shaped Gerrit's internal structure are not responsible, in part, for the way in which she "sees" the world and expresses that vision in creative behavior?

The creative accomplishments of both Gerrit and Victoria exist in the world; they have form, texture, and substance. Their works have been publicly recognized. Yet both these women remain humble concerning their own creativity. Gerrit does not view her photographs as creative works because, as she explains it, "I do not experiment. I do not see myself as an innovator. I believe that creativity has something to do with innovation. It is strange. I do think more than most people I meet. But that is more an intellectual exercise. I do not think it has to do with the photographs I take. The word 'creative' turns me off. 'Creativity' is such a weighty, important word." Taking a moment to reflect on the problem, Gerrit then addresses it differently. She believes her best work takes place in the darkroom. "I make the photographs. I love working in the darkroom. This is where my creativity comes in. When I am in the darkroom, that is where I can experiment, innovate, manipulate the image into many things. That is what I love to do. I work at night. I have the music, and it makes me happy beyond description." Gerrit adds, "When it comes to creativity, nobody knows where it springs from. It must be a form of self-exertion. I do not know. When I work, there is a moment when I am photographing, when I have it or not. It always struck me as mysterious. It is an intuitive knowing. My seeing is photography-directed."

It is striking that both Victoria and Gerrit speak of creativity with the same terminology and in the same context. Both women defer creativity to others because they do not see themselves satisfactorily as innovators. Yet they continue to work and create. They continue to search, like the Goddess, for the proper framing of their inner vision. If one picture could capture the inner truth that Gerrit wished to express, if one painting could say everything that Victoria believes to be true, neither of them would have to create again. Perhaps humility fuels their search to understand their expression better, to find the best image possible. Searching for truth brings a woman to a deeper level of understanding and to new physical manifestations of that truth. Gerrit and Victoria seek reordering, and they need to produce a product. Intuitive knowing and an intellectual questioning are part of the makeup of women artists.

As a child, Victoria dreamed of following her fantasy. After graduating from high school, Victoria followed her heart to study art in Europe. However, her mother's early death forced her to return to the states to take care of her family. In an instant, her life was thrown into chaos. Crisis can move us in unexpected ways. Being forced to reconsider her path,

Victoria shaped her dream differently. Back in the states, Victoria decided to go to college instead of an art school. She received a scholarship to a nearby college, where she studied fine arts and illustration, thinking there might be something practical she could learn. She explains, "I was not very good at illustration. I did not know I could paint. I discovered that I could. I had one very encouraging teacher. He was very strict. He taught me how to see color and value. He taught me how to think. When I graduated, I felt I could not do anything. To earn money I did portraits. I went to people's houses and charged ten dollars a day." That was the beginning of her painting career. There was never any question in her mind about doing it once Victoria found her passion in painting. The intensity of her commitment has remained throughout her life. Victoria never tortured herself about her ability, her worth, or her creativity. She wanted to paint and she did. She admits that not everything she painted was brilliant. That is of no significance to her. The act of moving through her process has fed her creative spirit. But ten dollars a day for a portrait did not bring the family enough money, so she found a job designing children's clothing.

She did not work as a designer for long. Victoria met and married a man she describes as a true Renaissance man, "a modern Leonardo da Vinci." He was a lawyer, a humanitarian, a marvelous musician, loving and supportive of Victoria's passion—her painting. He understood her need to paint. When their children were little, Victoria painted as the children played around her in the living room. She painted as dinner was cooking on the stove. She painted the family's portraits; she painted every conceivable scene out her living room window. She gave her children supplies and they painted with her. Finally, when her children were in elementary school, she decided that she wanted to do something else. She says, "I needed sociability. I wanted to do something that had to do with the world. I saw who was teaching my children art, people who were drawing on their drawings." She spoke to the dean at a college, and he assured her of her ability to teach. Her husband encouraged her. She went back to school at night. Thinking back, she states, "I had a wonderful time. I got so into it I took a lot of credits. I got my master's degree and thirty additional credits, and got a job right away." Victoria received her teaching certification before she received her master's degree and immediately began teaching in the public school system. She took care of her children, taught, went to school at night, and painted. She committed herself not only to her painting, but to living her life and enjoying it.

Victoria taught public school for twenty-four years until her husband's health failed. She retired from her teaching and attended to his needs. That was when she began teaching adults, both professionals and nonprofessionals, one day a week, which she continues today. Through the stress and upset of taking care of her husband, she continued to paint. As her husband lay near death in a hospital room, the staff allowed her to visit no more than a minute or two. She went home to paint. She could not bear to sit in a sterile hospital waiting room for hours, not being able to be with her husband, not being able to touch him. Painting offered her an escape; it created a space within her where she could find solace. Painting her way through this pain was productive for Victoria. It was an affirmation of herself and of her life.

One's development as a creative woman does not happen overnight. There are always life lessons to be learned and new paths to be taken. Like Victoria, Gerrit would have to find her path through the circumstances of her life. At nineteen, it was time for Gerrit to leave her father's house. She moved to Berlin to live with a cousin and study secretarial skills. She says, "Everyone had to learn something, so I was sent to business school. I learned typing and stenography. I hated every second of it. I was working as a secretary when I met my husband. I did not work in offices after we got married." In 1933 her husband lost his job. With only his camera in his pocket (it was his hobby from youth) and hopes of starting a new life he went to Palestine to look around, to establish himself. Gerrit was to follow him. But after two weeks he was back in Berlin. He had been horrified at what he saw; the difference in cultures was too extreme. Gerrit adds, "He came back with pictures. He developed them himself. I told him, these are fantastic. I have never seen pictures like these." Gerrit decided to take the photographs to the editor of a famous Zionist paper in Berlin. The staff was astounded and offered her money for the photographs. Gerrit was shocked; she did not know you could sell photographs. She told me her husband had no role models; everything he photographed came from within him, from his years of taking photographs as a hobby. He was, she says, a splendid photographer. The newspaper continued to assign Harold jobs and pay Gerrit. She explains, "I started as the go-between and then I became his assistant. I started to get into it, slowly. I took my first pictures in Berlin." That began Gerrit's lifelong journey into her creative expression.

Gerrit and Harold waited for a visa to leave Berlin as life in Germany grew more difficult daily. Harold continued to develop as a professional photographer, while Gerrit learned the craft of photography. Harold photographed life in the Jewish ghetto for the Jewish newspapers. They were finally granted their visas, after years of waiting. The war was intensifying. They had to leave quickly with only a few possessions. They were forced to leave half of their photo archives behind. In America, Harold was known for the quality of his photographs and for the subject matter; he continued to get work in the states from the Jewish community. By this time, Gerrit had also established herself as a professional photographer. She recalls, "After the war, I started getting assignments abroad ever year or two, and it has stayed that way till now. I came back this January from Israel. I still have my studio upstairs." Gerrit found her passion later than the other artists you have read about. But her age is irrelevant. It was her commitment to her essential creative nature that allowed her to respond to an opportunity when it was presented. Neither she nor her husband grew up believing that they would be professional photographers. But they did not turn away from the path when it presented itself.

Gerrit possessed a sense of herself that enabled her to make her art, despite difficult times. She spent a good portion of her life not talking and suppressing everything. She believes she lived this way as a means of protecting herself. However, instead of burying herself alive in her pain she converted that energy into the creative energy needed to make her photographs. Perseverance, goal-directedness, risk-taking, and passion have enabled Gerrit to work as a photographer. Though she learned her craft from her husband, Gerrit did not have a happy marriage. Her husband was "a womanizer." She was willing to tolerate this relationship because she felt marriage was not a prison. She did not realize until many years later how stifled this relationship had kept her. In trying to explain the truth of their relationship, Gerrit believes, "There was this thing between master and pupil. It was hostility, not enmity. He was a much better photographer; he was creative. I never tried to copy anything he did or copy anybody else. But there was hostility because there I was, this pipsqueak who came out of nowhere. Communication between us was very bad. But you do what you can in the moment."

When Gerrit was sixty-three and married for forty-one years, her husband left her. She states, "He was always punishing me; he was filled with extreme hostility toward me. But when he moved out, I started to breathe. I started to talk. I was liberated. I became a happy person at the age of sixty-three. I started to live and be happy when he left me, and my self-esteem came after. As lives go, I think my life is wonderful. I have had such satisfaction." Her husband did not go far, however. He moved into an apartment directly above Gerrit's. While Gerrit thrived, she says her husband grew tired of photography and stopped completely. He took up painting. I wondered, perhaps, whether he could no longer tolerate her success. A few years after their separation, he became ill with cancer. Gerrit was relieved and thankful when a woman he met in the hospital nursed him until his death.

Gerrit's definition of creativity as a form of exerting one's inner self demonstrates how a woman can flourish in an overtly hostile environment. If Gerrit had not exerted her "self" through her photographs, her husband's hostility might very well have destroyed her. Despite his anger and silence, Gerrit continued to develop as a photographer. She loved what she was doing and derived extreme satisfaction from it. Sometimes now, when she feels depressed, she goes to her studio and looks at her photographs. A warm feeling flickers within her knowing that she has produced something wonderful in her life. Her strong sense of self is not dependent upon the approval of others. She explains, "I never listen to what people are saying about my photos. Yes, I have an ego like everybody else. But I am not interested in the reactions of people. I like them to like my work. It comes from being a journalist my whole life. I have seen my name printed thousands of times under pictures. I do not have an ego to the extent that I believe I am terrific. I do what I do. I love what I do. I get my satisfaction from the work. When people praise it, of course it pleases me, but I am not dependent upon it."

Self-reliance and self-motivation buttress creative behavior. The Goddess could not tear down and rebuild the world without these qualities. Without self-reliance and self-motivation, a woman cannot follow her creative impulses. The motivation to paint has always been within Victoria, and that has been translated into real and tangible products. For one brief moment in time, Victoria put down her paintbrush. She had suffered from uterine cancer and was recuperating from treatments. Recovery was slow and painful. Victoria was depressed, uncomfortable, in pain, and unable to paint. Lying on her couch, she waited. Her commitment, made so many years earlier, to live her life in the now was reaffirmed with fervor during this painful, depressing time. I asked Victoria whether her work changed as a result of this experience. Laughing, she says, "I am the incurable optimist. No, there was no change. I was not going to paint my insides. I was not interested in that. I was just more determined than ever to produce something really good, and that is my eternal desire. I rarely achieve it; it is the quest for the unattainable." Feeling that her desire to paint something really good is unobtainable has not stopped her from painting and developing as an artist. In truth, her humility does not accurately reflect her accomplishments as a painter.

Inventing one's life is a lifetime endeavor. Victoria continues her search to express her essential creative nature. But life has changed and she continues her search for the appropriate expression of that which is within. Her life partner is no longer with her; her children are grown and have moved away. She has grandchildren now who give her much joy. Several years ago, Victoria visited her sons and their children in their homes in the southwest. She fell in love with the topography of that part of the country and decided to spend half the year near her children and grandchildren. She has successfully established herself there and teaches at a museum. Victoria has been invited to join several prestigious artists' organizations in this region and has ventured into new areas in making her art. This new avenue of expression has been exceptionally well received by the public and the art community. Her relatively new success as a watercolor artist has not slowed her impulse to explore, to listen, and to learn. She has begun working in monochrome. Victoria explains that "my work keeps changing because I am into different things. I am influenced. That is why I like to work in a group periodically."

Victoria offers us a lesson in approaching work, in approaching creative behavior. Her attitude of acceptance, her commitment to her passion, and her ability to maintain goal-directedness have helped her to live a happy, integrated, productive life in many respects. If you have a passion, a need to express yourself, you must follow that passion with regularity. Victoria states, "When I paint, I see beauty and drama. I am a realistic painter. I look and things grow from that. I like to travel. I see new things, new people, new ideas. It's horrible, but it's wonderful." Victoria understands, however, that seeking and growth are accompanied by chaos and uncertainty. The need to remain true to her vision and her process requires the knowledge and acceptance that creating involves pain, turmoil, and a type of spiritual death. The value of the process is understood at completion. Victoria declares, "I know from my teaching never to destroy my work. I go back to it—maybe tomorrow, maybe a year from now—and look at it. A whole new understanding will be there. I am in turmoil while I am working on it. With every stroke I am dying. Every stroke another death. I am always unsure. I do not know what I am doing, but I keep working. After all these years I know that."

It is only through vigilant work that one can grow as an expressive, creative human being. Perhaps you are not destined to be publicly proclaimed by the world. Does it matter? If you do not work at something, you do not produce. If you do not produce, you cannot learn to value yourself or anyone else. The discipline and commitment involved in pursuing your vision, which Victoria and Gerrit have demonstrated, can help to move a woman through difficult periods. There is knowledge to be gained in the process. Victoria and Gerrit have learned to exploit those qualities that help them create. They have learned to tame those traits that hinder or threaten their expression. They have learned there is value in simplicity and clarity.

The inner urging, powerful in its implication, demonstrated in the image of the Goddess and in the lives of these six women tells you that the essential creative nature cannot be quelled. Talent and support will not ensure creative behavior. Self-doubt and tentativeness will hinder the productive release of your creative expression. Still the call of your essential creative nature will not be silenced. The pain of ignoring the inner urging is greater than the pain of releasing and following it. Women will move through difficult and easy times throughout their lives. Creativity can help shape these experiences and the path to follow. Whether you are an artist, a businesswoman, a mother, or wife, the qualities that buttress creative behavior are within your grasp. You need only respond to purpose in *diakosmos,* the inner urging of the Goddess, and the calling of your essential creative nature.

## EMBRACING *DIAKOSMOS*

Perhaps you have resisted your essential creative nature, despite the sting of that action. Perhaps you know the path you need to take but have denied yourself the steps to begin the journey or the steps to continue the journey. Finding your essential creative nature in your inner voice can be frightening. The bravest woman may be reduced to quivering before commencing her journey into the creative process, into the realm of *diakosmos.* The traits required are accessible to you. Every process has a beginning. Every step leads you to the next one. If you have resisted your inner urging and have felt pangs of discomfort, you can do something about it.

In the last chapter, you made a list of things you do well. You defined creativity for yourself and you listed aspects of your behavior that are viewed positively by others. Take one of those things you do well. In the privacy of your own room, studio, even your bathroom, say out loud that you do this activity well. How does that acknowledgment feel? Does it scare you to utter those words? Say it again. Perhaps you need to give yourself a hug afterward. This may sound foolish, but I guarantee you that your body will respond to the experience. Commit yourself to a daily, weekly, or monthly regimen of doing what you do well on a regular basis. Take the activity to the next level. Learn more about it. Experiment. You do not need, initially, to share the activity with anyone unless you crave direction and guidance. If that is the case, you must seek the help you need to pursue the next level.

If you lose your courage at different times during your creative process, try formalizing the manner in which you begin. In other words, begin with a self-affirming ritual. Begin to explore ways in which you feel centered. If your problem is in sharing your work, start with someone you trust. Then you can try joining a group of people who are struggling with the same activity. Become part of a community that understands your form of creative expression. There is a wealth of knowledge to be gained by listening and watching other people challenge themselves. Find books that stimulate your imagination in your area of creative expression and try out some of your ideas. The path you want starts inside of yourself. But it moves from inside yourself to the outer world. Ultimately you must be willing to share your vision.

Self-doubting is based in fear. It is merely a feeling. We need to wrestle with our fears and our self-doubts, but they should not stop us. No matter how scared you may feel, you can move through that fear and produce a product. Do not get overly concerned with quality. If you cannot begin, you will never create. If you are too judgmental, you will never complete a project. If you determine that the sole criterion for producing a product is recognition, you will never begin. Dedicate yourself to your creative expression. Try it for a specific period of time. Develop a discipline that is important. Commit yourself fully. Then, at the end of the time, evaluate your experience. These actions develop the discipline to engage your essential creative nature and will lead you toward perseverance, inner-directedness, and tolerance for uncertainty. The more you learn about yourself, the better able you are to confront the qualities that hinder your creative expression. Remember that you are the center of your creative expression. What you feel and think, how you frame your vision, is personal and without need of approval from others.

CHAPTER THREE

# Fertile Lives:
## Heeding the Call of Your Essential Creative Nature

She was worshiped by the Greeks. She is the Mother Goddess, the Earth Goddess. To be creative is Gaia's very essence. Gaia means earth.

> "[S]he is not earth as an abstraction. . . . Gaia is the living presence of earth. . . . She reminds her worshipers that matter is still rebellious, alive and eruptive. Gaia is earthquake and volcano, molten lava and shifting rock. . . . She is goddess of all that grows but never the goddess of agriculture. . . . She is for life but for ever-renewing, ever-changing life, for life as it encompasses death. . . . Gaia is also the giver of dreams. . . . Her prophecies come . . . from her deep knowledge of what is really (and inevitably) going on. . . . [S]he is nature moving toward emergence in personal form. . . . It is in her very nature to create, to bring forth variety, heterogeneity. She is ever fertile. . . . Gaia's emanations are projections of her own being, each catching one

aspect of her own protoplasmic fullness." (*The Book of the Goddess Past and Present*)

There is a rawness in creation. There are no boundaries; change is ever-present and possible. Indeed, it is a fundamental principle in nature. It is just so in women's nature. You are capable of volcanic energy, of shaking the foundations of your own life and the lives of those around you. The essence of creativity is in the flow of change. Vital, productive lives of functioning, creative women demonstrate for us that all women are capable of pushing through the boundaries, of changing the parameters, of re-creating themselves and their environment. This idea sounds lofty, and perhaps unobtainable to many, but if you stop and look at the lives that touch yours, you will find Gaia's essence in action.

If you examine those qualities that move creative people forward, you see the volatile nature of creative action. Risk-taking, a tolerance for chaos, an openness for the unknown, disregard for certain rules, patience, and goal-directedness all comprise Gaia's volcanic power. In the creative process, the raw nature of the effort and the earthiness of the experience feed the inner being with renewed life. The earthquake or the volcano changes the terrain forever. The power in those natural occurrences is what assures the outcome. There is no stopping the process once it is set in motion. Gaia cannot hold within that which needs to emerge. Creative people cannot hold within their physical and psychological beings that which must be expressed. To do so means to suffer great pains and trauma at the energy turned inward. Its destructive force can be unrelenting until the energy is finally exhausted and the next eruption occurs. The women artists you met in the last chapter struggled to respond to their raw, earthy natures. While they struggled against producing that which was within, they yearned to release that which needed to be expressed.

In this chapter, you'll meet three women who have responded to the essence of Gaia. They are not women in the arts. But many women interviewed for this book, who were actively involved in creating productive lives, often incorporated the arts into their lives. Creation and change characterize their unique paths and reflect Gaia's volatile nature. Gaia's protoplasmic fullness engages women in multiple ways. Women express their essential creative natures even if they have not been professionally trained in that expression. Sometimes the manifestation of creative behavior is seen in more than one discipline. Each form of expression energizes life, and as a reflection of a woman's essential creative nature, each needs to be expressed. The rush of energy experienced when expressing this powerful force regenerates the source. It is necessary for survival. The inner essence that needs to be released into the world feeds the creative spirit and causes growth. Age, cultural background, and form of expression may vary for each woman, but not the need for self-expression. A woman's journey toward self-expression exposes the struggle she engages to release her personal expression and live a creative life. Edward S. Ebert II writes, in "The Cognitive Spiral: Creative Thinking and Cognitive Processing," "[O]ur function is not so much to uncover why some people are more creative than others, but rather to find out how we can make more of us use and develop the creativity we already possess."

## THE SOURCE DISRUPTED, THE MOLTEN EARTH BEGINS TO BOIL

Lilly has had to renew and re-create her life in her thirties. She has learned relatively early how misdirected a woman can become through avoidance and addictive behavior. A woman disconnecting from who and what she is, how she feels, and what she thinks leads herself toward earth-shattering experiences. Her creative expression is inner-directed toward destruction. Each phase of Lilly's life has been responsible for a new creation and a slightly different persona. The energy in each phase reveals the power of creativity used both positively and negatively. A woman's creative impulses are slowed, if not severely hindered, during a negative phase. Healthy creative products, thoughts, and actions require an awareness and a sensitivity to some internal order and process; substance abuse, addictions, and extreme psychological states block creative behavior. Through Lilly's story you learn how embracing your essential creative nature alters your choices and how that change affects the course of your life. Such alterations do not come without great fear, confusion, risk-taking, and perhaps pain. Once the choice has been made and the forward action has begun, a woman experiences her strength. The growing potential within is unmatched in its possibilities; it is a fertile time full of life-producing energy. The choice, if constructive, is a healthy, life-affirming, creative act.

Lilly is a bright, articulate, thirty-five-year-old white woman. Born and raised in the northeast, she is one of three children. She is the only girl, the middle child between two brothers. Lilly maintains close ties with her parents, her brothers, and their immediate family members. She delights in the presence of her young nephew and, recently married, looks forward to having children of her own in the near future. At the present time, Lilly is finishing her master's degree in divinity and hopes to be ordained a minister in the Unitarian Universalist Church within the year. She has been working hard in her church community, teaching religious education, preaching, visiting patients in the hospital, and working on the AIDS task force she started. Those are the present external manifestations of Lilly's life.

To understand what has motivated her journey, I asked Lilly to describe her guiding image for me. "I want more; I want adventure and more. I want to do more. I am always wanting to know more, to check things out." This desire for "more" has not always served Lilly well. In the past, it has pushed Lilly into obsessive behavior. This attitude has made it difficult for Lilly to experience satisfaction in her life. She says, "It creates such ambition in me it puts too much pressure on me. To get to one hundred percent instead of ninety-five, to do it better than the last time. I do not know if I call that creativity or whether it is self-will run riot. I do believe there is some creative impulse there. It's negative in that I have felt so much pressure."

Researchers believe that any personality trait in the extreme can work to a woman's detriment, especially with regard to creative behavior. The essence of your creative nature, as the image of Gaia reminds us, means extreme conditions cannot remain constant. An eruption of one sort or another is bound to occur, altering the terrain. Lilly tried to neutralize her emotional terrain with substance abuse and extreme behavior. The drive for more was found in her need to achieve. Even her "search for love" through "sexual promiscuity" reflected her need for more in the extreme. Such self-destructive behavior is the misuse of a woman's creative powers. Lilly understands the problems inherent in her desire for "more."

Her life, even through her addiction, has always been grounded in action. As a consequence, Lilly perceives creativity as active and engaging. She explains that creativity is "finding a new way to do anything, whether solving a problem or entertaining a child. It is connected with imagination." Transformations and the making of something new have shaped the path of Lilly's life thus far. Because Lilly is goal-oriented, she has a need to acquire understanding and a sense of control over her environment and ideas. She grasps onto the flow of her life through a variety of activities that commit her emotionally, intellectually, and spiritually. It is, she says, "seeking the creative impulse behind my wanting to experience. Whether that is through reading books or meeting people, traveling, writing poetry, or playing the piano. There is something about creativity, there's an element of surprise in it. It has something to do with not knowing. You do not know what the end result will be. But the minute I let go of the required creativity and the attitude 'if I don't figure this out this minute,' the minute I take that pressure off myself, the creative juices flow much easier." She experiences her essential creative nature through spirituality, community work, writing poetry, making collages, drawing, cooking, playing the piano, and nurturing relationships with family and friends.

Lilly is not judgmental about her abilities, or even her products, because they are not for "professional purposes." She allows herself the freedom to explore and work in several mediums, simply as a form of self-expression and pleasure. Her life in the present is enriched by her desire to be engaged and by her need for more. Now however, the motivation behind the "more" differs. Because she is learning to let go and allow the process to occur, Lilly is able to try different things and to approach a problem in a new way. By her own definition, this is creative behavior.

Lilly acknowledges that her personal creative expression is a gift to give back to people. "I have a great ability to be happy and have a good time. I think that takes some creativity. I also see the products of my creativity in the work I do, but those are secondary to the gift I have for relationships. I consider the friendships I have the result of many gifts, but one of them is some kind of creative thinking. When I answer someone's questions, my creativity is put to use. How do I address a problem in a way that will be nonthreatening, noncondescending, and helpful? The creativity is in how I keep the dialogue open." Lilly respects her ability to listen, identify, and solve problems.

Why has communication become Lilly's most precious creative expression? As a child, Lilly did not feel heard. She did not feel valued. Her relationship with her parents and her older brother helped to foster these sentiments. The household was filled with tension and unspoken demands and expectations. Her parents were "emotionally abusive, excessive drinkers, and emotionally removed." Now in her adulthood, Lilly is learning to communicate with them. She explains, "My parents were controlling, overly domineering, emotional cripples. They did a lot of damage to me. I could have been a squashed person. I dealt with it by getting high. I never felt my parents were real, that you could sit down and talk to them." To avoid her feelings of pain, isolation, disappointment, anger, and confusion, she began smoking marijuana and drinking alcohol at an early age. Lilly's path into self-destructive behavior actively began to manifest itself around the age of nine and thus began the first transformation in her life. Instead of the normal growth pains of adolescence, Lilly medicated herself to avoid her feelings. In so doing, she damaged the first important transformation into adulthood and hindered her growth as a young woman. Yet it was more profound than that; she altered her perception of the world and changed the inner flow of her creative impulses. Lilly was fortunate, however; her core being had been given support and love by her grandparents and younger brother. This love would serve as her foundation when she went into recovery.

Her relationship with her brothers was simultaneously loving, warm, supportive, threatening, and confusing. The impact of a tumultuous relationship with her older brother was offset by the relationship she had, and continues to have, with her younger brother. Her younger brother has "profoundly enriched" her life. She admits he "helped me to keep a more positive attitude toward men." At nine or ten years of age, her older brother sexually abused her "twenty to thirty" times.

What made this experience so difficult for Lilly were the mixed messages she received from him. He bullied her and teased her, yet he also sincerely gave her love, support, and aid. When she felt unable to speak to her parents about her needs, it was her older brother who spoke for her. Her older brother did not escape the pressures of the house either. He too has suffered much of his life from drug and alcohol abuse. While achieving career success, his inner life was dying. (Like Lilly, her older brother has since found a way through twelve-step recovery programs to rid himself of drugs and alcohol and reclaim his life.) Communication was at best difficult for Lilly, yet it is the essential context of how she negotiates her gifts in the world today.

Her choice to become an ordained minister simply illustrates how a loss experienced in youth can become the impetus for a creative gift in adulthood. In fairness to her parents, it also reflects positive qualities given to her through their moral underpinnings. Her mother managed the care of the children and the household, but always did community service. Lilly believes her mother and father are both creative. "My mother had wonderful things for us to do and make. She is a gourmet cook. I love her house at Christmas. I love the way she dresses. My father, who is a lawyer, is creative financially. He loves playing the piano and the harmonica. One of the few things I did solely with my father was playing the piano." But her parents expected creative behavior from their children. They were goal-oriented and expected their children to achieve career success.

Lilly's approach and sensitivity to the world are uniquely her own. "I have a joy of living, a great ability to enjoy my life. I have done the work that has enabled me to deal with those things that prevent me from enjoying my life. The fact that I stopped drinking has had a major influence on my life. I think my intelligence and, more importantly, my sense of humor have helped me. I find almost anything hilariously funny and that has helped me deal with things."

Creativity is clearly demonstrated through those activities a woman holds most dear. Joseph S. Renzulli believes "it is primarily in those areas in which one takes a deep personal interest and has staked a salient aspect of one's identity that the more individualized and 'creative' components of one's personality are energized." Like Victoria, the older woman painter in Chapter Two, Suzanne believes learning is of paramount importance in her life. The essence of Suzanne's desire to learn is fundamental to how she experiences life. Seeking, seeing, knowing—those are the qualities that compose her essential creative nature. Suzanne is a sixty-eight-year-old, white, upper-middle-class woman. She is married and has two daughters. She is a bright, articulate, opinionated, warm, friendly, approachable woman. She speaks easily of who she is and what she thinks.

Suzanne believes she has a good personality; she enjoys being with people, and she enjoys her life, despite her fears. She declares, "I love the things I do, and I never do things half-heartedly." Because of that trait, she is judgmental and demanding of others. Suzanne has an intense love of learning, though she sees herself as "a dilettante." She explains her sentiment, stating, "I love to learn, but it does not seem to have a place in the world." Suzanne characterizes herself as a "very moral person." She believes she lives and thinks in a moral way. She is "generous, dedicated, and devoted." She tries not to be trivial. The very idea offends her. She told me she does not see everything as equal. "Some people are better than others," but she views that perspective with regret.

Suzanne was born and raised in a large northeastern city. Her father and mother were Jews born and raised in Poland. Her father, though he had no formal education and could not write well, was literate. Indeed, he read very well and was a "good storyteller." Though he was demonstrative about his love, he also demanded performance. He was devastated when Suzanne dropped out of college. She was bright, and he expected her to perform up to her intellectual capacity. Her mother had a high school education and, contrary to her father, Suzanne says her "mother did not seem to be able to show affection; she expected obedience over performance."

In this country, Suzanne's father worked in the shoe industry, and before marriage her mother worked as a milliner. After marriage, her mother managed the household and did volunteer work at the hospital and as an election poll registrar. Suzanne felt love, warmth, and security within her home, but she was threatened by the world outside. The family had little money, enough for their housing and food but not much else. Her mother, Suzanne says, was determined to "provide a safe environment for her family." She describes her mother as creative "because she created the most beautiful home with little money. She was a wonderful hostess, baker, and cook. Her sewing was artistically done. But like the women of her time, she was very repressed." While her parents did their best to provide for their daughters, her parents' fears of the world infiltrated the home. Suzanne understands the influences that contributed to the source of her own internal fears. She states, "My sister and I were treated like princesses, but we had nothing. It was a fairy tale; it was not true. The environment my mother created gave us a sense of security when we were very young. We were very loved, but we felt uncertain of our future. It was a wonderful home, but there was a lot of fear. I was not frightened of people; I was frightened of 'out there.' I knew from my parents it was going to be rough. It may sound dramatic, but the fact that there was a war on as I was growing up had a tremendous effect on me. It was one additional reason I was so fearful. I cannot imagine how it would have been without that war. I felt personally involved in the war because my father had family in Europe. Also there was a great deal of anti-Semitism in my neighborhood. I think the world that you are brought up in affects you."

Protecting herself from "out there" became her guiding principle. This defensiveness has hindered Suzanne's personal creative expression and limited her possibilities for growth. As a child, Suzanne had a fantasy to be "a great thinker and influence a lot of people." Though Suzanne has continually underestimated her influence upon the world around her, she has fulfilled her fantasy in two ways, both nontraditional. First, Suzanne has for the last fifteen or twenty years led a Great Books seminar; second, she has acted as a docent in a major metropolitan museum.

Suzanne's quest for knowledge helps to frame her definition of creativity. Like Lilly, Suzanne understands creativity through the process of transformation and the making of something new. She says, "When you take a real thing and turn it in your mind or your hands, you make it into something that you perceive. That is creativity. In order to make it real for yourself, you re-create it. You turn it around in your mind first, before you do anything with it. For me creativity works mainly in the mind." Suzanne's creative manifestation or product, then, is expressed in the intellect. Her seeking, the very thing that stimulates, motivates, and thrills her, also drives her crazy. She says she is always second-guessing herself and her perceptions. Because of this pattern, Suzanne tries to weigh everything from both sides. But she gets lost in the process, unable to determine the best direction or to feel secure in her perspective. Suzanne never received the tools through formal education to assure herself that the concepts she arrives at are valid. She remains uncertain of how and why she reaches a specific conclusion. Without a formal process to guide her quest, Suzanne is left feeling insecure and tentative about her thoughts. It is a problem for her because she sees it as such. An article in *New Woman* in 1995 reported that "a study of several hundred people of varying age groups . . . [found that the] most common regret . . . was not getting a good education, followed closely by not 'seizing the moment.'" Had Suzanne finished college, her path would have been different. She might also have been spared several barren intellectual years. Had Suzanne found a mentor during her first year of college, I believe she would have formally studied the appropriate disciplines that motivate and shape her quest for knowledge. She would have felt her view had credibility.

Since learning and seeking are the paths to her essential creative nature, I wondered if Suzanne saw them as creative. "No, I am not creative, because I do not make things. People tell me how much I influence their thinking, their lives, their perceptions of things, of life. That is a creative kind of thing. I guess the role of mentor is a creative kind of thing." Then, "No!" she blurts out. "I could be a terrific critic. I can critique almost anything. I can get to the bottom of things. I can see the way it has been put together. I can go to a movie, read a book, see a painting, go to a city and see a building and I critique it. What is that?" Because she finds fulfillment in learning, Suzanne spends her time reading, listening to music, going to concerts, theaters, and galleries, and entertaining. She believes her strongest expression is leading the Great Books seminars. Suzanne's talent also lies in her abilities to speak to people and to help others find joy and satisfaction in intellectual seeking. The energy and drive that motivates Suzanne to conceptually seek out and understand new information is the same energy and drive that motivates a painter to paint, or a dancer to dance.

Suzanne's creative expression is in seeking, in moving through a maze of mystery and wonder intellectually. Lilly's creative expression is in connections and the ability to give spiritual support and understanding. Like Lilly and Suzanne,

Tonia, the third and last woman in this chapter, is always searching. Unlike Lilly and Suzanne, Tonia needs to produce a tangible product. At thirty-three years old, she is extremely productive. She is bright, articulate, highly energetic, and well-spoken. Her creative energy fuels her approach to life.

Born in Mexico, she was raised in a large metropolitan city in the midwest. She is one of four children, two girls and two boys. Her ties to her Mexican heritage and her involvement in the Mexican community have helped shape her vision and influenced her creative expression. By trade she is a journalist; that is the public demonstration of her creativity. Recently she has found a private outlet for her creative vision, which has grown more spiritual over the years. She creates altars in her home with her husband, who is a painter, and she builds public altars for certain religious holidays.

Tonia is driven to express her vision. That drive has helped shape her guiding image, which she describes experiencing on a "visceral level. My desire is to have recognition, to achieve. It has not been to prove myself because I've always believed I could do what I wanted to do. But it has been to be recognized." Tonia feels that recognition through creative self-expression would be the ultimate. She declares, "Then I would be recognized for being my true self. As a journalist, my biggest struggle is trusting my voice. My voice is an important one." Over the last few years, Tonia's understanding of creativity has shifted. Viewing herself as creative was inspired by her friends. She explains, "Not too long ago, in conversation with friends, many of whom are artists, I would say I am not creative, I am not an artist. They would say you are! You just create in a different space. That was the changing point in how I saw myself and creativity."

Tonia's need for recognition has its foundation in her cross-cultural upbringing. While the culture in her home was Mexican, the culture of the outside world was American. This presented a problem for Tonia. "Growing up in an immigrant family in this country, I was different and therefore needed to be recognized for who I was. As a result, I became competitive. Sometimes that is a negative trait." Most of Tonia's family still lives in Mexico. They are upper-middle-class and well educated. Her aunt and uncle are considered a bit odd because they are "intellectuals," but their influence upon Tonia has been great. "The happiest times in my life were spent in Mexico," she admits. Tonia's father moved to the states with his family when she was a year old. He is an ear, nose, and throat specialist. Though her mother was a high school dropout, she is now a well-respected social worker. Her mother has achieved recognition in her field despite her lack of formal education in her discipline. She specializes in dealing with problems affecting Latino women. Tonia views her mother's capacity to "re-create her persona" as evidence of her mother's creative abilities. One of Tonia's brothers is a professor. Goal-oriented behavior runs throughout the family profile. A confluence of influences may explain her need for recognition. The drive within the family to achieve and her experience as a petite immigrant child who felt different and needed to make her presence known may also have contributed to her need for recognition.

Whatever propelled Tonia to seek recognition and personal expression influenced her core personality. Her work has been her primary form of creative self-expression. It determines the shape and content of her work. Self-expression determines how she presents herself to the world. For example, she wears her hair, which is long, dark, and wavy, loosely around her face and neck. She was advised that her style was "too ethnic" by others in the television business. Similar issues arose around her choice of jewelry. But Tonia understood that these two images had political overtones. Rather than play down her ethnic origins, she wanted to highlight them. She won that battle. Publicly acknowledging her culture has helped shape her vision.

Tonia has always responded to her essential creative nature. She believes that her "innermost desire" was to have been an artist, but she did not trust herself to achieve in that capacity. Instead she channeled her energy into writing and producing. Though she has not professionally pursued the arts, she sees herself "as creative. When I do things, whether it is building an altar, or doing a radio piece or an interview, I trust myself. I can see my expression. I would say that in almost all aspects of my life I'm trying to be creative: when I'm writing and conceiving my stories, the way I interview people, when I dance, when I do my altars, when I cook, in my spatial concept of my house." Because Tonia commits herself to her actions, it is a natural consequence that she defines creativity as personal expression. She believes, "Creativity means to trust your inner passion, to express yourself in whatever it may be. It has a lot to do with having a sense of trust. For a long time, creativity for me was something specific, like being a dancer, or an actress, but now I think it is broader and more elusive."

In the book *Women Who Run with the Wolves*, Clarissa Pinkola Estés speaks of the river that flows deep within. It is the source that feeds us. The inner river is a powerful life force; as with any vital river, the energy in the flow keeps the river and the life supported by the river alive. "[C]reativity emanates from something that rises, rolls, surges, and spills into us rather than from something that just stands there hoping that we might, however circuitously, find our way to it. In that sense we can never 'lose' our creativity. . . . The only ways we can avoid its insistent energy are to continuously mount barriers against it, or to allow it to be poisoned by destructive negativity and negligence." Your connection to this powerful surge of energy happens when your river, metaphorically speaking, flows freely, unencumbered by your negative emotions. The flow can be altered or stopped by your own thinking and avoidance of your essential creative natures. Whether the image is of Gaia, the essential earth, or the powerful river, the message is the same—the vital energy that flows within must be released to create life.

Negative thinking impedes a woman's ability to respond to her creative impulses. Indeed, it may stop the impulses from happening at all. In the act of re-creating herself, a woman learns about herself and life. Lilly's essential creative nature needed to find its way out. Drinking delayed its healthy emergence. Fear and avoidance of who she was and how she performed in the world only limited the joy she was capable of feeling and the creative surge of energy she was capable of experiencing. Fortunately, Lilly responded to the internal earthquake when it shook her being. The pain and fear were becoming overwhelming; alcohol and drugs no longer worked. Scared and unsure of what she was doing or feeling, she let her earthly essence begin to emerge. For the first time since she was nine years old, she faced herself and the world without the use of alcohol or drugs. This approach, if open and honest, results in change and radical transformations. Success can be experienced on many levels, not just measured in monetary values or career success. For Lilly, the river has been set free through a series of risky steps, both large and small. The core of Lilly's creative being is still finding ways in which to manifest itself in the world. As long as Lilly allows the river to flow, or as long as the energy within the volcano is used in healthy, self-affirming actions, her journey will continue to be creative and productive.

Creative behavior takes time to be nurtured. Sometimes women are isolated from their own inner being, from the river that feeds their souls. Sometimes they subject themselves to negative thinking, neglecting their spiritual/creative sides and stopping the inner river and the flow of energy. Suzanne's fear of "out there" has hindered her ability to assertively respond to her creative impulses. It has hindered her personal creative expression in her intellectual pursuits. She struggles daily against her self-doubting, using much of her creative energy to overcome her fears. Suzanne's intelligence has helped her withstand the threat of losing herself in the process. She told me that she regrets not having gone into therapy years ago; then she would have a learned process to overcome her negative messages. From Suzanne's perspective, learning the lessons of life has been her path: "You must learn from whatever happens, and do the best you can. I think that is what life is—learning how to do the best you can and not become bitter and rotten to other people."

I believe that our lives, as Suzanne stated, "are always in process." The process and the path differs for everyone. Tonia lives a fast-paced life that she alone created. As the outside world moves quickly by her, and as she moves from deadline to deadline, she is learning to sit still and listen. She is learning to let her essential creative nature be revealed. Time is slowing down within her, allowing her to deepen her connection to her personal creative expression and making the most productive choices in shaping her life. In the past, when Tonia felt cut off from her creative impulses, she spontaneously picked up and moved. She has lived on the west coast, in Mexico, in Washington D.C., and in the northeast. Sometimes such changes are productive; sometimes they are a sign of internal discord. Tonia is now married, so her spontaneous responses have a greater influence upon the world around her. Because the vision of her world is different now, she is learning to sit with her impulses, learning to allow other aspects of her life to filter in and direct her choices. This shift in response pattern is in itself a creative transformation, a creative act. Tonia is learning to deal with problems differently. She told me that this process is teaching her that sometimes she needs to wait and not be spontaneous. Tonia is learning that sometimes creativity or creative impulses need time. Spontaneous responses are not necessarily the reflection of a completed creative process. First impulses are, after all, only first impulses. Tonia's ability to sit quietly is growing. As her vision broadens through the people and things that share her life, she becomes more deeply connected to her essential creative nature.

Perhaps a woman's path is straight and easily traveled. Perhaps it is frightening; the emotional and physical terrain may be rugged, the woman's vision blurred. Lilly, Suzanne, and Tonia have each followed a "unique" path. The knowledge they have gained from their journeys is personal. Their work history has reflected their ongoing process of becoming. Unlike many bright young women, Lilly was not lost in her career choice. She did not flounder when she graduated college. She did not take meaningless jobs, moving from one unsatisfactory experience to another. She was able, despite her substance abuse, to identify what she wanted to do and what she needed to succeed. Like many "functioning" alcoholics, she maintained her goal-directedness and drive. Though her profession has recently changed, the essence of her creative expression has not altered. Only the outward context for her expression looks different.

Lilly's involvement with her church and her desire to do work benefiting the community have always been constant. In college, she did volunteer work for her church with social service agencies and also worked with an agency that dealt solely with housing and planning. When it came time to make a career choice, her father, being practical and logical, sent her on several interviews where she could learn what was required to move ahead in her chosen field. The matter was approached in an orderly, logical fashion. Her choice was housing and real estate. Lilly decided to take a job as a loan officer in the real estate division of a major bank. After five and one half years, she went to work for a major developer putting together loan packages. That position was unsatisfying; her boss was extremely difficult to work with, so she changed jobs again.

She chose to work for a company that financed the rehabilitation of buildings for low-income housing. Lilly had acquired the knowledge and recognition needed in her field. She was fortunate to have had a mentor in real estate who believed in her talent and taught her what was necessary. That relationship, which was initially professional, became social. (This is a problem in male/female mentor relationships.) Full responsibility was given to Lilly for setting up and running a new office. She "got the office off the ground." First she scouted towns and cities for prime redevelopment areas. Then she worked with developers on loan packages to make the rehabilitations occur. In the ten years she spent in that field, she achieved an impressive position, an impressive salary, and her work had social merit. Yet something was wrong. She was no longer satisfied intellectually, emotionally, or spiritually.

Several years earlier, Lilly had entered a twelve-step recovery program for substance abuse, and that began another transformation. The process led to her wondering how she might alter the context of her work and her life. Communication and helping those in need had always been priorities. Her inner urgings impelled her to change. She decided to investigate becoming a CAC (certified alcohol counselor.) Beginning cautiously, slowly, as is her style, she did not leave her job immediately, nor did she enroll in the program full-time. Instead, she took one class to test the waters, to see if she liked it. Early in the semester, Lilly realized that she did not agree with what was being taught or with how the subject was being presented. She left the class. She was not daunted by this realization. She had long, soul-searching discussions with a woman friend who was a minister, as well as with the minister of her church. She decided to apply to divinity school. After ten years in real estate, Lilly did not expect a reputable graduate school for divinity to seriously consider her as an applicant. But remembering an expression from the twelve-step programs, "Feelings are not fact, they are feelings," she did not allow her fear or the negative messages to stop her inward journey. Lilly had been learning to handle those negative messages that can stop progress. She had been learning to value her inner voice and seek a healthy creative expression. The changes would be radical. Her life would alter, but she decided she would return to school. How would she cope? She would have to quit her job, letting go of a respectable position and a six-figure salary. How would she write academic papers after all these years? The force of Gaia's nature, represented in an ever-changing, ever-renewing life, was the same force driving Lilly to apply to school. She worked diligently and honestly on her application and the essay on why she wanted to be admitted. Her efforts were rewarded. She was accepted at two of the top divinity schools in the nation.

Lilly's recovery from substance abuse helped release the impulse for change. The time, thought, and emotion needed to make the change could not have been so clearly articulated had she still been under the influence of drugs and alcohol. She would not have been able to see a way to pursue a life based on process. Transformations helped her free herself emotionally. She also chose to become involved with a man who wanted to be in her life, a man who wanted to share love in a healthy relationship with her. She took another risk and committed herself to this relationship and married him. For Lilly, her spirituality had become her method of understanding and negotiating the world, her emotions, and her actions. It has become an integral aspect of her personal creative expression. Lilly sees this as her impulse for more. I would prefer to frame the creative impulse for more in the context of seeking something grounded in vision and personal expression.

Since the seeking of personal vision and creative expression are part of the essential creative nature, any action leading a woman away from her core results in psychological and physical discomfort or pain. Suzanne was isolated from herself and those who saw her gifts. Her choices were met by physical and emotional discomfort. She had betrayed her own essential creative nature. She had left college after the first year. Suzanne did not read the messages in her body, nor did she pay attention to the pleadings of family and friends to change her mind. "It was a terrible time for me, and I have never glossed over it." Self-doubting has been the long-term effect of that action.

Suzanne never returned to school to receive a formal degree. Nevertheless, her thirst for learning was insatiable. "I love not knowing. I love going back and finding out. I want to know why does something start. Why does something touch me? It makes me sleepless; it is wonderful." Concepts are exciting, and because Suzanne willingly shares this enthusiasm, she was and is naturally suited to leading the Great Books seminar and being a museum docent. Her ability to get others engaged in a sharing dialogue and learning from each other takes a particular talent. Suzanne diminishes these talents because she insists that she is learning too. I wonder why Suzanne believes that teaching excludes the experience of learning? As a docent, she receives weekly training at the museum and receives specialized training from time to time. When I spoke with her, she had just finished a six-week intensive course given by the staff of a well-renowned museum of contemporary art. The staff trained the docents, Suzanne recalls, on "how to look at contemporary art. Most people do not know how to look at it, understand it, never mind discuss it." Suzanne has been a docent for ten years, and though she has taken a break from the Great Books seminar, she insists, "I will go back to it, I need it. I know it is coming."

Painting a new picture, composing a new piece of music, managing an insufficient budget, or finding the solution to an intellectual problem are all problem-solving experiences. Suzanne searches for beginnings, for clarification and understanding in the metaphysical underpinnings of art and litera-ture. The excitement she now feels in this exploration did not occur until her thirties. She lived a comfortable life raising two daughters. Despite the outer trappings, she was bored by her life and did not know what to do. Her discontent was internal. She lacked intellectual stimulation. "I thought that I would go back to college and get a degree. Someone said there was a program where I could get credit for my life experiences. I really could have gone and gotten my degree in a very short time. I decided not to because I did not know what I would do with the degree. It has never been my family that has held me back. It has always been me."

When her youngest daughter was two or three years old, Suzanne became involved in a study group with a Jewish orga-nization. In a short time, she was researching topics and lead-ing the discussion groups with another woman. "It was very safe. That was the beginning of my saying I needed people to be intellectually stimulated. I began to reach out. But I could not find anything that I liked. I did not like women's organi-zations. I did not like the PTA. I am not an organization per-son. I did the discussion groups for five years. Then I moved." The inner pressure from years of repressing her essential cre-ative nature could no longer be quelled. The need to respond was too great to ignore. She could no longer stand still, hop-ing that something would happen. The study group was the impetus for what began her next transformation. That same year, Suzanne took a class in comparative religions at a univer-sity near her. She told me how difficult it felt, how she was floundering without direction until her instructor acknowl-edged Suzanne's essential creative nature. "This extraordinary woman came into my life. I had taken her class for a year when she asked me if I wanted to come to a Great Books seminar. I did not know what it was. She sent me information and I did it. I was lost. I am articulate, but I could not speak. I did not know what to say. I spoke to her about it, and she said, 'Suzanne this is for you; you should be a leader.' I told her, I cannot even speak, never mind being a leader. She told me I would be fine. She made me join a group as a participant. After two or three years, I took a training program, and then I led a group. That was my college education. That was the best thing I ever did."

Suzanne was serious about her effort. When she led a group, she would spend hours preparing for the discussion. She was moving through early middle age when the women's movement gained public attention; by that time her daughters were grown and in college. The women's movement, coupled with a different posture expressed by her daughters and their friends, struck a chord deep within Suzanne. "My children are very intelligent women. I am extraordinarily proud of their abilities. I think I felt I had to do something too. I wanted to be me, somebody that could do something, somebody who could contribute something, particularly because women of my daughters' generation were beginning to choose such wonderful things to do with their lives. I think that had a great influence. I do not know that, had I had sons, it would have been the same. The fact that they were women with choices made me more aware of things I did not think about."

After many years of leading the Great Books seminar, Suzanne began to grow tired and felt she wanted to do something else. A different woman came into her life and asked Suzanne if she would be willing to work as a docent at a museum. Responding from her fear, Suzanne rejected the idea—"It is ridiculous, I am not trained in art"—and just as it happened earlier, this woman told Suzanne she would do fine. "If you led Great Books, you will be terrific." Suzanne went for the training and loved it. "I went and came home and said they are willing to train me in art history. It's what the really good colleges would do. I took the training, and my eyes were opened to a whole new world." This time Suzanne was responding more quickly to her inner voice. She understood the impulse; she saw the opportunity, and she needed to act. She allowed her environment and those who touched her life to reveal the path to her. The way to a woman's path sometimes comes from other people or things around her. Sometimes the path appears in an unexpected direction, perhaps through a comment made in passing by a stranger. Suzanne never envisioned herself leading a Great Books seminar, nor did she envision herself as a docent at a major metropolitan museum. Yet she does both successfully and is filled with satisfaction. She is stimulated by her efforts and the interactions that occur, and her creative energy and her intellectual insights are given back to the world.

As you have read, Lilly and Suzanne have transformed their inner lives. That in and of itself is a creative act that many people, to their own detriment, shy away from. Both women possess the drive and the courage to proceed. The forward motion may be fast, or the pace may be slow and steady. As a woman moves through her daily life, I wonder whether the speed of the transformation is as significant as the transformation itself. Often in the quiet moments of life, a woman can hear her essential creative nature calling. Acknowledging those moments deepens her connection to her essential creative nature. Tonia juggles her "self-determination" and need for recognition with a creative source that is less dependent upon others. She believes in the importance of her drive and her "commitment to things." But that drive isolates her from her family and friends, and she and they suffer. She worries a lot.

Many women, like Tonia, Lilly, and Suzanne, begin a tumultuous inner journey in their thirties. I found that the women in their twenties, though creative and vibrant, did not possess a sufficient inner understanding of themselves as women in the world to thoroughly speak about creativity and their lives. The journey inward requires awareness. At a young age, a woman lacks a certain capacity or reference point for self-reflection. Perhaps the twenties are a time when women are still shedding their adolescent persona, trying on new ones and beginning to savor what it means to be an independent adult. I found shifts occurring in the thirties, late forties, and early fifties. The inner urging has to be strong enough to catch a woman's attention, but once that happens her life becomes fertile ground.

The transition Tonia is experiencing comes from a quiet, serene place. It is a place free of time constraints and fast movement. It is a place that demands inner recognition. This place is private but open, solitary but joyful. Tonia has worked hard to find this place. Her journey began right after graduating from a women's college with honors. After an internship with a radio station, she decided she wanted to be a reporter. Brief stints of intense political activism, working as a waitress, and free-lance reporting followed. She did not feel creatively fulfilled, so she found a job as a production assistant for a radio station. For a short time, she felt creative; her approach was new. She explains that she "was the first Latino to be hired in house. The impetus was to be creative, but I got tired. I was not recognized for my work." After a year, she quit and moved to the west coast. She then began producing a Spanish-language radio program. Regretfully she says, "I was not able to be as creative as I wanted to be because I did not have enough staff. But that is where I hooked up with all these Mexican artists. I did a few art exhibits; I did a few documentaries. Things were definitely boiling." Despite these activities, she felt constrained and moved back east to work on a prime-time morning show. That show was disappointing for her, but for the first time she had enough money to go to jazz concerts and the theater. Once again she grew restless and constrained. She quit her job and tried free-lance work again. It was an exciting year for Tonia, and she loved developing her own stories. She had become involved with a man who was, as she describes him, a "Mexican intellectual, an alcoholic and unfaithful." Despite the pain of such a relationship, she found the romantic notion of the sick, suffering, brilliant artist stimulating.

Alcoholism and infidelity are problems that can ravage individual lives and the lives touched by the problem. Artists may suffer, as do a large percentage of the general population, from substance abuse or behavioral addictions, but these addictions are not the source of creative behavior, nor are they the source of inspirational thinking. However, this relationship offered Tonia an opportunity to mingle with other Mexican intellectuals and artists. It was through these connections that she began building altars and discovered a sense of freedom in dancing to Latin American music.

Tonia's need to freely and fully express herself drove her from job to job. She changed jobs two more times before settling in her present job. She met a Latin American painter who was soon to become her husband. These last few years have been satisfying for her in her marriage and in her work. Her husband's work, which she describes as "kind of Caribbean pop, very angelic, very mystical, mythic. He works with Indian traditions of his country," has had a profound influence upon her and her vision. Needing to produce, still driven to be recognized, Tonia contracted to have her own television show. That experience was difficult, but it afforded her the opportunity to confront herself as well as others. She explains that the producers tried to create an image that was not of Tonia. They straightened her hair and made her wear suits. They tried to control the questions she asked. Over the years, Tonia had learned to value her voice and to respect and rejoice in her ethnic origin and culture. She knew what she needed to say. She fought for herself and won. She also began working on her first book. Currently Tonia works on her own writing, radio, and television projects.

Everyone's essential creative nature is unique. For Tonia, there has been much activity and a quick flourishing. This flourishing has been accompanied by high energy. But like Lilly and Suzanne, the time for quieter inner connections is beginning to take hold. Until now, outside recognition has been paramount. I believe that Tonia has shifted her awareness to an inside recognition, to an inner self-discovery. The altars, her cultural connections, her dancing, her spirituality, her efforts to have a family with her husband are part of her inner path. The fury of the volcano or the dynamic impulse of the earthquake come from within. The inner core helps determine the topography. Like Gaia's essence, impulses are the fervent beginnings of the process of creative expression.

Finding the inner voice for self-exploration is a creative process, which in turn produces creative products. Lilly, Suzanne, and Tonia have demonstrated how contact with the world can offer pathways to finding or enlarging a woman's creative expression. Lilly, Suzanne, and Tonia's stories illustrate how seeking openness through a willingness to see, hear, and feel their inner urges leads women into exciting, intellectually, emotionally, and spiritually challenging experiences. According to Anne Roe's study "Painters and Painting," there are four ways in which an artist initiates work: the stimuli come from within, from an idea or an emotion; the precipitating stimuli come from without; the external and internal are closely interwoven in a combination of idea or mood and a visual experience; and finally, the artists can begin work using either internal or external stimuli. The impulses for change, whether it is a career change, a vision change (as Tonia experienced), or a life change, are all around and within. A woman's life is fertile with possibilities, she need only listen to the inner calling of her essential creative nature and feel the clues in the shifting forms of the world around her.

The following exercises offer you the opportunity to review your own path and to place it within a conceptual framework. It is my hope, especially for those of you who have never looked at your path, that you will discover something new, something that may spark an impulse within to explore your essential creative nature.

In the first series of exercises, you identified how you define creativity, what your guiding principle has been, things you do well, and in what context others tell you that you are creative. Now look at your lists again. What messages about creativity have you been given by others? Is there a common thread running through your lists? Is your essential creative nature thoughtful, practical, methodical, intellectual, emotional, physical? Are you talented at communicating, the arts, listening to and identifying problems, sports, handling budgets, or organizing?

Whatever you find, value. It is yours. It is part of your essential creative nature. But perhaps you need to open the path to your essential nature. Perhaps you need to revitalize your vision and your personal expression. Do things you do come easily to you? Are they done without much effort or thought? The time to challenge yourself may be now. You can begin with a small challenge, or something that arouses tremendous fear. It depends upon what you want to accomplish. Consider taking the following simple actions to stimulate the impulses within:

1. Take a different route to work. What are the different sights, sounds, feelings?

2. Take a class. If you have always wanted to take a calligraphy class, do so. If you have always wanted to take a philosophy class, enroll now. Whatever your fantasy wish has been, follow it.

3. Change your hairstyle, your makeup, the colors you usually wear or some other aspect of how you physically present yourself to the world.

4. Keep a daily journal, noting your thoughts and feelings, and the sights, sounds, and physical sensations you experience during the day.

5. Get a massage, exercise, or do some other new physical activity.

6. Get help for an addiction or an emotional problem.

7. Ask someone you admire and trust to mentor you in something they do well, something you would do if you let your restraints go.

8. If you are not organized, organize your day. If you are too rigid, be spontaneous. Once a day do something small on impulse, then gradually add to the risks. Make your choice a healthy reflection of your creative experience. Perhaps you have wanted to see an exhibit at the museum, but normally you would not go alone. Now may be the time to test yourself. See the exhibit on your own.

9. Identify how you approach the world. What perceptions rule your behavior and your emotions?

10. Try using daily affirmations every morning before you begin your day! An affirmation can be as simple as, "All is well. I am good. I am enough." There are a variety of women's daily affirmation books available at most bookstores.

11. Become involved in a community group or a political organization you believe in. Volunteer to work at an organization that you feel reflects your principles.

CHAPTER FOUR

# IN HER IMAGE:
## CREATIVITY AND GENDER

❧

Demeter was the Greek Goddess of the Grain. She was responsible for everything that was born and grew.

> "Greek *meter* is 'mother.' *De* is the delta or triangle, a female genital sign known as 'the letter of the vulva' in the Greek sacred alphabet. . . . Demeter was what Asia called 'the Doorway of the Mysterious Feminine . . . the root from which Heaven and Earth sprang.' Doorways were generally sacred to women." (*The Woman's Encyclopedia of Myths and Secrets*)

> "The mother archetype was represented to Mt. Olympus by Demeter, whose important roles were as mother . . . provider of food . . . and spiritual sustenance. . . ." (*Goddesses in Everywoman*)

Without Demeter's attention nothing could grow. The lives of the gods and humans alike were touched by her domain. In her temple, overcome with sorrow by the abduction of her daughter Persephone, Demeter refused to see the world around her. Hades, the god of the Underworld, had abducted Persephone. Demeter roamed the earth looking for her daughter until she learned of her whereabouts. Demeter, angered at Zeus's part in her daughter's abduction and his refusal to return Persephone to her mother, left the place of the gods and neglected her responsibilities; instead she intensely grieved her daughter's absence. In her grief, the world was cast aside, the earth grew fallow, and famine plagued the people. The gods implored her to act in accordance with her godly domain. She refused. Only after the return of her daughter and their physical embrace did Demeter lift the weight of grief from herself and the world; the earth was renewed and the corn grew again.

Demeter's power was reflected in the impact she had on the world around her; it was embedded in her feminine aspect. This aspect defined her expression as a Goddess; she was mother, wife, and giver of life. Demeter acted out of her essential creative nature; nourishing the world fulfilled her need to express herself in her style. She did not need to throw lightning bolts to demonstrate her strength. Her actions were tied to the expression of self, to her inner essence. She was in all things a mother. This image is significant in looking at women and their relationship to creativity. It is significant in analyzing the factors that shape a woman's response to the world and the style by which it is revealed. In their perfect form, women express their essential creative natures through the doorways of the mysterious feminine. Women create the world around them. Those doorways do not just exist within the vulva; they exist within her emotional, intellectual, and spiritual being. Those doorways are the pathways through which a woman receives sustenance and inspiration for, and understanding of, her essential creative nature. The inextricably feminine aspect of Demeter is translated into form through the beauty of giving the product (grain) nourishment and love.

Women and men are endowed with both "feminine" and "masculine" traits, but in our culture those traits and what they represent have grown distorted. The images we are bombarded by daily are weighted with darkness and violence, aggression and the acquisition of power. The pursuit of control has led us all down the path of destruction—physically, intellectually, and spiritually. The masculine presentation of self has dominated for centuries. It has infiltrated the psyche of women and has left them disconnected from their own essential creative natures. It has perverted the image of those qualities labeled as feminine—softness, roundness, emotionality, and fullness of life-giving capacities—as inferior, though necessary for man's continuance. Many women misunderstand the power of the mysterious feminine. They see themselves as less than if these qualities are exposed. They struggle against themselves to bury that which is theirs by birth. They become burdened by negative value judgments erroneously attached to their feminine aspect. As a result, many women do not believe they have the capacity to succeed in the world. They do not attempt personal expression, and they shy away from being public. In an attempt to deny the mysterious feminine, those qualities defined as masculine—those that are logical, practical, aggressive, hard, and active—also become inaccessible to women. The irony is that now when women need to claim both sides of their nature, young women seem to be rejecting the masculine qualities for only the feminine. In *Women's Ways of Knowing*, Mary Field Belenky and her co-authors discuss the trend in academia: "Because of the high value Western technological societies have placed on objectivity, rationalism, and science, women and modes of thought cultivated by women had relatively little impact on the values and directions of modern society. . . . [T]here is a temptation for feminists to 'abandon their claim for representation in scientific culture and, in its place, to invite a return to purely "female" subjectivity, leaving rationality and objectivity in the male domain.'" The problem then compounds itself: as a woman, how do you define yourself? How do you create in the world without touching that which is inherently part of your nature? Demeter did not label her powers of mothering, or her role as guardian of and provider for the earth as feminine. In other words, she saw the world through her essential creative nature and acted according to that nature. She was who she was because she comprised masculine and feminine qualities. The configuration of those qualities varies within each woman and is responsible for her style.

The problems associated with understanding gender and its effect upon a woman's full expression of her essential creative nature are complex. The need to acknowledge the legitimacy of rationality, objectivity, softness, life-producing capacities, and emotionality is necessary if a woman is to find her own "voice." In *Writing a Woman's Life*, Carolyn G. Heilbrun implores women to share their stories with other women, to validate their stories by publicly acknowledging their voices, and to provide other women with a model for creating their own lives. The stress between possessing masculine and feminine qualities and rejecting them has yet to be resolved for many women and men. Without unity and wholeness of spirit, women can display only a portion of who they really are—a loss the world can no longer afford.

I believe issues around gender must be examined in order to fully understand creative behavior. A woman's perceptions about gender will influence the manner of her creative expression and the resultant product. Gender perceptions received early in childhood exert an influence upon a woman's essential creative nature. They affect the way she responds to the world around her: her view of the nature of men and women and their approaches to the world, and her style of expression. The influence of gender upon creative behavior has received little attention from researchers. It is not enough to just look at an end product to evaluate creative behavior. As a woman, I want to know what makes me behave as I do. What influences my creative expression? What inspires me? What interactions serve me positively? My gender is certainly one of those things that exerts an influence.

I cannot separate out my background, beliefs, and physical existence from who I am and how I express myself. Being female shapes my reality. It feeds my vision. I believe the mysterious feminine, those doorways into and out of my being, are the channels of my essential creative nature. Do all women hold perceptions of gender that filter down into their work and personal relationships? Do all women separate out gender from their work and their lives? These questions must be explored in order to understand women and their essential creative nature.

I asked the women I interviewed a series of questions about gender, gender perceptions, and gender roles, and about gender influences upon creative expression. Certain images and terms were repeatedly used in the women's responses. Most of the women were hesitant to make generalizations about gender and gender perceptions, and rightly so. No generalization accurately describes an individual. But a woman's perceptions are not solely reliant upon her individual experience. Perceptions form an overview of the world and are usually acquired or learned early in life. Rightly or wrongly, women and men use generalizations to inform their sense of truth about the world, about life, and about creating. Do these generalizations have biological origins or are they imparted by society? For the moment, it is of no importance. Perceptions in relationship to creativity need to be examined before tackling the problem of origins. In fact, the precise origins may never be proven.

I have chosen not to become entangled in polemic about defining femaleness or meanings of "womanhood" or "gender." As Elizabeth V. Spelman wrote in *Inessential Woman*, ". . . [I]f we examine the use of 'woman' in particular contexts, then we might be encouraged to ask when descriptions of what-it-is-to-be-a woman really are descriptions of what-it-is-to-be a woman in culture X or subculture Y. Being a woman, as we surely know by now from cross-cultural studies, is something that is constructed by societies and differs from one society to another." In an attempt to address this problem, without engaging in the discussion directly, I have tried to share the lives of women from different cultures throughout this book. Class, race, cultural, and educational differences among the women, including those chosen for this chapter, are part of their stories. It could not be otherwise.

Inner awareness broadens a woman's concept of creativity, opens her to change, and helps to actualize her essential creative nature. The deeper one's awareness of self is, the better one is able to approach creative behavior. This awareness does not equate with complexity. You need only recall Victoria and Gerrit's stories to understand the value in approaching creativity with simplicity and clarity. With simplicity and clarity of direction comes awareness and acceptance. Do you hold views about gender that isolate you from one part of yourself? Do you hold views about gender that stop you from acting upon your creative impulses? Do you hold views about yourself as a woman that diminish or negate that which is productive and active in your life? Do you know the dominant qualities that characterize your life? The three women you are about to meet have all struggled with the question of gender and the expression of their essential creative natures. Each one of these talented women has chosen to express herself differently, but all have been undeniably influenced by gender.

FIGHTING "HER" WAY OUT

Kathleen Noble published the results of her study on gifted women in *Psychology of Women Quarterly*. She wrote, "[W]hat little data exists suggest that at the elementary school level, at least one-half of all children 'identified' as gifted/talented/highly capable are girls; by junior high school, less than one-fourth are still so identified. . . . By adulthood, it is likely that the majority of gifted women will settle for far less than their full potential." To struggle against one's own essential creative nature is painful, debilitating, and time-consuming, as you have already seen. Yet many women do just that. A rebuff to your inherent femaleness further debilitates your creative energies and impulses. Financial success does not mean an absence of internal discord stemming from gender perceptions.

Nancy is a musically gifted, forty-two-year-old African-American Episcopalian minister. Her "calling" came to her in high school. Her path to ordination and her career as a teacher of theology has been strewn with personal trials. Like Lilly, Nancy has known the betrayal of self through drugs and alcohol, and the miracle of recovery. The reasons for Nancy's self-destructive behavior are to be found in part in her early-childhood and adolescent experiences. Valuing and cherishing herself as a woman has been difficult. She has known degradation and humiliation through her father's verbal and sexual abuse, being raped twice, overeating, racism, and the terror of never-ending depression. Her spirit, though still somewhat troubled, is beautiful and vibrant. Her essential creative nature is expressed in her feminine approach to her work as a minister and in her music; she gains power from her creative self-expression.

Nancy's mother was a strong role model of a professional woman. After practicing as a doctor of osteopathy for several years, her mother went back to college. She received a

Fulbright scholarship for economics, which was then followed by the birth of three children, all girls. Shortly after the birth of her youngest daughter, Nancy's mother went to work as a teacher of mathematics. Despite her mother's professional agility, she had unresolved personal problems and drowned her feelings with food. Nancy learned this model of behavior early in her youth. For her mother, food was a pacifier. Nancy's over-consumption of food is a defense against her body: being female has been dangerous. Any attention Nancy has received from men seemed bad. She has blamed herself, explaining, "I developed early physically. I was bigger than other girls. I ended up deciding that I was fat and ugly." She took responsibility for the sexual abuse inflicted upon her and nurtured the blame, shame, and guilt. Nancy's inability to feel good about her body and to be physically fit has distracted from her creative potential.

Despite negative feelings and behaviors, Nancy was grounded in the image of her mother's public productivity. That image has helped her to become a woman of moral and cultural stature. Nancy's battles to survive reflect basic problems women face growing up in a culture hostile to their full development. Unfortunately, Nancy has not yet come to closure with these early childhood experiences, nor has she completely reclaimed her emotional and physical life.

Despite the energy spent overcoming her barriers to self-worth, her essential creative nature, vitality, and faith have helped her survive. Music, one of her primary creative expressions, has been crucial to her well-being. In fact, music and her faith in a "supportive, caring, loving God" have been the two fundamental experiences that have kept her alive. When I asked Nancy what her guiding force had been, she explains, through tears, "I guess what has kept me alive is music. I was most at home when I was making music, and since my actual home was not comfortable, a lot of my life has been about finding home. Music has always provided that."

Fortunately, Nancy understood and valued her gift for music. Her singing has helped move her out of difficult, dark, and painful emotional places. In high school, Nancy always sang. Despite her superior voice, she was never given a lead in the school musical. Believing this reality was motivated by racism (she was one of only a few African-American students), her parents hired a lawyer and sued the school. That was a terrible year for Nancy. The school settled with the guarantee that Nancy would receive the lead in the next year's musical. Nancy's tentative sense of self and her struggle to see herself as good and worthy received another terrible blow. The part she was given was written for an alto, while Nancy was known to be a soprano. To further insult and hurt Nancy, the young female lead was a prostitute who was killed at the end of the play.

Music, teaching, and preaching, the expression of Nancy's essential creative nature, have helped her understand and define creativity and her connection to her God. She says, "Creativity is my most basic connection with the creator, with the creative force of life, and that connects to me with the music. The music has kept me alive. My music is my way of giving back to that which has kept me alive. It is like participating in a dance, a responsive singing. It is a give and take. For me it is tied up with spirituality and my relationship to God. Creativity has to do with energy, that which makes me feel most alive. There is always a sense that creativity comes from outside of me, but is at the same time most me."

The harsher realities of life pursued Nancy. In junior high school, within one year she experienced the loss of both of her dearest friends. One died a horrible death in a fire; the other moved away. The result of these experiences was, as Nancy frames it, "a core feeling that the people I loved the most would abandon me." However, Nancy has not abandoned others. She finds personal fulfillment of her essential creative nature in giving comfort and encouragement to others. Providing for, like Demeter, is part of Nancy's creative expression.

Others readily acknowledge and celebrate her creativity as a teacher, minister, and musician. Nancy recounts with pride that professional musicians have told her that she is "truly a musician." She puts passion into her life and her work. She believes that she is creative because what she does "elicits passion. I associate passion with creativity and a willingness to sacrifice other things to do them. There is something about these activities that I feel called to do them, to put it in religious terms. What happens as a result of them very much has my own stamp on it. It is particularly mine, identifiably mine. I am most myself when I am doing these things."

When a woman responds freely to her essential creative nature, there is an experience of wholeness within. Sherry feels most herself among women. She is a small-framed white woman who is vivacious and speaks easily of herself and her perceptions. At forty-two years old, she is a free-lance trainer and consultant for third-world women's organizations with a master's degree in international administration. Cross-cultural communication has had a significant place in her work. She develops fund-raising and marketing modules for women's economic development projects. She speaks more than one language fluently. Most of her working life has been for and about women. She believes gender issues have not influenced her choice to focus her career around women, but the intensity of her commitment to women and the path her life has taken are incongruous with that statement. She told me that she does not compartmentalize her life, and at times work has taken over, to the detriment of her immediate family (her husband) and her friends. Her desire to have an impact upon women's lives can be traced to her early experiences.

Sherry comes from a family environment cloaked in depression, fear, isolation, and fighting. The most profound traumatic influence upon Sherry's life occurred the year before she was born. Her mother's brother died of natural causes, and the impact of that death devastated the family. It plunged her mother and her grandparents into depression, intensifying their already heightened sense of fear. It was common to find her grandparents sitting in a darkened house in silence. Her mother never spoke about her brother or his death—all traces of his existence were hidden. Sherry believes her mother would "sneak peeks" at his pictures. Her mother's family was from Germany, and two other brothers had been killed in Germany during World War II. When her uncle died in this country, the family could no longer negotiate their grief and fear. They tried to escape their pain by wiping out his existence. But hiding from their pain simply caused it to control their lives.

The quality of Sherry's early years was further diminished by her parents' unhappy marriage. They fought constantly and threatened each other with abandonment. Her parents were frequently so "distracted with their arguing" that the children were ignored, although they knew they were deeply loved. Sherry had to negotiate and integrate fear of loss, fear of abandonment, and fear of sickness. Her father scared the children with his violent displays of anger (breaking furniture). He was sarcastic and undercutting. But nothing is just as it appears. Like the onion, there are many layers to be peeled away to understand the composition of the whole. Sherry's father also instilled in her a sense that she was smart, that she could do anything—within certain parameters. Despite his praise of her intelligence, his expectation along with her mother's, was for Sherry to "marry and have children." They demanded absolute loyalty to family and made Sherry feel that even friendships were an act of disloyalty.

Sherry holds on to a guiding image that is not fruitful for her as an adult. She admits, "I have talked about this over time with my therapist, so these ideas have been constructed over time. They haven't just popped into my head. One idea that has ruled my life is to leave while you're having a good time. I do not like to wear things out. In my life, I have made a decision about people who like to suck blood (they demand my life), and those who do not. I am in the latter category, although I can be a blood-sucker. I am aware of it, and I do not like it." "Getting out" through indirect and hurtful behavior has characterized her pattern of behavior in significant relationships. Staying and working problems through or ending a relationship openly and honestly has not been her style. She has been addressing that issue in therapy as well.

Sherry used her girlfriends as a means of holding on to the outside world in her youth. With her friends, she found a means of moving through her daily fears. Her friends, usually one "best" female friend, were viewed as her "window out." Sherry has always wanted to be with women, in work and in love relationships. She believes that she is a lesbian because of her deep connection to women, and because as she says "I truly love women." The word "lesbian" may be misleading. Sherry is married now, to a man, and that relationship is very important to her. I asked her why given her feelings about women, she would marry a man. She explained, "Max is very lesbian in his way. [He has] a sensibility, a sense of vulnerability in the world that most men do not have. That lets him relate to me. I appreciate him enormously because he is a man with that vulnerability." This feeling was expressed by other women about their husbands or male partners as well. The soft qualities, sensibilities, and vulnerabilities in men's personalities, or the "feminine aspect" of their beings, were the most endearing qualities for the women I interviewed.

Her parents influenced Sherry's creative expression in two other respects. She learned from her mother and father a particular approach to creating and thinking—one destructive, the other productive. In describing her mother's relationship to creativity, Sherry says, "Yes, she has creatively boxed herself into incredible misery. It is her ability to imagine things, to develop a cause-and-effect relationship between things that do not exist. Some people might call it nuts, but it is a kind of creativity." Her mother's use of her creative energies, as Sherry describes it, has no productive, life-affirming public expression. It is inner-directed and destructive in its intent. However, her mother's process also mirrors in reverse the one Sherry's father uses and the one Sherry herself uses. Her father demonstrated how one could explore the world through a game they called "what if. . . ." He trained her to use her imagination. Sherry plays the "what if . . ." game continually; it is how she approaches her life. She told me that people see her as creative because she looks at situations and problems and says, "What would happen if . . ." This technique is recommended for problem-solving. Sherry believes, "People confuse imagination with creativity. Just imagination is not enough. There must be an act." Sherry does not credit her ability to engage others through her imagination as an expression of her creativity or as a creative act. She minimizes her achievements as a professional trainer and attributes her accomplishments in her field to "being nice." After fourteen years working as a trainer and consultant who specializes in analyzing problems in women's economic development programs, I believe she brings more to her work than her pleasant personality. Her approach has been sought after by national women's organizations, international women's organizations, and federal agencies. Being able to work with others is certainly a talent. Since her seminars heighten the ability of women in third-world countries to solve problems concerning survival, Sherry's work requires more than mediocrity. Her method is based upon seeking and change. She possesses a never-ending desire to find a new way to approach a problem. For Sherry, the answer is not found within a textbook. Her concern for others, her choice to search for the answers through a communal process of exploration reveals a sensitivity toward a feminine orientation to the work. Though Sherry may diminish her creativity with regard to her work, others do not.

Not surprisingly, overcoming fear is an integral part of her definition of creativity. She defines creativity as "an absence of inhibition and the ability to get in touch with the space behind inhibition. To let it come out. Confronting your fears. You have to produce a product, but it does not have to be public. I leave before I can get in touch with that place. I have a memory which symbolizes the way I view my own creativity. I took piano lessons for years. I got to a point where I knew if I could get beyond that point I could play extraordinarily well. But I could physically feel the curtain go down, a block, a barrier. I could have broken through. I did not feel it was the limit of my capacity. It was the limit of my will! In a popular sense and not in an artistic sense, I think I spend a lot of time working through my inhibitions and blocks, to let things happen, to force myself to do things. Confrontation requires some creativity. The ways in which I confront my fears on a daily basis require a lot of creativity! I write, I create training, I am involved in creative processes."

As Sherry pointed out, dealing with her fears on a daily basis requires an act of creativity. Nurturing fears that no longer reflect the present reality demands a good deal of creative energy. Though Sherry has acquired a certain standing with her professional community, she holds herself back emotionally, spiritually, and professionally. Her life, like her mother's, is ruled by the negative attention and validation she gives to her fears. Her attachment to those fears is clearly articulated by Sherry: "I'm energetic, I'm analytical. I think through things, maybe too much. I'm neurotic. It is not a problem for me, but for everyone else. It absorbs me, it's where my creativity comes out. I analyze my neurosis, I ponder it. It's okay for me." It is my concern throughout this book that women embrace their essential creative natures through healthy, life-affirming creative expressions. The energy that Sherry places in cherishing her neurosis does not serve her well. A healthy, life-affirming choice would be to go "to the place behind the inhibition" and find the full expression of her essential creative nature, perhaps by playing the piano.

Performance is important for Marissa. She is a thoughtful, provocative Latino woman. She is thirty-seven, single, has no children, and describes herself as a poet, fund-raiser, and advocate for Latino women and children's needs. Her path to her creative expression has had twists and turns, but advocacy has shaped a large part of that journey. She was born in the Dominican Republic but was raised in Puerto Rico. Her childhood home was "wild." Because she was one of eight children (five brothers and three sisters), the children competed for attention. Being "noticed and heard" became a primary need and drive. When she was four years old, she fell out of bed and seriously injured her leg. She could not walk well. She recalls, "I did not play much, and that forced me to try to do better in other things like school. That marked my life. I needed to compensate, to prove that I had value."

Women use their creative energies to find ways to survive in most conditions. Sometimes the survival mechanism they create exerts a positive influence upon them; sometimes it does not. Until recently, the memory of being fondled by her father's friends has been repressed. That repression has complicated Marissa's life and has unwittingly sapped her creative expression. Her father was an evangelical minister and because he trusted his friends, he gave them a good deal of power in the house. Only recently has Marissa learned that one of her sisters has quietly dealt with this same violation of trust. Marissa told me that in adulthood she had been "emotionally abused" by men. With this awareness, Marissa can stop the pattern in her adult relationships and create a new, healthy context for her male/female relationships.

Marissa's lack of control in her childhood environment, the threatening nature of an older male presence in the house, and her physical disability in her youth caused her to develop a guiding force that was grounded in the need to be independent and to maintain a sense of control. As a result of this drive, Marissa says, "I became very hard. I became conservative because everyone in the house was so wild." In order to survive in that environment, "I was really controlling. I suffer when I have to relinquish power, when I have to stop controlling." Being heard and being in control have become the leitmotifs in her life. In her drive to be independent, Marissa has developed an understanding of herself and her personality traits. "I have a good sense of humor; I understand people; I am open and supportive. I support myself, and I think that is positive. I do not dislike myself, but I can be moody and very negative. I am not tolerant, but I am gentle, loving, and generally responsible, and I am a good friend."

Her journey to find and identify her essential creative nature led her through many stages. These stages can be best understood in the jobs she has held. But she says, "In my search, I have had to create certain things. For the last six or seven years, I have opened a new door." Marissa has grown more focused. She has identified what is important to her and how she wants to express herself. Not unlike Cari, the mother of two in Chapter One, Marissa is skeptical of her ability to "easily go all over the place." This problem "of going all over the place" affects many women who are bright and interdisciplinary and who have not had a role model or a mentor for guidance. Their lack of focus is usually accompanied by depression and confusion about themselves, their abilities, and their value in the world.

The issues most commonly mentioned by women in the study I conducted for this book, those that hindered creative expression and creative output, were:

fear of failure

fear of success

time needed to be with family members, usually children

being responsible or obligated to others—at one's own expense

other people's judgments

conflict

an inability to prioritize

fear of not being accepted

negative voices or "tapes"

feeling overwhelmed and inadequate

financial insecurity

being unable to give oneself time

With one or more of these negatives operating together, a woman's ability to freely pursue her essential creative nature can be marred.

In "writing her own life" and pursuing her passion, Marissa has come to understand and value her need to create and share her creations. Not unlike the women artists in Chapter Two, Marissa exclaims, "I must make something or I will get depressed." The act of physically making something is a significant part of how Marissa experiences and defines creativity. She understands creativity in three ways. First is the traditional way, the need to create something new. The second is her understanding of creativity through the sensation of the creative process. Creativity, she says, is "the moment when I can let go and find the space that is perfect. I throw away a lot of stuff. It is like a trance." Her third understanding of creativity is in the context of surviving. You have to be able to survive, she declares. The expression of creativity on a basic human level, experienced as the act of surviving, was mentioned by many women. It was most keenly expressed by women who have moved from one culture to another. Marissa says surviving is grounded in "how I become an independent thinker." She writes poetry and short stories; she paints and sings. People are important in her life. She has had success as a union organizer and as a fund-raiser, because as she frames it, "I am the resource person." Like Demeter, Marissa's career has been shaped by providing for the needs of others, and setting up the channels through which the help may flow.

The image of Demeter hovers above Marissa, Nancy, and Sherry, giving context to their creative expression. Work experiences have played a significant role in shaping their concepts of gender and the integration of these concepts into their creative expression. Nancy came to understand that she was "called" to the service of God in high school, though it would take her many years before her path to ordination was complete. Nancy's journey through college was disjointed. She was unable to stay focused and found herself at various times in extreme emotional states. It was during her college years that Nancy was raped, twice. She declares the only thing that kept "me alive was knowing I had a God who could suffer with me, because I felt totally alone. It was only through the grace of thinking, feeling, and knowing that God loved me that I stayed alive." The results of those long years of trying to complete college were several. First, Nancy's desire to become a minister was renewed. Second, there was a heightened sense of herself as an

African-American woman. Third, her pattern of struggling with completion became apparent. Even now, she struggles to complete her Ph.D. after having started that process in 1983. Nancy is, of course, not alone in her inability to complete this degree. Women lag far behind men in earning doctoral degrees.

In her first two years of college, Nancy took time off to work for a black media company. When she returned to school, she organized a reading tutorial program and did research projects. In her second year of college, she was paid to sing in churches. She continued earning money that way for eleven years. Nancy did a number of things simultaneously as her schooling was continually interrupted. During her next leave of absence, she went to work, first as an admission's officer at a college and then as a curator for a collection at an African American History museum. While at the museum, she became a consultant for a multicultural education program. Nancy was part of a team that conducted teacher-trainer workshops for multicultural classrooms; she was the African-American specialist. Finally she finished her undergraduate work and went on to complete a master's degree in divinity. She began teaching New Testament theology, Greek, and Hebrew. She became the coordinator of Christian education for children at a parish and the coordinator of counseling at a soup kitchen in a major metropolitan city. Working with children, a later phase in her professional development, has been important to Nancy. She admits, "I take it for granted that personal relationships are creative, but with children in particular I have a sense of who I am. Children are spontaneous. They are creative in ways adults forget how to be—or train themselves not to be. With children there is a connection to creativity that is special for me." Nancy's sense of completion, ease, and freedom with children is not uncommon.

Sherry also views playing with her niece as a creative expression; she feels a freedom of spirit with her niece that is not easily duplicated in other areas of her life. The spirit of an experience is crucial for Sherry. It colors who she is and what she does. Sherry did not know when she went to college that she would work with women. She did not know then the importance women held in her life. After graduating from college, she had difficulty finding a job. She was hired to assist a marketing director of a publishing company but quickly realized that she did not fit into the organization. With some friends, she started a newspaper. Three and a half years later, she left the paper to begin work as an associate editor at an international magazine. For the next couple of years, Sherry worked and traveled. She explains, "I wanted to do international work. I knew I was good in languages, so I felt the best way to do that was to be an interpreter." She applied to graduate school to study languages and was accepted. But first, before going back to school, Sherry decided to study in Spain on her own.

While in Spain, however, something crystallized within her—she wanted to work with women. She recalls, "I wanted to do something more abstract than translations." She returned home and got a master's degree in an experimental program that "combined cross-cultural human relations and human potential courses." She quickly found a job as a fundraiser with an international women's organization. Finally, Sherry and another woman at the organization began developing training programs for women in third-world countries. Their product created a rift within the organization. Two other women who had also been doing training became peevishly petulant about Sherry and her partner's work and refused to do any more training. Sherry and her partner were hired out through the organization to run the programs they developed. The key programs they developed were modules to be used in raising money for women's projects, marketing women's economic development projects, and one about feminist consciousness in a Latin-American context. These programs were all "participatory, problem-solving processes." Sherry stayed with that organization for many years, longer than she should have, until she left to be a free-lance trainer and consultant. Her work now involves setting up training conferences for women's foundations, working as an analyst reviewing programs for women's economic development that are in existence, reviewing project planning for training and economic development for an international women's organization, writing reports, writing training directions, and conducting training in economic development for a federal agency.

Being able to analyze and appropriately frame a problem so that a new solution may emerge is a creative talent. Problem-solving and problem-stating have characterized Marissa's work. Her journey began as a beautician when she was sixteen years old. She worked part-time and went to college part-time for seven years. Feeling restless and bored at her beautician business, she decided to visit her brother, who was in the army in the United States. She planned to stay only a short time and then visit a friend in Mexico. She remained here instead. Her money ran out, and finding a job became problematic. Though she could read and write English, she could hardly speak a word. She states, "I had trouble because of my problem with the language and because I did not have a college degree. I found a job taking care of children at the army base." The wages did not cover her living expenses. Marissa is very friendly, and she began meeting people. She met a family from Puerto Rico and was invited to come to live with them; they gave her a room and got her a job at a factory. A friend of Marissa's introduced her to some community activists. They were interested in where she worked. What they said stimulated her intellectually. Wanting to help her fellow workers better their jobs and secure their futures, she tried her hand at organizing. But the woman she lived with was having an affair with the boss and turned Marissa in. Though she was fired, she was not sorry for the experience, nor did she remain unemployed for long. She went to work as a reception-ist at a law clinic that helped with workers' rights. Her English had greatly improved, and she quickly became involved in everything the lawyers were doing. She acted as a translator in court, mostly in landlord-tenant cases. Marissa loved the work and wanted to become a lawyer. She applied to a special pro-gram at an experimental law school that accepted students who had not finished college. They would begin as first-year law students. Staying in school was contingent upon passing an exam at the end of the first year. Marissa was unable to pass the exam. She got another job with the union, as an organiz-er. She remained at the union for several years and loved it. Marissa had learned a lot since her first attempt. As a woman in a male-dominated environment, she learned how to capital-ize upon it. She explains, "My job was to bring in union mem-bers. Then I tried to organize seven hundred men." It became rough. She held secret meetings at three A.M. at different bars to "get to the issues."

Also during this time she became involved with a human-itarian organization that addressed the needs of women and children in Central America. A delegation was coming to the United States, and Marissa organized the tour and the other needs of the visiting women. The tour was a success, and Marissa was offered a permanent job. The prospect terrified her because, as she explains, it was "such a big job. I never thought I would be able to do it. It was a high-visibility job, with a lot of international work, and I was still committed to seven hundred men at the union. Finally I decided to go for it; I said yes. I worked at that job for two and a half years. I orga-nized health professionals for out-reach programs. I traveled so much I didn't know where I lived. I took another job, which was created for me at an organization that also helped women and children. I did fund-raising. Now I work part-time as a free-lance fund-raiser. Fund-raising is very intense. I do not know how long I will last. I am also doing publicity translations for a children's television show, I recently published a book of my poetry, and I paint."

Gender themes run throughout these three women's experiences. It is not an overstatement to say that their experience of gender has profoundly shaped their lives and their personal expression. Historically the helping professions have been dominated by women. But the role of minister, priest, rabbi (whatever name you wish to give to the role of preacher and teacher) has always been the domain of men. The position of spiritual guide and counselor in organized religious communities has been available to women in this country only in the last twenty years or so. Nancy's choice to be a minister, while perfectly logical on many levels, is a bold and unorthodox act for a woman. She found the ministry through her own need to be optimistic in the world. To overcome the pain caused to her by others and to express God's place in her life, she has a desire to help others.

Nancy states, "I am very relational in what I do, and I think that comes from being female. I do not care if it is inherent or if it is cultural. It is definitely related to gender, and to allowing myself to be passionate about what I do. It is much easier for me to show my connectedness to what I'm doing in an emotional way because I am female. I see nurturing as part of my role as teacher, preacher, and musician. Part of what I am there to do is to sustain and support people in their lives." Her focus on women, women's history, and women's culture was of great significance to her while she was teaching college. She began to understand the place being female had in her work. Her awareness was altered and heightened through consciousness-raising groups and her focus on feminism. She explains, "It built into me a sense of my working with my femaleness and my African-

Americanness. A major part of my working life would be dealing explicitly with those parts of my identity. I cannot separate out my femaleness when I sing. It comes out in the quality of my voice and the material I sing. It is very much a gender connection. My preaching is very feminine. Other people have said that I am seeking to make an effective connection with people. I rarely deal with abstractions."

In relating her thoughts about women, men, and work, Nancy states, "I think, by and large, women are more concerned with the process of interaction and therefore whatever they produce is something that expresses that concern. Men are not as concerned with that. They possess a sense of privilege, particularly in academic work. Men are comfortable with ungrounded abstraction. Men are always described as abstract and women as concrete. There is a ranking system which says abstract is smart, and concrete is not as smart. Women's ways of dealing are concerned with quality of the interaction. Women tend to be more open to intuition and do not see feeling as the enemy of thinking."

Through their feelings, women are often led to a new and useful awareness. There had been moments leading up to this one, but on this day it all crystallized for Sherry at a women's conference in Spain. She recalls, "There was a woman; she had brown curly hair. She was a fiery speaker. I could speak Spanish, but not with great fluidity. Watching her, listening to her passion, her anger, her body, did it for me. I instinctively understood everything she was saying. I did not understand the words, but I felt all she felt. It was a powerful feeling of oneness. I could imagine my work needed to be that." She continues, "My work is like working with a mirror. It is outside and inside all the time. It's different because I have a different relationship to the issues than men would. I have different emotional reactions, and a different understanding of the issues." Sherry feels the answers are still to be found. The seeds of truth are buried within. They have not been fully revealed. Significantly, Sherry does not feel compelled to articulate as truth that which has not sprouted yet. Her slow pace of constantly reexamining satisfies her. By way of contrast, she relates her experience of working with a young male trainer. "He has been doing this work for eight months, and he's developing a paradigm to describe what happens in feminist organizations! That's alright. Maybe it will be useful. He is on the outside looking in, so it will be interesting to see what he thinks and how he makes sense of all of it." In contrast with her male counterpart, Sherry believes that her work is a lifelong process of exploration. "The dynamic is going to keep changing, and we are going to keep looking at it, trying to understand it and write about it. We are not looking for the answer, for the framework that it fits into, and then we can close the book!"

Sherry is angered by a new and troublesome element of training that has invaded the community through "the men I meet who do training. They are the ones who have introduced the notion of 'intellectual property' of our training approaches. What has been exciting about being a trainer is sharing techniques and approaches. Increasingly, I hear men do not share anymore. You want my training approach, pay me! I should be licensing all my training approaches. I think men gravitate more toward ownership. Men are more involved with themselves as 'the trainer,' the deliverer of information." She sees her role differently: "I try to be situationally appropriate. I am more comfortable as a facilitator. I am willing now, to be a trainer. After all these years, I am much more willing now to be authoritarian and provide more content, rather than saying all the learning and knowledge has to come from the participants. I see things in shades of gray. Men see things in black and white. It helps them have a greater sense of security. Training is detail-oriented. I need to prepare a lot. Most men wing it. No problem, they say, look relaxed; cross your legs; tell a joke; you'll be fine. For me, that is like flying without a parachute. I cannot work that way."

If Nancy and Sherry's complaints have a familiar ring to them, it is because they are regularly expressed by many women. Marissa does not wing it, either. She pays great attention to detail as an advocate, a fund-raiser, a writer, and a painter. Marissa's willingness to put herself on the line challenges her essential creative expression. Her willingness and boldness may be perceived as masculine traits, but they are merely part of Marissa. They are part of the whole that allows her to get to that place she describes that expresses her feminine aspect. Together these parts of her innermost being make her creative expression possible. She continually needed to negotiate issues of gender as a union organizer. She was not just a woman, but the only Latino woman organizer. She explains, "My approach was different. I did not act like the men. I had to learn how to talk the way men talk." Marissa decided to capitalize upon the differences. "I used to visit the shops in high heels. They did not allow people inside without the guard. I started talking to the guards, and they let me go in by myself. Part of it was that I was a woman, part of it was that I was nice. When you are around men, you become aware of who you are, and you have to fight."

Marissa has had the opportunity to see the differences in male-dominated organizations as compared to female-dominated organizations. Working with women presented her with different issues, no less daunting. There were unexpected power struggles, along with the awareness that they were all women engaged in a common struggle. She believes, "In general, in a corporate setting there is competition. Though women compete, they see it as wrong. If I compete, I am not doing it to other women. We compete all the time. I am always trying to do it right, to improve something. I think most women do that. I take it so personally. Men do not take things so personally. Men delegate more; they always find someone to do it for them. I do not think men have the concern about the details, about making people comfortable, about making people happy and relaxed. Women are more open. We bring everything to the job. Women are supportive. We share much more of our insides, our pain, our happiness; we are more open."

Communication, caring, and relationships are crucial elements in Nancy, Sherry, and Marissa's work, including their "artistic expressions." In two studies conducted twenty years apart, the following results were found to be common among women. Lois Wladis Hoffman, in a 1972 study published in the *Journal of Social Issues*, wrote, "[I]t is suggested that females have high needs for affiliation which influence their achievement motives and behavior, sometimes enhancing and sometimes blocking them. . . . [W]hile boys learn effectance through mastery, the effectiveness of girls is contingent on eliciting the help of others. Affective relationships are paramounts in females and much of their achievement behavior is motivated by a desire to please. If achievement threatens affiliation, performance may be sacrificed or anxiety may result." In 1992, the results of the study "A Longitudinal Examination of Life Choices of Gifted and Talented Young Women" were published. Constance L. Hollinger and Elyse S. Flemming reported that "[w]omen's orientation to the world is relational in nature, an orientation which influences academic, career, and all other life choices. For women, the impact of decisions or choices on significant others plays a central role in the decision making process." The authors felt that "diversity of life pathways needs to be recognized and valued. . . . [H]elping professionals . . . need to emphasize the development of strategies for coping with multiple role demands . . . [and] that concepts such as 'achievements' and 'realization of potential' must be clarified, . . . if they are to be congruent with women's worldview. . . . [Furthermore] 'achievement' is not limited to educational degrees and career status but includes personal and interpersonal or relational achievements as well."

Despite the gains obtained by the women's movement, women still sacrifice. They manifest greater anxiety in choosing to respond to their essential creative natures than men. Societal expectations placed upon women from infancy are part of the contributing outside influences. For example, Sherry's father, despite his affirmations and proclamations of her intelligence, above all else expected her to marry and have children. Relational demands are then pitted against one's essential creative nature. Personal expression usually loses. These two needs should not be at odds.

None of the qualities associated with being "female" are essentially, biologically, or naturally negative. They are, in the image of Demeter, the pathways to the mysterious feminine. They are also the doorways to your personal power and expression. Nancy, Sherry, and Marissa's creative expressions reflect the positive power of gender influences when used in a life-affirming manner. These pathways to the mysterious feminine add to women's effectiveness in the multitude of roles they must play. They add to the quality of a woman's creativity.

I believe women are bound to their creative expression through their gender and are nourished in that expression through their femaleness. It is important to recognize that feminine aspects of a woman's essential creative nature are a powerful force within her being. Gender is part of being a woman; it is contained within her thoughts; it compels what she has to say; it defines the quality and tenor of her voice and the manner of her physical movement; it shapes her unique response to the world. A woman's ability to nurture, to give birth, to be emotional and rational is connected to her femaleness, to her womanhood, and that, positively or negatively, shapes the expression of her essential creative nature.

Change is part of awakening the creative spirit and of deepening your connection to it. There is no one path to finding your inner voice, no one way to express your creativity, your vision, your passion. What is revealed in the stories of these three women are the ways your environment can give you information about your creative path. Being open to the clues around you makes finding your path and pursuing your creative journey possible. Sometimes these clues are influenced by gender, as Nancy, Sherry, and Marissa found out. If you are closed off to that part of your essential creative nature, you cannot receive the information you need. If gender perceptions can deepen your connection to your essential creative nature and can shape your creative expression and bolster the power you feel within, as I believe they can, then they are worth exploring.

## FINDING THE PATH TO THE MYSTERIOUS FEMININE

If you have not already done so, make a list of ideas that characterize men and women. Do you attribute positive or negative value judgments to these ideas? Which gender qualities are given negative and positive values? Do you believe men and women approach life and work differently? Do you assign value judgments to those differences? You can use the thoughts about men and women that Nancy, Marissa, and Sherry expressed as a starting point. Your views do not have to be in agreement with theirs. Now make a list of what you believe to be your dominant gender qualities, the ones you use most frequently. Are they qualities that serve or hinder you? Look at those you have placed negative value judgments on. List a few ways in which those qualities can be transformed into something positive for yourself. Remember, any trait "masculine" or "feminine," can be detrimental if carried to an extreme. Keep a notebook of the experiences and feelings you have during the day that are influenced by gender.

Try making a collage by cutting out images in magazines that stimulate you. What does your collage say? What are the dominant themes? Create a quiet space for yourself where you can concentrate upon your positive feminine/masculine qualities. Read about women who are inspiring. What qualities of those women do you respect and wish you possessed? Make an action plan to encourage the growth of positive qualities, and always remember that moving into creative behavior requires self-affirmation and respect.

## CHAPTER FIVE

# SHE WHO BRINGS ORDER AND LIGHT FROM DARKNESS:
## TRAUMA AND CREATIVITY

"Inna or Ishtar (the composite image of the Sumerian Goddess of the Great above and the Great below) was one of the three great goddesses of the Bronze Age." (*The Myth of the Goddess*)

"Ishtar, Queen of Heaven, said to have descended from the planet Venus, thus arriving upon earth accompanied by the Ishtaritu, Ishtar's holy women, was revered as Mother by Semitic peoples who lived along the banks of the Tigris and Euphrates." (*Ancient Mirrors of Womanhood*)

"As the Great Mother, [she] is both the radiance of the luminous dew-bestowing moon and the diminishing and vanishing of that radiance in the darkened moon. . . . She incarnates both generous and wrathful feeling, both love and rage. She is ever changing yet ever the same; by turns 'radiant, thundering, destructive, defiant, judgmental, kind, generous, peaceful, healing, erotic, decisive, discerning, wise, transcendent, loving, fertile, joyous, and ever youthful.' . . . She is the implacable Law of Life. . . . " *(The Myth of the Goddess)*

"It is you who changes destiny
to make what is bad become good.
At your right side is justice,
at your left side is goodness.
From your sides emanate life and well being."
*(Ancient Mirrors of Womanhood)*

Ishtar is the essence of the creative spirit, of the creative process, of the creative woman. She is ever-changing, volatile, alive with being. She enfolds you with possibility. Ishtar offers you the image of one who moves in many directions, whose powers are great, whose love is magnificent and nurturing, whose wrath is devastating. Tied to the cycles of the moon, as all women are, she is felt in her fullness as light and in her limits as darkness. She is the rhythms of the universe. As a model, she gives you the choice. She offers you the prerogative to bring light and order into chaos, violence, and confusion. It is within her power to create her environment, to guide the light or break the order. But she must be honored or she will become wrathful and heap pain upon those who have transgressed.

Ishtar personifies the need to honor the creative spirit within women, especially in daily life. Women are confronted with the choice to negotiate their lives, their pain, their pleasure, their sorrow, their joys, their fears, their wonderment on a daily basis. That is, I believe, the meaning of Ishtar. A woman can try to retreat from the "implacable law of life." She can try to deny the darkness, ignore the chaos, and be insensitive to her own confusion. The obvious result of such behavior is time lost, opportunities missed, and the continuance of pain—powerful negative influences. What can a woman see if she is in darkness? What can she produce if her process is chaotic? Where can she go in her blind confusion? Ishtar's ability to be ever-changing brings to her environment a transcendental unity and the manifestation of the creative power. For many women, negotiating life requires the ability to transcend the reality of the moment, the experiences of childhood, the pains of womanhood in a culture dominated by a male vision.

What does it mean to bring light into darkness, order into chaos, and understanding into confusion? It requires moving through and surviving trauma. The word trauma is weighty. Its magnitude is great and its effects far-reaching. Trauma is associated with shock. The aftermath may be physically and emotionally life-threatening. When a woman faces her inner darkness, she uses her power to move through the trauma, strengthening her essential creative nature. Choosing light and order represent a permanent change within a woman forever. Embedded within her choice is her capacity to accept all that attends living a life. Acceptance does not imply impotence or victimization. A woman's acceptance of the "implacable law of life" leads her to seek, to define or redefine her essential creative nature; it helps her survive trauma.

Ishtar can make bad things good. To face severe trauma—such as the loss of a loved one, loss of self through addictive behavior, sexual abuse, depression, anxiety, tentativeness, or unhealthy relationships—requires the Goddess power within. In the likeness of Ishtar, negative experiences can become strengthening growth experiences, muting the shock inflicted upon a woman's psyche. A woman's uniqueness embraces these painful intrusions, translating and integrating them as part of the shape of her life. Every time she responds to the circumstances of her life, she demonstrates her creative abilities. Her commitment to herself and trust in her essential creative nature is revealed in her healthy actions, in moving toward the light.

The three women in this chapter have had the opportunity to look at themselves and their emotional makeup through the shock of trauma. Each one has found the power of Ishtar, the creative power to bring light and order to their personal darkness. Their traumas have been different and difficult; the depths of their pain and anguish have been intensely personal. Choosing to live her life by utilizing her essential creative nature, each woman has made the choice to honor herself and her capacity to cope with her trauma.

## DARKNESS CONQUERED, LIGHT AND ORDER RESHAPED

Anna is thirty-six years old. She is one of nine children, five of whom were born in Puerto Rico. In Puerto Rico her family was very poor. Her maternal grandfather was a well-known "scoundrel." She says he "made me fearful of men, until I worked it through in my twenties." In the states, Anna's father worked in a factory. At home he was an abusive alcoholic. He treated her mother poorly. Anna recalls, "Even when he was not drunk he was pretty awful. I prayed daily that he would die." Anna's parents were unhappily married, but they have remained together. They moved back to Puerto Rico many years ago, and her mother thrives on working with plants. Her paternal grandmother was mentally ill. Anna became fearful that she might inherit some of her grandmother's or father's madness.

During Anna's youth and early adulthood, her mother was seriously ill and nearly died. Anna speaks fondly of her mother. "Mom is kind of magical. She had a real rough life. She is a farmer. She embroiders. My mother has a way with colors and textures; she embroiders the same way." Her mother's means of expression had two outlets: making objects with her hands and creating an environment through plants. Anna explains, "We were surrounded by chaos, but she created a space with plants. She plants everything. She walks with seeds in her pockets, and she plants wherever she walks." Later in Anna's life, her mother's creative expression would become a path back to mental health for Anna.

Anna's journey into darkness began when she was young, though her most challenging fall did not occur until she was a young woman, in her twenties. As a child, life was scary, not only because her father was an abusive alcoholic, but also because her mother was so often sick. While Anna felt loved by her mother, she was also keenly aware of her mother's fragile condition. Anna was fortunate in receiving loving care from her older sister. A foundation built on love in a woman's childhood helps develop a sense of worthiness within her that can aid her journey through darkness. Anna's older sister, Noel, functioned in many respects as a surrogate mother. She was the person Anna was closest to. When Anna's mother was too sick to demonstrate love, her sister Noel stepped in. When Noel decided to enter a convent to become a nun, Anna was devastated. She blamed the church for taking Noel away. Anna recalls, "It took a long time for me to forgive the church." Noel is no longer a nun, and she and Anna are still very close. They live near each other and spend a good deal of time together. On the weekends, Anna and Noel garden together and find pleasure, fun, and creative expression in cooking wonderful meals.

Anna was twelve years old when her mother became seriously ill. Reminiscing, she says, "I became a truant when my mother was home. I stayed home, to be with her. When my mother was not home, I went to the library. I went to the library a lot. To cope I read. I felt like me and my little brother were left to take care of my parents and to intervene." It was not until her twenties, when she felt despair from being clinically depressed, that Anna realized that she had buried the pain of being sexually abused by one of her brothers as a child. She explains, "I thought I had dealt with it. As a child it was not at the surface but it was a big part of my depression, of who I became and what was wrong with me. It influenced how I felt about myself. I never confronted my brother because he is still one of my favorite brothers. Looking back, I understand how it happened. The family was in chaos."

Anna is thoughtful, sensitive, warm, and caring. She is a caregiver. Like many children of alcoholics, she has struggled to understand the meaning of personal boundaries, and to identify her own needs. Among the nine children, six are in the health-care professions, taking care of the needs of others. Anna has struggled to tear herself out of the brutal grip of severe depression and emotional breakdown. She has learned the devastating effects of emotional darkness and despair. She knows now that the power to produce emotional light and order come to her through creative self-expression. When I asked her to describe her guiding force, she declared, "When I wake up in the morning, I don't know whether to save the world or savor the world. I feel the world is very rich and that there is tremendous beauty and opportunity. There is so much work to do, and I try very hard to balance my life—to do good things and to appreciate the things around me. I feel very lucky to feel that way after going through depression. I am in social change work. I am the director of training for home health aids and also for training of our staff. Our company trains people to be managers of socially conscious work. I need very much to be connected with something that I feel is moving people forward."

Anna is committed to helping people progress. That commitment has been a key to her personal and career success. She explains, "I also feel that I need to take care of myself or I cannot help people move forward." Anna is able to express excitement about life. She has a good deal of creative energy and works well as a team player. She works hard to acknowledge her wrongdoing and to resist being judgmental or mean. Because of the personal work she has done, she prides herself as being a person you can talk to. She has learned, since her breakdown, to protect her boundaries and maintain her health. She guards against overcommiting herself and becoming isolated from the world outside of work, yet she muses, "I can spend weeks by myself and forget to call people." The ability to maintain boundaries, to stay focused and goal-directed, have been mentioned before. Without these qualities a woman cannot and will not sustain her commitment to creative behavior. Anna struggles to maintain her focus. "I have a gazillion ideas and I have a real hard time getting them to fruition because the excitement is in the thought. I can let things go if something more exciting comes along."

She fills her time creatively at work with training and staff development and at home baking, and making things for her home and for other people. She vividly described how she likes to make pillows, decorate objects, make collages, work with fabrics, and paint things. She is constantly redecorating her home by creating new spaces for people to explore when they visit. She also engages her guests with projects such as making dinner or baking cookies as a group.

Anna is also intensely involved with flamenco dancing, which she feels is the key to her spiritual and philosophical approach to life. She believes it is an activity that best expresses who she is, declaring, "I am Puerto Rican and we dance. We dance in couples. In celebration. I take flamenco lessons; that helps me to be more expressive. I try to live the values represented in the philosophy of the dance. One is passion. A passion for life and for struggle and what you have to learn. You have to control the passion so it comes out beautifully. The way it is portrayed in the media is wrong. It is not sexual. You cannot just go and lose it. You have to be centered.

You have to be open and growing to the sky while being grounded. The passion is the tension between reaching and being grounded. I feel the reason I need to dance flamenco is because of the struggle with my own personal stuff in trying to find the balance. It puts me in touch with duality and contradiction. I wanted to dance initially like the men because I did not acknowledge that the feminine was beautiful. Then I started taking lessons. I go to flamenco activities; I read flamenco; I talk to people about flamenco."

The level of her output is dizzying. I asked Anna if she thought of herself as creative. She explains, "I did not until people started defining me that way. I was intrigued by it, and now I am comfortable with it, because I am happiest when I am allowed to manipulate things and things are new. I need things around, or I become unhappy. I need my work to involve the things I am creative with: color, people, games, art, and poetry." Work is creative because, as Anna explains, "it is part of why I do what I do. It gives me the opportunity to do something for others which is also for me. I create something which has meaning for a large group of people." Anna's teaching methodology is reminiscent of the approach of Rose, the woman in Chapter One who is director of education for an RN program. Teaching is participatory and exploratory; it presumes that the student is responsible for learning and learns best through that responsibility. Anna's classroom must reflect excitement; it must be a safe place in which to grow and change. There are ever-changing colors and textures on the wall, and the tables and chairs are always being rearranged to accommodate an interactive exercise. Personal creative expression ensures Anna's ability to choose the power of light and order.

Life as we live it in the twentieth century can be busy. As women, we often have multiple roles to fulfill. Our essential creative nature is woven through the actions that fill our days. Jackie's life is crammed with the business of being a single mother, working full-time, and going to school. She is a middle child of fourteen children. She lived down south until she was fourteen years old, when she moved up north. Her childhood memories are clouded with visions of an abusive father. She reflects, "When I was young, my father would beat up my mother. Mother would run out of the house with no clothes on and hide in the cornfields. We used to take her clothes to her. It hurt me bad." Those were her formative years.

Jackie is a thirty-seven-year-old African-American. She is a quiet, soft-spoken, reserved woman. She possesses a clarity about herself and what she wants out of life. She is not tentative or shy about her dreams or the work required to achieve them. Above all else, Jackie is optimistic. Her optimism and her willingness to take risks have helped her move through the pain of humiliation, physical abuse, and abandonment that she experienced in her childhood and her early adult years. She appreciates her talents and shares them with others in her family, at work, and in her church community. Her belief in her God gives Jackie, like Nancy the Episcopalian minister, a strong foundation.

Jackie's fortitude is part of her guiding force. It has enabled her to express her essential creative expression. She says, "I have this will power. I can do it. I will pursue it until I am successful, until I overcome the obstacle. It is about doing something to make me feel good, that I achieve something." Her perseverance, determination, self-reliance, and goal-orientation reflect the traits described in Chapter Two. Jackie has taken adversity and creatively found a way to use those experiences to learn something about herself. She continually moves forward. Jackie is not unlike Anna in her desire to help other people. She thrives on meeting a challenge. Her guiding principle, "the need to overcome," is also embedded in her concept of creativity. She explains, "When you have an idea and you get focused on that idea, you can bring it into being. Whatever it takes to bring it up to its proper level, even if it means you have to over-come the obstacles, you have to have a mind to do it."

Taking care of business is not a novel concept for Jackie. The goal of holding on to her life was the business of life during her adolescence. When Jackie's mother left home, Jackie was a girl entering puberty, a tenuous time for many girls. Because she physically resembled her mother, Jackie's father would fly into a rage and beat Jackie. He would say, "You look like your mommy." Jackie states, "He would take the money in the cash box and beat me. I was little and though I was sad, I was also happy when they locked him up and my mother was coming to take us away. I would be free of him."

By the time Jackie was eighteen, she was married. She thought she had married someone who was nice, someone who was helpful, until her husband started drinking. At first he controlled his drinking and generally managed his money and the business of life. Soon, however, problems began when his pay-check was given over to "his friends" for partying. "I was working; he was working. I believe you take care of home and family first." Jackie was angered. She demanded control of her husband's paycheck. She recalls, "He started coming to me, with his friends, for money. I had bills to pay. Then his friends introduced him to a girl. They had more influence over her than me, and so he started going with her and not coming home." Jackie's husband, the father of their two children, did not care emotionally or financially for his family. Jackie only asked that her husband take care of his family. His response was that he wanted to live and have fun in his life. Periodically he would appear and demand money. Then he began to physically abuse Jackie. One morning while Jackie was preparing to leave for church, he started fighting with her. She states, "The kids ran out of the house to call the police. That day I got an order of protection and he had to leave the house. Soon after, I came home from work and he had taken everything out of the house. I changed the locks. I was not going to take him back. My father beat my mother, so when my husband hit me, that was it. There was no process to decide. I had to protect my kids."

Her path was not without pain and hard work. She lost over thirty pounds when her marriage ended. She was depressed, angry, hurt, and alone with two little children. A church member who saw Jackie wasting away told her, "You are going to be dead, and he will be alive and still doing the same thing." That thought shook her deeply. The image of her two children left to someone who did not care about them was more than she could bear. Her inner voice called to her. She could not surrender to the darkness; she needed to extricate herself from this mess. The saying "You must live in the solution, not in the problem" seems to exemplify Jackie's approach. The search for the solution is always the impetus for creative behavior. Whether the problem is framed in aesthetic terms, like the arts, or in emotional terms, the process toward creative thinking and doing is the same.

It is not just the way in which she manages the business of her life that expresses her creativity, it is also Jackie's ability to find her vision through her dreams. Jackie can conceptualize her goals and go after them. Her capacity to organize, which is a finely developed skill, reflects her creative style and is, she believes, the best expression of who she is. People tell Jackie she is creative because "I am always doing something, because I am always coming up with a new project." The need to create something is central to many women. That urge is ongoing throughout our lives. Creative impulses are nurtured when a woman routinely acts upon those impulses. Jackie did see creativity manifested in the activities that touch her life, but she was uncomfortable about labeling herself as creative. To try to demonstrate how she interprets creativity in her activities, she relates these examples: "We go on trips at the church. I had an idea that we could go on bigger trips. I was told it could not be done. But I got fifteen people to go on a cruise to the Caribbean that year. It was a success, and the church got money from it." Jackie organized the trip, planned the schedule, made the arrangements. She had never done anything like that before, and she thoroughly enjoyed it. Over the next few years, the trips were bigger and better.

Jackie's church is large, yet they had no church journal; that bothered her. "Other churches, much smaller churches, have journals. I did the first journal by myself, and each one after that got bigger and better. I am most creative anywhere when my mind starts going. It can go anywhere. With my kids, I try to be creative to show them they can be successful." Without the ability to bring an idea to fruition, creativity goes unnoticed. Connections are imperative for Jackie's essential creative nature. She experiences connections through ideas and through people. Jackie also enjoys traveling and being out. Because she is goal-directed and a hard worker, she is impatient with procrastination and last-minute changes. Boundaries can still be a problem for Jackie; as she explains, "I am too nice, I should say 'no' more, but I do not. I try to please people, even when I know I cannot, and it has gotten me into trouble. I will speak to you no matter what, even if you are angry with me."

Jackie's drive to succeed and her need to overcome keep her in school. As a child, she decided she wanted to be an accountant. It is still her goal; she loves accounting work. To enable her to achieve the appropriate level, as she sees it, she has gone back to school to get an undergraduate degree in business administration. Jackie then plans to go on for her master's and her Ph.D. She has already earned a bachelor's degree in religious education. Her ability to communicate with people has also helped Jackie commit herself to furthering her religious education to get a Ph.D. in theology. Jackie has been told that she is a good teacher. She demonstrates that weekly when she teaches Sunday school and when she works in the counseling program sponsored by her church.

What drives Jackie? Her dreams symbolize her guiding principle of overcoming and becoming the most she can become. Jackie is not daunted by the prospect of so many years of hard work. "School is exciting. It makes me think; it pulls something out of me," she declares. It helps her re-create who she is and where she is going. Challenging herself moves her beyond herself; it gives her a path to her future. Jackie does not have time to linger in fear or depression. She sees herself as the loser when she gives herself and her life up to pain caused to her by someone else. She chooses light and order and seeks her personal style.

Mercedes tries not to lose very often. She is a strong, articulate, extremely bright, thoughtful, innovative forty-seven-year-old woman. She is divorced and a mother of two children. Mercedes has witnessed great sadness and experienced the depths of pain. She has also worked hard to achieve success. Her experiences have been used to gain a deeper understanding of herself. They have helped define a direction for her life, and have given form to the manner and style of her creative expression. Working with women has been part of that expression.

The world she grew up in contained double images. Mercedes was born in Puerto Rico, and throughout her life her parents moved back and forth between the United States and Puerto Rico. Most of her youth was lived in the United States; her family was the only Puerto Rican family in a middle-class Jewish neighborhood. Her father was an apartment-building superintendent, and the family lived in that building. Family life for Mercedes was peaceful. She felt loved, cared for, and safe. But she simultaneously felt the pangs of rejection. "We looked Puerto Rican. We knew it, and they knew it." The neighbors denied her ethnic origins by refusing to acknowledge her background and her culture. For Mercedes, it was a "different experience of being 'other than.'" It was difficult and complex to sort out." The struggles of adolescence were heightened by this confusion in identifying her place. Notwithstanding the sense of isolation and rejection Mercedes experienced, she pursued creating her life with ardor. Her vigor, her intelligence, her lust for knowledge, and her need to produce have always moved her through the hard times.

Mercedes's mother offered her one model of personal creative expression. She honors her mother's ability to make things. Mercedes believes her mother is a "wonderful artist." She explains, "When I was little, mother sewed my clothes. She would embroider and paint on the skirts. My mother wallpapered and upholstered. She designed stuff for father to build." Mercedes's sense of the visual, taught to her by her mother, has stayed with her throughout her life. It has become an active part of her essential creative nature.

Mercedes exhibits a goal-directedness in her search for meaning. Her need, like Jackie's, to challenge herself had been used as her guiding force. "I think for me it was about overcoming fear." She continues, "I always think of myself as someone who is enormously fearful and very courageous. It was always about pushing myself. The image I had was almost like jumping off cliffs." She pushes herself to leap into the unknown despite her fears. Being scared is her feeling, but she does not allow such feelings to stop her from taking the necessary life-affirming steps. Mercedes respects and values her urge to push ahead into the unknown. This helps her understand and define creativity. She believes that "creativity is mysterious. But you open yourself. You are motivated by curiosity, and you take in what you see. It's like a 'snap'. You ponder it, and 'snap,' something perks up. You think about things; you make connections. More than anything else, it's about making connections." Mercedes believes that in searching for the information, one finds the connections. There is an "intellectual and intuitive process" through which a woman moves that leads her to something new. Mercedes states, "My creativity comes out in ideas, whether they take the form of drawing and painting, writing a story or whatever." Openness, observation, seeing (as in understanding), and connections characterize the steps for Mercedes. She states, "The result can be new just for me, as with an insight. Curiosity causes me to make the leaps, to close my eyes and jump. Curiosity and seeing are tied. I am creative because I make these connections. I revel in new ideas and sometimes I love thinking with people. Collaborative thinking. I do a lot of collaborative creativity in my activist work."

Mercedes, like Anna and Jackie, functions at a high level of doing. Her creative expressions are interdisciplinary and multifaceted. Mercedes's collaborative work, her problem-solving, painting, drawing, parenting, writing, reading, cooking, her visual presentation of self, her house, and her office decor are the elements that give form to her creative expression. Mercedes believes the eclectic mix of things she does best expresses who she is. She understands creativity as "the way you live your life." She states that creativity "is about an approach to the long-term living. It is creating your life." She tries hard to be active, thoughtful, and concerned about others. But in her unrelenting drive to move ahead she becomes, in a sense, blind to those around her. Her drive to get things done can be misinterpreted as aggression. It is this drive that has saved Mercedes.

Creating a life entails negotiating the pain that is part of life. Since it is Mercedes's nature to be involved, she does not and cannot isolate. She declares, "I do know people who pull the covers over their heads and stay in bed for a week. They come out and the problem is all solved. I do not have that process." Though childhood experiences were a powerful influence upon Mercedes's personality, the death of her baby was to help shape her personality in the world and deepen her understanding of herself and of life. Her baby was born with a rare genetic syndrome. She lived for four months before she died. Mercedes was grief stricken, but in the midst of her despair and mourning, she chose light and life for herself and her family. A month after her baby died, she moved the family to a new apartment. Three months after her baby's death, still intensely grieving her loss, Mercedes opened her own law practice. Feeling her presence in the universe helped Mercedes move through trauma. Chaos and darkness may weigh upon her, but her positive spirit and essential creative nature have a stronger hold upon her. Mercedes's need for action, especially in difficult times, is not a reflection of avoidance. She did not move her family or open her law practice as a means of avoiding her pain. She told me she was in full mourning, but her creative instincts urged her to "pull herself through" and that meant doing something. Plans had been made prior to her baby's death, and her plans needed to be carried out. Mercedes acted in a life-affirming manner through her anguish. Her drive, her goal-orientation, her perseverance and self-reliance made creative behavior possible.

Sensations of pain differ for all people, as do the experiences that cause pain. The facts of the trauma are not as significant as a woman's ability to weave the experience into her life. In sharing their stories, these women demonstrate how they bring light and order to the internal darkness and chaos that once bore down upon their essential creative natures. These women are strong, vulnerable, courageous, and productive. They share a strong drive to understand their place in the world, to learn about themselves and their environment, and to declare their presence in the universe. You can interpret that declaration as a means of honoring the Goddess within them. Without some public declaration, women can easily become invisible. When women feel invisible, they feel helpless, hopeless, unable to cope, and uncreative. Anna, Jackie, and Mercedes are goal-directed and possess an intensity about the idea of connections that helps them frame their essential creative natures and share the product of their expression. The power of their essential creative natures can be found in their approach to work and to negotiating traumatic experiences.

Anna's mother was close to death as Anna entered college. Her mother was also on a restricted diet. Anna felt compelled to help her mother; she chose to study nutrition. But she found it difficult to concentrate in school. The depth of her anguish was not to emerge for several more years. Unresolved experiences of youth that filled her with anger, shame, and guilt would continue to torment her until she brought them into the light. Twice Anna dropped out of school and traveled across the country. While finishing her degree, Anna worked part-time in a "fine" restaurant; the chef considered himself an *artiste*. He treated people poorly. It was horrible. He would throw pots at people, Anna recalls. This blatant disrespect for others, as well as the tragic waste of food, greatly disturbed Anna. A friend told Anna of a job opening for a person with restaurant experience, a background in nutrition, and an interest in adult education. Anna applied for and got the position. That was fifteen years ago. She recalls, "I became a cook's trainer. We offered a program for hardcore unemployed people. We were teaching them to cook fancy foods, to do this work in restaurants for high salaries. We ran a very successful program. We were de-funded when Reagan came into office and tourism dropped off. We could not place as many people. Now we are training people as health-care home aides." Anna has remained with her company all these years. The program has changed over the course of the years, but the vision remains the same. She explains, "We are still taking people who are unemployed or who are on welfare, and we help them make the transition. We are a women's company now." Anna has helped women move from unemployment and welfare to the status of trainers within her company. The challenges at work deepen her commitment to herself, her essential creative nature, and her creative expression. She has gone back to school for her master's degree in public management.

Sometimes, in the midst of a trauma, it feels that the only person a woman can rely upon in the world is herself. There was a time when her vision, not fully formed yet, was deeply threatened by meanness and cruelty. Around Jackie's twelfth birthday, her mother left home rather than face certain death at the hands of Jackie's father. Jackie swallowed the pain of her loss; she understood her mother's need to survive as her father continued to drink and to be abusive. Jackie was left to care for her younger brothers and sisters. School was no escape from mistreatment. One teacher was particularly cruel toward Jackie. Motherless and with a drunken father, Jackie became the target of her teacher's ridicule. Yet Jackie liked school, and her grades were good. Fortunately, there was another teacher who inspired her. He was the closest Jackie would come in her youth to a mentor. This teacher, a math teacher, asked the children on a regular basis, "What do you want to be when you grow up?" That was when Jackie decided she wanted to be an accountant. Her teacher, taking the children's answers seriously, told them to think the question through carefully. It was as if the children were making a pledge to do something with their lives. They were committing themselves to the concept that they could achieve. Jackie's teacher supported her idea to be an accountant; he told her she was accounting material. If the children worked hard, he told them, they could achieve. That concept has stayed with Jackie throughout her life. He helped Jackie believe in herself.

Two years after her mother moved north, Jackie and her brothers and sisters were taken by court order from their father and placed in the custody of their mother. Jackie finished high school, married young, and went straight to work. Her first job was as a receptionist in a law office. Once again, she faced humiliation when one of the lawyers sexually harassed her. She left that job and went to work on an assembly line at a factory. At the factory, she was moved from the assembly line into the office. She wanted to do the accounting, but she was told she needed to go to school first. Dissatisfied at the factory, she got a job at a fast-food restaurant for a brief time until her first child was born. After the birth of their son, her husband did not want her to return to work. She remained at home until her second child was two years old. Then she could no longer bear "sitting still." Her marriage had fallen apart. She found herself separated and on welfare. She hated where her life had gone and what she felt like. Nonetheless, she believed that there was more to her life than this. She believed her children needed a stable, healthy role model. She got a job with a women's organization, running errands, filing, and typing. Her capabilities were more than what was being asked of her, but the bills were paid and her self-esteem was returning. Now, Jackie says, "I'm in charge of sales of publications and the invoices. I do the mail, order the supplies, and maintain the office equipment." She is confident her dream of being an accountant is closer to being realized and so she is patient.

Jackie was only twenty-four years old when her marriage fell apart. She suffered great emotional pain at that loss, but she found support and comfort in her church community. She began to attend bible study classes. In religious school, Jackie met a woman minister who encouraged her; she urged Jackie to continue her education. Jackie decided to get a degree in religious education. Though Jackie remained active in her church, with her counseling, teaching Sunday school, and singing in the church choir, her dream to be an accountant pulled at her. After finishing her degree in religious education, she returned to college, this time for a degree in business. Now

Jackie insists that she perform at her highest level. She must achieve her potential.

Fulfilling her potential through relationships, work, and self-knowledge are part of Mercedes's ever-emerging persona. It is a way of life for her. I choose the word "emerging" because change is inherent in how Mercedes lives her life. In her seeking, she has generally changed careers every five to seven years. Often in someone's work path there is a through line, the obvious connections from one job to another. The link between jobs in Mercedes's past has been the social activism crucial to the performance of those jobs. Activism helps Mercedes shape her life. Her own discomfort as a youth, her need to overcome fear, the sense of being "other than" have influenced her choices and drawn her to social activism. Mercedes went to college in the United States; during this time her parents returned to Puerto Rico. Upon graduating, Mercedes joined her parents. She had difficulty in obtaining work and took a clerical position for which she was overqualified. She then found a job as a psychologist's assistant, working in a drug treatment center at a hospital. She also led group therapy sessions in a prison. Feeling restless and uncomfortable, she decided to leave Puerto Rico. She returned to the United States to work for the federal and city government. She moved from program evaluator to program developer, and worked her way through the city agency until she was working with the assistant commissioner. After three years, the feelings of restlessness and boredom began to reappear. She had met and married her husband. Given her propensity for change, she decided to return to school for a degree in law, to do civil rights and public interest law. After law school, she worked for a Puerto Rican organization as a litigator. It was exciting, intense work for the first few years, but again she grew tired. The intensity and stress associated with litigation work no longer enthralled her. During this time of discontent, she gave birth to her first child. She decided to take several months off to be a "stay-at-home mom" and then returned to work one day a week. This time she worked for a program that helped young Puerto Rican students get into law school. Then she had her second child; the baby died at just a few months old. Mercedes knew she wanted more children, but she also knew she wanted to work; she never intended to be a stay-at-home mom indefinitely. She opened her own law practice with another woman and worked part-time. Money was not a worry, so she did not work full-time. The focus of her law practice became family and matrimonial law. Mercedes wanted to represent women. She explains, "I wanted to help women who were involved in separation or divorce and in custody disputes. I also did small business law primarily with women." In matrimonial law, Mercedes states, "the line between counselor and lawyer is not so clear. So I got to do both. I found that with a little guidance as to what the possibilities are, it can be an enormously empowering experience for a lot of women. I have been a feminist since I came back to this country." Seven years went by when the need to change was urging her on, tugging at her serenity. She had her third child. Mercedes was invited to join the development committee of a new women's organization. Her time as a volunteer adviser kept increasing, and her commitment and involvement with this organization kept growing; she became part of the board of directors and a member of the executive committee. Mercedes was spending far more time volunteering her expertise at this organization than working at her law practice. After seven years, she felt restless, bored, and burnt out. Her marriage had failed, and the stress of the separation became too much. She decided to close her practice. The executive director of the women's organization left, and Mercedes was asked to take over as the interim director. She needed and wanted to change the direction of her work. "I wanted to write and work with women's issues. Now I am a V.P. of a woman's foundation. I run the place; I supervise the managers. I oversee the finances. I do not practice law. I have the opportunity to do many different things in this position. The organization is changing and getting very big, and it all feels new." Addressing the numerous issues facing women and girls, educating the public about women's issues, implementing and funding new programs, and running the foundation challenge Mercedes sufficiently. She has not yet experienced the restlessness and boredom that can invade her psyche. As long as Mercedes feels challenged and able to make significant connections, there is no inner urging calling her to move on.

For Mercedes, personal meaning and satisfaction is derived from meeting the challenges presented throughout a woman's life. Her inner voice is solidified through the process of following her essential creative nature. Meeting the challenge of trauma brings a woman closer to her essential creative nature as well. Commitment to self is entwined with honoring the essential creative nature and steadfastly seeking the light rather than faltering in the darkness. Sometimes the choice and the process of moving toward the light takes months, sometimes years. Sometimes it is a lifetime before a woman is ready to hear her inner voice and respond to the pain of trauma. However, once a woman has emerged from the darkness and chaos, no confusion exists about where she has been. No doubt lingers that she has fallen, gotten up, and stepped out of the darkness and chaos and into the light. Her steps may have been taken haltingly at first. Perhaps they were barely noticeable, but even tiny steps continually taken produce forward movement. With time and practice, small steps turn into a strong, even gait. Even if the rhythm is momentarily broken, it is easily picked up again. The strength of a woman's essential creative nature enables her to negotiate the next fall, the next trauma, the next journey through darkness, with a degree of certainty that she will emerge into the light.

Once Anna went away to college, she became clinically depressed. After graduating from college and joining the company she presently works for, Anna's depression intensified. She describes that time: "I could not get it together. I felt any mistake I made meant I was not able to save the world. Here I was so smart and I was not able to get myself organized, to be of value to anyone. I did not have a right to exist." Despite her positive performance at work and people who were supportive of her talents, Anna was extraordinarily unhappy. She could no longer muster the energy or the courage to continue on in the darkness alone. Her fears and negativity were too great to mask and too powerful to ignore. She decided to go to therapy. She describes how "they put me on all different drugs. The drugs affected my speech; they affected my energy. They scared me, and after a time I refused to take the drugs. But I feel the medication saved my life." The medicine helped buy Anna time to fight the overwhelming despair that had engulfed her. She was working in therapy on the issues that had shaken her sense of herself. Her father's abuse, her mother's illness, being raped by her brother had left her deeply injured. The medication and treatment led her through a process that brought light to where darkness had reigned. She began, in her own style, to take control of her recovery. She says, "I reached a moment when I knew what I had to do to protect myself and take good care of myself."

Part of Anna's style is her need to understand and assimilate intellectually whatever is occurring to her. Anna read about depression and alcoholism. She followed suggestions: she pampered herself, read, took saunas, rested, ate well, and made sure she spent time with people. She declares, "When I knew what to do to guard my rest and guard my space, I knew that depression would never happen to me again. A lot of the problem had to do with organizing work and thinking my main role in life was in taking care of everybody else."

Creating a healthy life free from her crippling depression was also grounded in her being able to stop racing and make something with her hands, like collages, pillows, or bread. This is reminiscent of the way her mother expressed herself through a difficult marriage and a debilitating disease. Anna chose the path by which she could emerge from the darkness and chaos. In years past, Anna made things as a means of isolating herself from the world and from her feelings. Now she creates as a means of expressing herself, of grounding herself in the here and now; it brings her back to herself. The motivation for creating with her hands has changed. Now Anna wants to share her creations with the world. Anna explains, "I do not get depressed now. I am very clear about the distinction between feeling sad and feeling the world is fucked. I can be sad, I can be worried about a relationship, but I have not been clinically depressed again."

Recently Anna had to open a new training center for her company in another city. She was organizing the center as well as training new staff members. The pressure felt enormous. Her anxiety about performance was intense; she felt solely responsible for the success of this center. Anna became emotionally and physically exhausted. She began drinking too much, and her fears and her stress kept increasing. The warning signs were before her; she read the clues in her internal environment. In a strange city, isolated and alone, Anna was vulnerable. She stopped everything. Gathering the materials necessary, she spent the next week redecorating a piece of furniture for her home. She calmed herself, stopped drinking, and let go of her fears. She reminded herself: Anna was the priority, not work. If Anna could not succeed in taking care of herself, how could she take care of business?

Taking care of business entails a thorough evaluation of the internal and external realities affecting your life. Jackie evaluates the situation, examines her choices and their ramifications, and decides how to overcome the obstacle. She believes in the power of praying for guidance. She works on her relationship with her God on a daily basis, and takes whatever steps necessary to keep moving forward. Involvement with her church helps her stay grounded. To take control of her life, Jackie had to force her husband to leave and had to return to work. Leaving her children all day was difficult, but she knew that, for everyone's well-being, she needed to work. She explains, "When I started back to work, I had a problem. The children were very upset when their father was not around. I had to get organized." Getting organized is a manifestation of Jackie's creative expression.

Years later, Jackie counseled a young woman with a small child at church. The young woman was in great torment: her boyfriend, the father of her small child, had just left her. Jackie heard the young woman's thoughts of suicide and recalled her own experience. She presented the same issue to this woman that had been posed to her. The image still possessed the same power. With consolation and support from Jackie, the girl saw her way through the trauma. Jackie realized how much she had grown in her own life since those days. Life, Jackie believes, is meant to be lived to the fullest. That means she must do what is before her to the best of her abilities. If it is not done to the best of her ability, "Why bother?"

Jackie's ability to cope is, like Anna's and Mercedes's, dependent upon taking action. Jackie's creativity is contingent upon connections to both ideas and people. She is attentive to her performance, open to new ideas, and grounded in the experience of actualizing those ideas. Jackie tries to live a simple life. She tries to be helpful because it is how she makes her presence known in the universe. It is a unique expression, one that only Jackie can create. She does not accept avoidance as an appropriate response; fear and challenge do not stop her. Her guiding image of "overcoming" ushers her out of the world of darkness and into the light.

Mercedes believes that "moving through trauma is associated with pulling yourself through." She says, "When I think of the worst of traumas, I think of my growing up Puerto Rican and having it ignored, the death of my child, and my divorce. But I am a problem-solver. I am a doer." Mercedes is not a passive observer of her life. Her reality is framed in the physical and intellectual sensations of her process. Mercedes, like Anna, enjoys producing tangible products with her hands. For Mercedes, the combination of making things, like a painting or a drawing, the act of overcoming fear, and intellectually challenging herself reveal the style of her essential creative nature. Mercedes says, "I will read. I will talk to people. I will try to process the experience. I am not someone who thinks bad things happen so that we can benefit from them. I take bad things and can say, I am who I am because of them. Like my daughter dying. It has made me a much more wonderful person than I would have been. But there are a lot of ways I could have become this wonderful person that would not have required such a terrible thing to happen. I am very persistent. I think that is a characteristic of creativity and problem-solving. If you struggle with something, you will eventually come out on the other side. I approach my life positively." She explains her perceptions further: "My family can be characterized as very 'stiff upper lip.' When my daughter got sick, my husband withdrew. I was with the doctors and dealing with the nurses. I was reading the scientific articles. I would get in the shower and scream and cry for an hour. But I have to do something. It is how I deal. It is how I process. Then I back off. I will be miserable, but I am more in the doing." Her optimism is contained within the act, within the doing, which gives her the strength to move into uncharted territory, to take risks when she is most vulnerable. Mercedes is nourished by the challenge to overcome. It gives her spiritual and emotional sustenance. Meeting the challenge strengthens her sense of self and stretches her perceived limits of her abilities.

The key to dealing with trauma is always found in a woman's personal, creative approach to life. But it must also be grounded in optimism. Anna, Jackie, and Mercedes are not perfect; they are not without their neuroses. But they honor their spirit to create their lives. The lives of these three women are testimonies to the power contained within. A woman's reliance upon her essential creative nature enables her to approach life from a secure stance, allowing her to negotiate the hard times. Moving through trauma may inextricably change a woman. Reliance upon that which is positive, her essential creative nature, enables her to transverse the darkness. She reaches a deeper understanding of herself as a woman capable of action. She will emerge as a woman whose presence is felt in the universe. At times of trauma, the creative woman becomes, like the image of Ishtar, she who brings light and order from darkness and chaos.

## FINDING AND STRENGTHENING THE PATH TOWARD LIGHT AND ORDER

One of the first questions you will want to explore for yourself is: am I optimistic or pessimistic in my approach to my life? The answer is crucial to the task of bringing light and order from the darkness. If you answered "pessimistic," do you understand the source of the pessimism? Perhaps it is time to release that connection to your past. Can you change your attitude and gain access to a more creative and productive image of life? Yes!

If you answered "optimistic," can you identify how you have used that optimism to move you through difficult times?

If you cannot identify the manner in which you have used your optimistic perspective during hard times, perhaps you need to evaluate your answer again. If you answered "optimistic" and you can identify the way in which you have moved yourself productively through trauma, you must then ask yourself whether you honor and value that achievement and that approach. Without honoring that strength, you will not trust yourself to meet the challenges of your life creatively.

Think of a trauma you have lived through. What was your emotional and physical response to the circumstance? Can you think of ways in which you might have acted differently, ways in which you would have felt the pain and yet would have grown? Make a list of your thoughts. As you review your list, does a pattern emerge? Is your personal style obvious in the actions and thoughts written on your list? For example, the women in this chapter used their need to gather information and to learn as a path to help propel them into action and out of darkness. They also all had a range of activities that brought them joy and that they believed expressed who they were. Do you know which activities, such as gardening, cooking, volunteering your time at a school or hospital, fill you? Are you able to continue giving yourself joy when trauma and crisis occur? Do you cut yourself off from those things that will secure your survival? If you learn to pamper yourself through actions, you will strengthen your essential creative nature.

Return to your list. Can you think of things to add to your list that would have led you more quickly through the trauma and lessened the pain? If your style is to make something with your hands, honor it. If you feel secure in gathering data before you take action, do it. Regardless of your fear, the intensity of the pain and the seemingly powerful grasp of chaos, you can trust yourself and your essential creative nature to lead you into the light and to shape order in your life.

---

CHAPTER SIX

# TIME OF EMERGENCE:
## YOUR CREATIVE PROCESS

❧

Aphrodite was a Greek Goddess. Her origins are several; her domain included at different times being Goddess of the sea, the animals, fertility, heaven, and earth. She embodied the union of nature and culture, beauty and love. Sensuality was the love she expressed in her Goddess vision. She was drawn to renewing life through the pleasurable experience of living life; she represents beginnings.

> "Heavenly Aphrodite was the figure who inspired the possibility of comprehensive love, including the passion for ideas and suggesting ultimately the passion of the soul wherever it may fall." (*The Myth of the Goddess*)

> "Aphrodite 'cultivates the ephemeral beauties,' reflecting the divine in its daily aspect." (*The Myth of the Goddess*)

> "[She] is a tremendous force for change. Through her flow attraction, union, fertilization, incubation, and birth of new life." (*Goddess in Everywoman*)

The mystery of life is found in the endless, timeless, limitless processes that we must as human beings move through. We are continually reborn spiritually, intellectually, physically, and emotionally. Our personal re-creations occur daily, weekly, monthly, yearly, generationally. These processes are the methods women use to negotiate decisions and achieve transformations. Transformations enlist our faculties, senses, spirits, and essential creative natures. These processes are the union of the heaven and the earth; they symbolize Aphrodite in their essence as beginnings. These processes entail breaking apart the present reality. This disruption is followed by a space between releasing the known and conceiving the new reality. The time of emergence encapsulates and frames this space. It is the context for the process of becoming.

Aphrodite has been, since her time as a revered Goddess, reduced to a Goddess of superficial beauty and sexual pleasure. In her original form, she was a profound female deity. Her elegant being and her passion for beauty were intensified by the exquisite joy she experienced in nature and life. Through her seeing, through the sensuality she experienced in the sights, sounds, smells, and sensations around her, Aphrodite found the union of heaven and earth. She found the origins of her beginning and her essential creative nature. Today she represents for women unlimited possibilities contained within the joy of experiencing the sensuality of one's physical and perceptional environment.

Aphrodite is the child of union, thus the symbol of beginnings. Every transformation, regardless of size, is the beginning of something new and potentially profound—for the larger community or, on a smaller scale, for the individual. Aphrodite represents the bringing together of the emotional, spiritual, physical, and intellectual aspects of a woman. By bringing these original aspects of her being together, Aphrodite avails a woman the opportunity to re-create herself. Aphrodite's love of life, and the joy she finds in the beauty and sensuality contained within life, symbolize a renewed longing for life. For every woman, the act of bringing together the separate and original aspects of herself (the emotional, intellectual, spiritual, and physical), stimulates her love for life, invigorates her senses, and energizes her existence. This interpretation of Aphrodite's image is a testimony to the power, the pleasure, and the significance contained within those states that comprise the creative process.

What do I mean when I use the term "creative process"? Without a process, nothing moves, nothing changes, nothing is understood. All is static, dead. The creative process is defined by a series of steps, stages, or phases that a woman passes through to make something where nothing existed before. The creative process contains spaces characterized by emotional, physical, intellectual, and spiritual experiences. These spaces enable a woman to journey through her life, move through her work, and form relationships. She engages her transformations while simultaneously shaping, creating, reshaping, and re-creating her life and the manifestations of her essential creative nature. Successfully moving through the creative process avails a woman that which feeds her life and gives her the energy to continue.

The creative process is motion. It is active, vital, difficult, painful, stimulating, and sensuous. The results of the motion can be viewed narrowly, as in relation to creating a specific product, or it can be viewed more broadly, as in shaping the internal life and vision of a woman. There is value in looking at a woman's personal creative process, both in the narrow and the broader context, for that is where a woman finds joy, sensuousness, and wholeness with herself and her world. There is value in crediting a woman's process with providing her a way of seeing, a manner of feeling, and a path to understanding. In analyzing her own process, a woman may be released from inhibitions and psychological blocks that impede her progress and hinder the flow of life-fulfilling energy. The significance of the process, far more than the end result, is in having shaped the product. Through the creation of a product, a woman recreates herself, as does Aphrodite in bringing together those original aspects of her beginning (the heaven and earth). Reaffirmation of self and empowerment are the rewards that exist far beyond the completion of the creative process and the product.

In this chapter, you have the opportunity to examine the meaning behind the phrase "creative behavior" and "creative process." The framework through which a creative thought or creative product emerges is found within the creative process. You will learn how some scientists describe the creative process. This information provides those of you who are unfamiliar with the concept of a creative process a context and a framework within which to place your thoughts. Though general concepts about the creative process have been described in similar ways by various scientists, most individuals understand the experience of their creative process through their own intellectual, physical, and emotional facilities. On a personal level, the creative process is unique to everyone.

The creative process involves many aspects of one's being. Isolating these various aspects becomes problematic. As a result, a researcher of the creative process is forced to examine undefined areas. In reality, these areas can never fully be described or quantified because they are not reachable through a scientific examination. They cannot be articulated. These aspects or levels of creating are beyond language and are outside of the scientific approach of looking at physiological or neurological reactions within the body and the brain. These areas of the creative process occur deep within the psyche. These experiences have no definable boundaries and cannot be framed by words. Indeed, articulation of these aspects, in some respect, limits them. Language is never all-encompassing. Sometimes the mere use of language reduces that which language seeks to define and understand. All the creative process researcher has of these metaphysical states is the knowledge that something occurs. In the end, after all the research and models of the creative process have been argued, redefined, diagrammed, and described, the best we are offered are flawed, unemotional descriptions of the intimate states of being that comprise the creative process. This problem, while worth noting, is more of a scientific dilemma than a problem for a woman looking to explore the unique configuration of her own creative process. One's own personal exploration does not have to match the scientific approach. (Nevertheless, it is helpful to have a reference point on the subject.)

A woman's process can be interpreted only through a personal perspective. The words used to describe the process have meaning solely for that woman, though we can learn and identify aspects in ourselves from listening to others express their views and experiences. In order to give you both an "objective" perspective and a "personal" perspective of the creative process, I have chosen one woman's story. After a review of some of the best creativity research, I have enlisted Moria's thoughts, feelings, and life experiences to help personalize the idea or concept of the creative process. Moria's story can be viewed from two contexts: first, the creative process as it applies to developing a specific product, and second, the creative process as it has been used in shaping a life and expressing a woman's essential creative nature. My hope is that you will understand the concept of the creative process in such a way that you can begin your own exploration without feeling lost.

Do you know what your creative process is? Do you know the manner or style by which you shape your life? Do you know when, where, why, and how you can begin work on a problem, be it internally motivated or externally motivated?

Do you know where in your process you tend to get blocked and overcome with fear? Do you know what actions or environments help you to move through those negative states? Do you know what internal and external conditions encourage you to respond to your creative impulses? These questions are posed as a starting point. They are the impetus or motivation behind the first step in identifying your creative process, especially if you have never sought to understand it before. The better acquainted you are with how you work, the more freely you will move through those difficult spaces that occur during the creative process. Indeed, such knowledge can help remove insidious judgments that have been subsumed within the creative process. Knowledge of your creative process can place the inner critic in perspective. That critical voice, a necessary aspect in the creative process, must serve you as a positive influence rather than as a negative one. The inner critic is not there to beat you down, to burden you with fear, or to question your integrity or your worth. Rather, the internal critic's role is to improve upon your thinking, to help determine what needs refinement, or to lead you to a new connection.

Theories about creativity and the creative process abound. Each theory is grounded in a different orientation, whether psychological, behavioral, or holistic, to name only a few. My position through this book has been to borrow a little from many perspectives. Irving A. Taylor has written a retrospective of a few of these theories. In his article "A Retrospective View of Creativity Investigation," he examined seven directions that creativity research has taken. Several of these have been used thus far: the psychological (the emotional and mental-health reasons for creative behavior), the humanistic (which implies self-determination and self-actualization), trait-factorial (the personality characteristics of creative people), and association-istic (making new associations and combinations to arrive at new understandings and solutions).

For your goal of understanding and fully utilizing your creative process, the concept of self-actualization plays an important role. It is used in evaluating and completing the creative process. Scientists whose fundamental perspective is grounded in the humanistic approach believe that self-actualization is the primary motivation behind the creative act. Taylor wrote in his retrospective that self-actualization was understood by some researchers as "a process of realizing and completing one's self by an integration within and between one's self and the world. By this process, the person becomes unified, more open to experience . . . and more fully functioning."

Further insights into the nature of creative behavior and the creative process are often found within various definitions of creativity. Donna Y. Ford and J. John Harris offer a context for the creative process through their definition of creativity. In "The Elusive Definition of Creativity," they wrote, "[C]reativity is those attitudes by which we fulfill ourselves. . . . Creativity is the actualizing of our potential. . . . It is more than originality which may only express the bizarre. . . . Creativity is an advance and change as well as an expression of continuity with the past." Words such as "choosing," "change," "fulfill," "generating possibilities," and "deliberation" are active words. They elicit images and meanings of engaged and focused states of being. The intensity of a woman's commitment to her creative process equals the intensity of the process and the outcome. If you are dedicated to solving the problem, you will find a solution.

Over the years, researchers and theorists have tried to describe the various stages that characterize the creative process. But the process is complex, and disagreement arises among researchers as to the names and breakdown of these various states. These disputes and differences are not significant for your purpose. Knowing that the creative process moves freely between the intellectual, the emotional, the unconscious, the spiritual, and back again, in a consistently changing order, enables you to examine the various stages of your creative process. The struggle among scientists to name these states does not add or detract from your awareness that transitional stages occur. You may call the stages of transition and transformation anything you like. Ultimately your own perceptions and meanings, in your own language, will best identify these stages.

In 1926 a man named Graham Wallas tried to analyze the creative process through four distinct phases: preparation, incubation, illumination, and verification. These four steps have been briefly and succinctly described by Mel Rhodes in "An Analysis of Creativity": "[T]he preparation step consists of observing, listening, asking, reading, collecting, comparing, contrasting, analyzing, and relating all kinds of objects and information. The incubation process is both conscious and unconscious. This step involves thinking about parts and relationships, reasoning, and often a fallow period. Inspirations [or illumination] very often appear during this fallow period . . . [illuminations are insights which suddenly appear. They are the answers which lead to the production of the product.] The step labeled verification is a period of hard work. This is the process of converting an idea into an object or into an articulated form."

In *The Courage to Create*, Rollo May vividly described the creative process, while remaining within the broader parameters of Wallas's four-step process. The vividness of his descriptions makes the process seem less rigid, less "steely." He wrote that the encounter, or engaging the creative process, is significant in the intensity and level of absorption with which it is experienced, and that "[p]urpose in the human being is a much more complex phenomenon that [sic] what used to be called will power. Purpose involves all levels of experience. We cannot will to have insights. We cannot will creativity. But we can will to give ourselves to the encounter with intensity of dedication and commitment. . . ." This encounter and the level of intensity demanded produce a kind of ecstasy. This ecstasy is part of the joy and sensuality experienced by a woman during the creative process. It is the result of the union of "form and passion with order and vitality. Ecstasy is the technical term for the process in which this union occurs. . . . Ecstasy is the accurate term for the intensity of consciousness that occurs in the creative act. But it is not to be thought of merely as a Bacchic 'letting go'; it involves the total person, with the subconscious and unconscious acting in unity with the conscious. It is not irrational. . . . It brings intellectual, volitional, and emotional functions into play all together." You can understand through May's description of ecstasy that the sensuousness of the process is not relegated solely to sexual experience. Indeed, sexual experience may be either heightened or hindered during an acutely active period in the creative process. Instead, the sensuality found in the creative process is found in a multilayered series of sensations: intellectual, physical, and emotional. The work of the creative process is arduous, at times emotionally painful and/or confusing. A woman must develop a level of tolerance for a wide range of feelings, both negative and positive, in order to successfully move through the process. The process is not static. It is fluid. It is constant in its motion.

But the whole of the creative process is not composed of an intense sensual experience. At varying times, after making hard, concentrated, vivid connections, the mind needs to rest and rearrange what it has been working through. Wallas called this stage "incubation." May referred to this as "the moment of relaxation." While the conscious mind no longer works to solve the problem, the unconscious is working out new configurations and understandings. The problem is shifted to the psychic realm, where possibilities are limitless and time is endless. This state of being supplies us with concepts and connections not readily available on a daily basis. It is the playland of new formulations, of new ideas. It is the land of original concepts and connections, of bizarre, wonderful, frightening, useless, and humorous images. Incubation or relaxation is a necessary step toward arriving at inspiration or illumination. Have you ever faced a perplexing problem and, upon reaching a point of intense disappointment or frustration, put the problem aside? Perhaps you made a phone call, began work on something else, or took a nap, when suddenly the answer appeared to you. Something stimulated you and the answer or the path to the answer appeared in your consciousness. That is how the incubation state works and how the inspiration stage is generally experienced. These are the "eureka" or "ah-ha!" moments. The incubation phase can last a brief time or a long time. It can last a few hours or years. At the moment of illumination, a woman has consciously engaged the problem again through a new perspective.

There is no preordained length of time that determines when one phase of the process begins and another one ends. A woman may move back and forth several times between emotional, intellectual, and unconscious phases before the connection needed to solve the problem reveals itself. There are three possible outcomes: resolution is reached, the problem is placed aside for a time (hours, days, weeks, months, years), or the problem is abandoned. In creative behavior nothing is final. A resolution reached at one time may be reworked at a later date. Every visitation of the problem alters the woman's perspective of the problem, changes how she defines the problem, and transforms the resolution to the problem. Regardless of how you order these shifting phases or label these states, nothing is birthed fully formed without first having gone through change, transformation, and maturation.

Because these intellectual, emotional, and physical sensations are experientially different, one woman may understand her process in broad strokes while another woman understands and senses the subtle shifts within her being. Do these differences matter? No. Regardless of the sensation of these phases, the process is not complete until the woman has articulated her understanding in some tangible fashion. Her new idea must be given a form and context. No matter how nimbly a woman moves through her process, without the act of giving form to the idea, or without verification, the creative process remains incomplete. Rollo May believes that "escapist creativity is that which lacks encounter." Do you have trouble following through on your ideas, and allowing them to come to fruition? This is not the root of your problem; it is the expression of a problem. If you can trace the reasons for such self-deprivation, with a certain degree of desire, commitment, work, and perhaps even therapy, you can free yourself from engaging in escapist creativity. You can move yourself into actualization. (Just moving through blocks into actualization is a creative process.)

Several years ago, I had the opportunity to explore my creative process through the use of a journal. During that time of exploration and examination, I actually freed myself of certain negative feelings and anxieties that were a hindrance. The knowledge I gained in examining my process helped me overcome those same fears. I did not articulate or frame my own process with the language used by researchers. I did not need a scientific model to analyze and understand my process. But once I saw the path I took and understood the emotional shifts that occurred on my path, my process altered. It became cleaner, easier, and more direct. The confusing times and frustrating phases were shortened because I understood what was happening. I was no longer as threatened by these stages once I understood their place.

Without immersion into the process, without following your commitment through to self-actualization, there can be no experience of beauty, no sensation of sensuality or pleasure.

A woman's sense of herself, her world, her joy, her sensuality, and her essential creative nature can be found only in the engagement with her creative process.

## SHE ALIGHTS IN HER OWN CREATIONS

She stands tall, though she is not above average in height. She is of slight build but fills a space beyond her size. She is energetic and lively. Moria is a fifty-year-old white woman, the only child of an unhappy union. She is single, has not been in a committed relationship for some time, and has never had children. Her childhood was a mix of the positive and the negative. It was a childhood that gave Moria the opportunity to develop an aesthetic sensitivity to the world around her but also gave her the experience of negotiating emotional pain and a sense of isolation. The positive experience of seeing both her mother and father through their creative endeavors developed a sense within Moria that she too could create. Her father loved to do woodworking and to draw. Moria found her most keenly felt connection to her father through sharing creative activity. In this realm, there was blissful agreement between the two of them. Moria states, "I was always encouraged to be creative by my father. I got a lot of acknowledgment when I would write stories, and he liked to draw. This was something I could share with my father. It gave me the feeling of being close to my father. I think that stimulated my inclination in that direction for the rest of my life. I felt valued for myself in this area." Moria's mother has always been involved in the making of things. She was and is an "exquisite seamstress" and loves to knit, crochet, and paint.

Where Moria's father withdrew emotionally, her mother freely expressed her unhappiness through her anger. Her mother verbally abused Moria. As a result, Moria was left with conflicting feelings of love, feelings of being overly important to both her parents, feelings of being ignored, abandoned, hopeless, and ultimately lonely. Moria was placed in an untenable position of being between her parents' joy and anger and of negotiating their emotional roller coaster. The approval Moria received for her creative efforts from her father angered her mother. In return, her mother rejected Moria and disapproved of Moria's creative expressions. Moria was a pawn in their anger game. She understands now that "the loss was the lack of emotional nurturing, understanding, and validation from my parents on a daily basis. They were not in touch and were so needy. Their relationship was so off-kilter. I was unhappy and constantly felt like I was wrong. I had the sense of not being heard and being wrong. Therapy teaches me that it was a form of annihilation." Moria's story reinforces the concept of creative behavior as a means of survival. It proves that a woman or a child can find the ability to fill a void through personal validation. Like other women you have met, Moria lived an active and vivid inner life to cope with her outer reality. At least that was how it all began. Moria took that impetus to create her world and worked with it. She developed it, cherished it, and later translated that impulse into a public expression of her essential creative nature—an expression that has led her to self-acknowledgment.

Moria experiences her guiding image as "this incredible discomfort at keeping ideas, thoughts, and visions to myself, in my imagination. It makes me feel unwell. I am always finding ways to expel what comes up." Moria has success and trust in publicly expressing her essential creative nature, which she developed in her youth. Her need to publicly share her visions and her ability to do that indicate the level of achievement she has in negotiating the world around her. It also feeds her ongoing urge to shape and reshape her life. Her guiding principle, giving form to her vision and sharing it, defines Moria's concept of creativity: "I think creativity is that thing that we name, that act of putting into form that which is within. I think my inner yearning to 'do' is what that is about. I know I have to act out, dramatize, write, or do something with what I see in my mind. Creativity is the act of expressing in form that which is within." Moria's definition of creativity also offers us an illustration of what is meant by researchers when they speak of the last stage in the creative process: verification, the stage of actualization. The strength of her need to move into actualization is directly proportional to her experience of being "unwell" when she engages in "escapist creativity" and does not give form to her ideas.

Moria understands creativity as an active state. Indeed, she feels compelled to make a "statement" about her inner vision in everything she does. She can look at herself and say without hesitation that she is a creative person, whether in dressing or decorating a room. She says, "Whatever I do, it is about expression. I never get any pleasure unless I do things in that way." Aphrodite's nature can be identified in Moria's conceptualization of herself as "passionate," "intense," and stimulated by nature. Moria explains, "I am fifty, and I am extremely happy in my body. I have worked extremely hard to make my body healthy. I love my body and love that it is there for me. I think it is essential to my being creative." Moria is sensual, excited by beauty around her, excited by sights, sounds, smells, color, and ideas; she is extremely unhappy in a "negative" surrounding. What a wonderfully vivid portrayal of the image of Aphrodite as it applies to creatively living every day. What a glorious example of the results of moving through the creative process.

As you can imagine, living a vital creative life has always been significant for Moria. When she was a young child, she dreamed of being a writer, a dream that she is beginning to seriously explore now that she is in her fifties. That dream was replaced in her teenage years by the desire to be an actress. She immediately began acting and studying theater. She worked in summer theater and was accepted by a college that had a highly regarded drama program. Upon completing college, she moved east. She recalls, "I could not get enough acting jobs to support myself so I did thousands of jobs only to pay my bills. That way I could continue to act even if it was in workshops, and I did summer theater. It was what I did in my twenties and thirties. Then I decided to move to California. I really wanted to earn a living at acting. A transition occurred. Just making the move in the direction was some kind of internal saying to myself, 'You have a right to live better than you are living now. Do you want to live better than you are living now?' That was a way of loving myself and raising my self-esteem. The courage that it took for me to make the move raised my self-esteem. When I came out here I began to work almost immediately, and that raised my confidence."

She manifested creative behavior early in her life that was nurtured and supported by her mother and father's positive creative expressions. But Moria intuitively understood from an early age that life was a creative process. She has always been influenced by her inner reflections. Like Aphrodite, Moria cannot escape her inclinations toward wholeness. She longs for the pleasure found in experiencing her life; she relishes the sensuality present in that engagement.

Moria's creative process has helped shape her decision-making process. Her words signify the place sensations have in her internal makeup and how she uses them as a guide. Describing her process, she says, "I will hang out with as many points of view about a thing as I can think of. I will spend a day absolutely not going to do something, then I will spend a day absolutely going to do it. I will explore all the points of view, and I will always talk to my friends. Ultimately, my decision is based on these questions. If I do this thing, do I feel enlivened? Am I moving forward? Do I get a feeling of lightness? Or if I do this thing, does it make me feel concave? Do I have an inner dread, a darkening? If I feel a contracting rather than an expanding, I will not proceed." This heightened sense of herself and her environment during the decision-making process is a creative process.

Moria does not run away from feelings or sensations. She has developed a tolerance for the unknown, for confusion, for pain and joy. That tolerance enables her to complete her decision-making and work process. She describes her working process as "an emotional, intellectual, and spiritual process. It is everything. An idea will come that will not leave me alone. Something will get hold of me. It is as though I become a vessel for everything in the universe that can feed this idea. It does not take place in a methodical linear fashion. I will see a book; I will take it and read it. I will go and look for material that will give me information about an idea, or the information will just 'appear'—sometimes a conversation will come up or I will see a picture on the wall that will give me information. Everything in my life is about this. There is an information gathering that just takes place naturally. If it is an acting role, I go into rehearsal and try it out, the idea and the interacting. When I am writing, after the information gathering has taken place, I will sit and see what comes up. I will type it. It is like being a channel. It is taking my own self and making a tube out of it. It is not like thinking. I ask that I get used as a clear and unobstructed channel for inspiration to come clearly, cleanly through. That creates a sensation in myself of being not in my personality and my thought. It happens when I am writing, performing, or taking photographs. That time in the process is undefined. When I am trying to be open and something will come up. There is a time when I write a lot of things down. Then I organize my notes. I think of structure when I am performing. I think of what happens and what emotions arise. Then I throw it away. I do not think about it.

It is scary; it is like jumping off the cliff. The completion time is painful but rewarding." Moria has just described her experience of Wallas's four steps of the creative process.

Do her words seem familiar? You have read them before. If you think back to the last chapter, Mercedes, an advocate for women in a women's organization and the mother of two children, described her process in a similar way. Mercedes told of an information-gathering time, and of a moment when action was needed. Mercedes also used the words to "jump off the cliff." Mary, the landscape artist in Chapter One, spoke of being a vessel through which the images of nature could move—through her and out her hand into her paintings. Whether the image is the moment of jumping into the unknown or becoming a vessel, these women are referring to a moment of complete commitment and abandonment of prohibition. It is enfolded by risk, which moves a woman into actualization. It allows her to test the validity of the structure she has created. Does it work? Is the context right? Is the form appropriate? Willingness to explore the possibilities reveals an openness to see the unexpected in the result. There is, as Moria referred to it, a need to stay open, to allow inspiration to move into and through her. Other women in the book have described similar feelings and images. These times when emotions, sensations, and intellect work in unison are times of actualization.

Following the actualization stage of the creative process, a natural "let down" occurs, especially if there is completion or resolution to the problem. Moria spoke of this stage as the "pain of completion." That pain is the result of the emotional, spiritual, and physical commitment exerted on her being during the process. Robert Grudin, in *The Grace of Great Things*, wrote that in the creative process there are four "distinct types of pain . . . pain of perception, pain of expression, pain of closure, pain of self-suppression. To each of these pains is attached, as though in a fairy tale or moral fable, a special pleasure rewarding the brave sufferer." I am speaking here of the pain of closure. When a commitment of such intensity has ended, there is an energy shift within the body and the psyche. This last phase, which Wallas did not include in his paradigm, is the cessation of the motivating drive behind the creative process. A woman experiences this cessation as a release, but it is usually accompanied by sadness, and sometimes even depression. It is unavoidable. It is the inherent consequence of the joy of completion. Because these emotions at the end of the process can be intense, moving through actualization to resolution can be frightening. Sometimes a woman will not move through this phase because the act of completion demands responsibility for the creation. Sometimes she is not willing to move through this phase for fear of success, or for fear of rejection. Sometimes a woman will not move through this phase because of the void felt immediately following the joy of completion. This void is potent. It can feel like a dark abyss. A woman must trust her ability to survive the depression or sadness of the void. She must believe there will be other engagements, other processes to challenge her and transform her. The inevitable question "What next?" arouses powerful feelings. As with everything else presented to you in this book, there are degrees of experience attending this last stage. Not everyone will be thrust into despair upon each completion. The paradox of creating, the highs and lows, the loss and the gain, must be personally understood to diminish the fear that accompanies it. Awareness and tolerance can lessen the negative influence that this phase may exert upon you.

Transitional periods, or transformations, as I have maintained from the beginning of this work, are the results of a creative process. If you were to look exclusively at Moria's acting career, you would be able to trace the transitional periods that have shaped her life and strengthened her creative process. But

I want to focus on the latest transformation that has occurred in her life, one which has had a profound impact upon her vision. It began around the time Moria's body began perimenopause. Five years since the beginning of menopause, Moria's perception of her life and the manifestation of her creative expression have altered. The vision she pursued all these years, which defined her relationship to the world, is losing its glimmer and appeal. She told me, "When I am performing, that is me. But there is so much around performing which is not me that I am losing interest." Her loss of pleasure has been accompanied by pain and confusion. The changes occurring within her body focused her attention, with great intensity, on how she defined herself and on the manner of her personal creative expression. She viewed confronting her physical discomfort as a reflection of her creative process, and as part of the exploration of her personal creative expression and her public persona. Moria felt these years were not creative. Ironically, she filled these last few "uncreative" years with studying the German language, German art, traveling, and learning photography. There was a seriousness and commitment with which Moria pursued her seeking. Her study of German and German culture has become a passion that brings her much pleasure and joy. Photography has emerged as her primary means of creative expression, and in keeping with the inherent nature attributable to the creative process, Moria has altered her vision.

Because of her shifting vision, her unwavering commitment to her creative process, her desire for wholeness through Aphrodite's urges for beauty and union with nature, Moria has had to re-create her public persona. A woman's public persona is reflected not only in her career, but in how she presents herself to the world, through her physical appearance and her relationships. For Moria it has been a time of emergence. She told me that for the first time in her life, dressing is significant. She sees it as a public statement. Moria states, "I never regarded dressing as important. I guess I did not regard myself as important. But as I began to think of myself more highly and more importantly, and as having an impact in the world, I began to dress myself with pleasure and enjoyment. There was a consciousness that it actually made a difference." Moria's time of physical transition has set off a chain reaction, one which beautifully exemplifies the creative process as it applies to shaping and re-creating a life. Though her physical changes have been difficult, her emotional and spiritual core have been strengthened. She has broadened the expression of her essential creative nature and has again chosen to share it in a public fashion. Despite the pain and depression she attributes to her hormonal changes, Moria has found a way in which to bring joy, pleasure, and sensuality back into her life. New experiences and perceptions afford her that experience. She says, "I am very excited by all the possibilities that have opened up to me. Prior to this I had tunnel vision!"

A woman must feel the need deep within her physical and spiritual core to form a confluence of aspects: her essential beginning, heaven and earth. The union of these original aspects of a woman's being flowing through the creative process bring her to a never-ending process of becoming. There is beauty, magic, mystery, and love for the woman willing to engage in her own time of emergence.

## MOVING THROUGH THE CREATIVE PROCESS

The following techniques are commonly used and can help you remain open and receptive to your creative process. This openness is crucial to the flow of energy of the creative process. These techniques are like a road map; there are many paths to get to where you are going. Not all of these will work for you. Perhaps you will need to improvise. Knowledge of your process will give you a pathway and sense of security during the confusing times. They can be adapted for use on personal problems, business problems, or artistic problems.

1.  Use free association. Ask yourself what is the problem you are confronting. Allow your mind to wander. No judgments, please. What images are conjured up? What colors accompany these images? Examine these images, colors, or words closely. Where do they lead you? You may feel the need to write the words, images, and sensations down. Explore the possibilities of what has emerged. Are there new understandings? Perhaps the words keep indicating that you need to shift your perspective on the problem to find the solution.

2.  If you like to make lists, use the lists to help free your thoughts instead of restrict and narrow them. Make lists categorizing negative and positive aspects of your idea. List the thoughts and feelings that accompany those categories. Then analyze your lists. If you do this properly, new categories will emerge. Remake your list. What may have appeared to you as a negative may suddenly hold the key to your solution, but only if you explore it completely. You must honestly and openly explore the negative list for its possibilities. Do not allow your negative judgment to stop the process of exploration.

3.  Mind maps are visual diagrams. They are a visual exploration of an idea. On a piece of paper, write words. They can be randomly placed. The words will emerge as you think of your problem. Then draw lines to connect words that seem to be associated. Maybe it is the feeling the words evoke. Perhaps it is a color that means something to

you. The words are associated with the problem. You can free-associate within the context of the mind map. Your words will give rise to new concepts, to new associations.

4. Examine all sides of the idea and explore what comes up for each side. This is a several step process wherein nothing is rejected or discarded. It is not very different from the list approach. You list the problem. What are the positives and negatives associated with the problem? Carefully examine the negatives. Why are they negative? If they are negative because they are different and far afield, allow yourself to follow them for a while. What would happen if you approached the problem from one of these wild and outrageous positions? These negatives may be the path to a new and better solution or product.

5. Gather information to stimulate ideas. You read in the last chapter how the women used information-gathering as a time for understanding the problem, moving through their fears, and gathering strength for the leap into the unknown. It is the preparation that gives you a solid foundation for your leap forward. Synthesize the information into an articulated concept. You may need to incorporate another technique to move to the next step if you get stuck.

6. Visualize. (A) Can you visualize your problem? (B) Can you imagine yourself doing some activity in which the problem has been solved? What are the steps you need to take to move from A to B? What is stopping you from placing yourself in the picture of B? What does visualization B tell you? If B seems unrelated to A, explore it further. What connection is being made that needs to be clarified? Sometimes people do these visualizations through images in their minds. Sometimes they make collages and look at what the collage says.

7. Engage in ritualistic activity as a means of opening yourself up. This technique can be used as a preparation state or to help you move through a block. Rituals are personal. Sometimes they are complex; sometimes they are simple. It can be a prayer, or a routine such as sitting in a chair and having a cup of coffee before beginning. During that time you are thinking of yourself in a quiet, centered manner. Perhaps your ritual is in reading a meditation, a poem that speaks to you, listening to a particular kind of music, or even sweeping the floor. If you find serenity in the use of ritual, embrace it. Use it to your advantage. Incorporate the ritual into your routine; it is part of beginning work on a problem.

8. Meditate. Meditating, like performing a ritual, can place you in a quiet, productive space. You must find a way to quiet your mind and your body. You cannot meditate and answer the phone. You must also be judgment-free. Meditating can be done in many ways. It can be done the traditional way, or it can be done by writing poetry, listening to music, or exercising. The meaning of meditation is also as personal as ritual. You can combine meditating and visualization. For example, lie on the floor, close your eyes, and imagine tracing the shape of your body. Watch your breath move in and through every part of your body. Watch it expand your limbs, and watch it move slowly easily back out. Once you are relaxed and centered, envision the problem. Can you see it with a clarity you did not have before? Can you see yourself doing an activity that feels as if the problem is solved? If that is too much, try to continue visualizing yourself in a quiet, comfortable environment. What happens when you find a quiet, relaxed posture and then begin work on the problem? Is the path into work easier? Are you less rattled by unforeseen problems?

Does it help you to immerse yourself into your creative process?

More information on a variety of techniques can be found at your local bookstore. You can look in several places: creativity in business, self-help books, creativity workbooks using the arts, and meditation techniques. The list below is a representative example.

Judith Morgan, *Creativity Therapy, Tools and Techniques for Personal and Professional Renewal* (New York: The Center for Innovation and Creative Thinking, 1994).

Edward De Bono, *De Bono's Thinking Course* (New York: Facts on File Publications, 1982).

Adriana Diaz, *Freeing the Creative Spirit: Drawing on the Power of Art to Tap the Magic and Wisdom Within* (San Francisco: HarperSanFrancisco, 1992).

Julia Cameron, *The Artist's Way: A Spiritual Path to Higher Creativity* (New York: G. P. Putnam's Sons, 1992).

Michael Michalko, *Thinker Toys: A Handbook of Business Creativity for the 90's* (Berkeley, Ten Speed Press, 1991).

Sidney J. Parnes, ed., *Source Book for Creative Problem Solving* (Buffalo: Creative Education Foundation Press, 1992).

Robert Fritz, *Creating* (New York: Fawcett Columbine, 1991).

## CHAPTER SEVEN

# THE REALM OF THE HEARTH:
## INFLUENCES ON THE ESSENTIAL CREATIVE NATURE

Hestia is the Greek Goddess of home and hearth. In her domain she ruled the household, childbirth, and motherhood. Her Roman counterpart was called Vesta. The women who tended the sacred temple of Vesta were the well-known Vestal Virgins. Though Hestia's reign was of the utmost importance to her society, she is frequently neglected in the literature on mythology.

> Hestia: "Greek [word for] 'Hearth' [is] one of the oldest matriarchal Goddesses. . . . She represented the home place, every man's 'center of the world.'" When the matriarchs ruled, "The hearth was in the midst of the dwelling; that hearth was to each member of the household . . . an umbilicum orbis, or navel of the earth. . . . Pythagoras said the fire of Hestia was the center of the earth. . . . Romans had the same idea about the altar of Vesta, with its perpetual fires. . . . Cicero said the power of Vesta extends over all altars and hearths, therefore all prayers and offerings begin

and end with her, 'because she is the guardian of the inner-most things.'" (*The Woman's Encyclopedia of Myth and Secrets*)

Symbolically, Hestia guards the well-being of the community and the internal structure of the individual as well. The home fires burn bright. The center of the household offers a pathway to other rooms and to the entrance and exit. The fires of the hearth provide warmth and a sense of security. This place comprises those objects that are used for one's survival and comfort. Hestia is powerful because her realm, as the Greeks believed, is the center of the world. She is not only the provider of warmth and security, but also the guardian of the innermost things. The hearth also exists outside of an archi-tectural domain. It is that place within the center of each woman that provides her with options. Figuratively, within each woman's internal household rests those aspects of her being—physical, psychological, intellectual, and spiritual—that affect her essential creative nature and her ability to nego-tiate the experiences of her life. As its guardian, each woman acts as Hestia over this domain. In Hestia's light, the inner-most things help to shape a woman's internal and external real-ity. The aspects that comprise the realm of the hearth provide a woman with a particular manner of seeing, feeling, thinking, and doing. These aspects exert a profound influence upon a woman's creative expression, shaping her essential creative nature. Hestia's realm is sacred, personal, and unique.

Through her essential creative nature, a woman feels the constant flow of the internal aspects of the realm of the hearth, or the physical, psychological, intellectual, and spiritual influ-ences that act upon her. This sphere of influence is deep within her center. Each aspect changes the dynamic or the intensity of a woman's perception by exerting, if only for a moment, its presence until another aspect comes to the fore.

The realm of the hearth, or the gateway to a woman's innermost being, provides her with a way of understanding her shifting moods and visions. The impetus for transformations enter and exit through the realm of the hearth. The innermost things, like the force of the moon, take a woman's awareness and pull her outward one moment, only to push her inward the next. Under the guidance of Hestia, and in an aura of light and warmth, all is secure and protected.

The quest to understand creativity has led you into the realm of the hearth. Within the realm of the hearth and under your protection exist those aspects that influence your everyday life and feed your extraordinary creative actions. Though the power of the individual elements of the hearth is fleeting, they do nonetheless color your perceptions and influence your creative expression. Women do not create in a vacuum. Their vision comes from the realm of the hearth. Unfortunately, the scientific community has paid little attention to how these aspects, which comprise the realm of the hearth, influence creative behavior. In this chapter, you will read about some of what shapes the realm of the hearth, including the relationship of creativity to: gender and role, environments, leisure-time activities, mentorship, biological changes in the body during phases of the menstrual cycle, pregnancy, early infant care, menopause, and sexuality. In my mind, these are the flames of influence that emanate forth from Hestia's realm. All creative expression is burned into a shape by the flames of inspiration within the realm of the hearth.

## GENDER AND ROLE: PERCEPTIONS THAT SHAPE CREATIVE BEHAVIOR AND PRODUCTS

Gender, as we explored earlier, has a direct relationship to a woman's creativity. It can exert pressure upon the manner and style of how a woman manifests her creative behavior.

Knowing that gender and perceptions of gender roles exert an influence can help a woman channel those perceptions in a positive, productive way. Those perceptions are part of the hearth; they are part of a woman's internal environment. Women are bound to their creative expression through their gender, and their femaleness feeds that expression.

Recall the discussion on gender earlier in the book. Remember how gender operated in shaping the views and paths of three women's lives. Those women claimed their essential creative natures and defined their personal creative expression through the powerful pull of gender. Most of the women in this study support the findings that women have a tendency to see and understand their vision through connections. This sensitivity toward connections, physical and emotional, is perceived in general as having greater importance for women than for men. Repeated references by the women to being emotional, being open to change and committed to process, indicate a natural creative stance.

Most of the women artists I spoke with believed that other women artists demonstrate a willingness to move through process more readily than their male counterparts. Women artists were seen as having a tendency toward agonizing over the validity and worth of their work far more than the male artists they knew. Dora, a forty-three-year-old painter and mother of two daughters speaks of gender roles and outside pressure on gender perceptions. She says, "The media message is destructive. There is an emphasis on men doing things and women as ornaments. I believe, in general, that men expect to be in control. They are less tied up in emotional stuff. Women are rational, organized, loving, understanding, nurturing, supportive, insecure, and bitchy; they assert power by manipulation. Even if you do not buy into gender roles, so many other people around you do. In my work I am totally apolitical as an artist, but I am female. The older I get, the more of my female-ness I feel."

Women in business reflected similar sentiments when they spoke about how their male counterparts were apt to adopt a posture of expertise even if they did not know what they were talking about. The women felt, in general, that men were concerned more with themselves than others. Eileen, a seventy-year-old widow, mother, and grandmother, who is now retired but who worked in a public school system as a supervisor of guidance counselors, states, "I internalized a lot about roles of what men and women were supposed to be. All during my career, I saw men of lesser ability get better jobs. The men I knew in guidance were wonderful, but my orientation was female. Women are intuitive and feeling. They are more expressive. I never wanted to be a male. Men are concerned about the nuts and bolts of things. But I do say it is a man's world; things are interpreted differently when a man acts a certain way and when a woman acts that way. Most male counselors were more concerned about their role and their image. The women were concerned about their clients."

While most women appreciated their feminine approach to life, their orientation toward process, and need for communication, they also felt they were far more tentative about being public with their creative expression than men. Lisa, a forty-four-year-old small business owner, actress, and divorced mother of two children, declares, "I compartmentalize. Men have power. I thought I did not have opportunities and so I have gotten stuck. The beliefs I hold shape what I manifest in my life. So I am choosing to hold different beliefs. Now I do affirmations. Everything comes from me. Part of it has to do with my being female. My intuitive sense is strong. My ability to connect with people is also strong." Many women indicated that they struggle with feelings of unworthiness and achieving a sense of value in the world. Feeling valued and being open to take risks directly relates to the health of a woman's internal structure or the state of being found within her realm of the hearth. This in turn affects her ability to take risks and pursue her essential creative expression.

## PERSONAL ENVIRONMENTS THAT FOSTER CREATIVITY

What conditions established by the woman herself make creative behavior possible? These states are contextually the internal and external environment, the psychological and physical environment by which a woman embraces her creative process. Beth A. Hennessey and Teresa M. Amabile examined environments and motivational qualities that move people into creative behavior. In their article "The conditions of creativity," they wrote, "[O]ur research demonstrates that social and environmental factors play major roles in creative performance. We have found that there exists a strong and positive link between a person's motivational state . . . and the creativity of the person's performance. . . . [P]eople will be most creative when they feel motivated primarily by the interest, enjoyments, satisfaction and challenge of the work itself—not by external pressures." They also found that if a person was "trained to deal effectively with extrinsic constraints and to focus on intrinsic reasons for doing work . . . overall intrinsic motivation would be increased."

If you can manage your outer environment comfortably and learn to accept and incorporate external constraints in a way that can be used in your work, your creative output will benefit. More importantly, learning to thrive and express yourself in difficult environments will build self-esteem and your sense of worth. Being able to turn adversity to your favor is, of course, a creative act. Intimate knowledge of the internal and external environments that constructively influence creative behavior gives you power over a crucial element of the creative process. All creative behavior begins with trust and an inner sense of security and safety. Feelings of security and safety are, in the absence of abuse, the domain of your innermost being. Those feelings help to frame your inner environment and your response to the outer environment and physical world around you. They feed the flames of inspiration in the hearth. How do women establish environments that allow their intrinsic motivation to blossom? This question is important. Knowledge of positive internal and external environments allows a woman to structure a space through which her imagination can sore. It can help assure that when she works, she will feel as secure as possible given the risky nature of creativity. You need to know what stimulates you, and what makes you feel secure and safe.

A majority of the women experienced a strong sense of comfort in a physical environment that had: natural light, soft music, objects hanging on the walls, and lots of color. These sights and sounds that stimulate supplied the women with a natural feeling environment. There was a strongly expressed need for the environments to be nonthreatening. The need for connections referred to in the women's earlier comments on gender was repeated in their desire to work in teams, to work in an environment filled with other people, and to work in an environment that allowed them to connect to and be internally fed by something outside of themselves, like the natural light, color, sound, and other people. Some women preferred silence. Most women expressed an overwhelming need to feel that their work space was organized and clean. An organized, clean environment meant the space was ready to accept the woman's presence, to accept her process. In preparing their space, these women enabled their product to emerge unfettered by unrelated outside clutter. (Clutter created during work on a project was different than preexisting clutter.)

A majority of women felt they liked working in teams with others, but within that framework they required a quiet separate space of their own to think and work. This combination of connecting to other people's energies, thoughts, and feelings, as well as having a quiet space to be alone, was necessary for different aspects of the creative process. Several women expressed a need to have a large, clean work table and materials of all kinds readily available to them. The materials most frequently mentioned were paper, pencils, pens, books, pallets, and computers. Lest you be deceived and think this list pertained mainly to women working in an office environment, it did not. Women from every field, including art, expressed this same need. In fact, several women artists used paper and pen to write down their thoughts before beginning a new work. Others used images from magazines and photographs, while still others sketched first before beginning to paint or sculpt.

The outer environment, that which makes a woman physically and visually comfortable, is only half of the picture. Many women paid serious attention to establishing an inner environment through which intrinsic motivation could be channeled. The outer environment without the inner environment cannot serve creative expression. How did these women achieve their positive inner environment? Several women spoke of having a ritual that they would use before beginning work. This ritual would help them move into their creative process. Sometimes the ritual was manifested in the need to clean the outer environment, which in turn helped prepare the inner environment and create a new order. Sometimes the ritual was cloaked in the pattern of gathering and setting up materials. This not only made the women feel comfortable in the space but helped prepare them emotionally to begin work.

Several women spoke of having a morning coffee ritual. The structure of this ritual was different for each woman. For example, one woman would get her coffee and place herself in a particular spot. This then helped her prepare her mind, body, and spirit to begin work. One woman spoke of starting her day by sitting on her bed with a cup of coffee and listening to the world around her. She was absorbing the sounds of the day while also listening to the rhythms of her innermost being. She was making contact with her Hestia and the state of her realm of the hearth. Sometimes women spoke of assuming a meditative stance. This meditative stance might have been used while looking out the window or walking. Walking was used by a good many women as a bridge to connect them to creative behavior and process. Walking in this context was used as a form of meditation, as a centering device. A variety of rituals were used by women to prepare themselves to begin their creative work. One woman, and I suspect she is not alone, shaped the appropriate external and internal environments that moved her into her creative process by composing and recomposing lists. If you recall the exercises listed in the chapter on the creative process, this is a commonly used technique.

Whatever form the ritual may take, whether it is meditating or sweeping the floor, women use ritual as a means of preparing their minds and bodies to begin their creative work. It is translated into a signal that creative work has begun. Rituals are valuable because they set up a discipline. Sometimes a woman needs a powerful outside framework to help her engage her creative process. Ritual structures the external environment and provides the path inward. The key to environments is the physical, psychological, and spiritual stance that allows the intrinsic motivation and freedom to flow outward. In preparing her environment, a woman affords herself the opportunity to become stimulated by the world around her and inside her. As she is present to respond, her creative impulses can flow, using the energy from the flames of inspiration, which burn bright within the realm of the hearth.

## LEISURE-TIME ACTIVITIES THAT STIMULATE AND EXCITE THE INNER BEING

The concept of leisure-time activities was difficult for most women. First responses were usually based upon the feeling that there was little or no time for leisure. Despite their feelings, most women readily acknowledge engaging in activities that provided them with spiritual fulfillment and creative impulses. Occupations that provide fulfillment and that are not bound to earning a living are what I consider leisure time. These activities stimulate a woman's internal environment and fan the flame of inspiration in the realm of the hearth. Providing yourself with some time for pleasure is part of being creative and guarding the realm of the hearth. Taking the time for yourself is a life-affirming action. Carla, a thirty-six-year-old single woman who designs, manufactures, and sells her own handbags, says, "Walking best expresses who I am. By being with nature and seeing the world around me, I become relaxed. I breathe differently. I always find something, like an animal, that makes me smile. Walking clears my head. If I am tired or sad, I walk to get out of the feeling."

Positive stimulation helps to keep the creative energies flowing and the creative impulses coming. All activities mentioned by the women I interviewed held a place of great importance in their lives. The list of activities they gave reflected agreement among the women. The flames of inspiration that fed these women's realm of the hearth and their creative expressions were cooking, walking, reading, parenting, entertaining, gardening, sports, and feeling connected to nature. Some women regularly engaged in a variety of activities. Eileen, the retired guidance counselor, describes her interests thus: "Now I do things like painting. I am on the solid-waste task force, the school committee, and the town beautification committee. All have a common denominator for me—meeting people and having fun." Sometimes leisure activities are used to help women work through their fears or their sense of isolation. Sonia, a thirty-eight-year-old woman, separated, mother of two daughters, who runs her own photographic research firm, says, "Reading challenges me. I enjoy it and I get so much out of it. It actually frees me in some way more than other things. I feel less fearful when I read."

The need to feel valued, the desire to freely express themselves, and their longing to feel part of a larger community were the feelings addressed in the women's choice of leisure activities. Motivation in this instance is internal. It comes from a desire to identify one's place in the universe. As Mary, the painter from Chapter One, believes, painting, going to galleries, hanging out with friends, reading, and taking pictures, all help "break down the separateness" she often feels. The need to be heard and recognized also motivates women to create. For the continuation of creative behavior, a woman must therefore find those things that feed her innermost being. She must engage in an action that stimulates and excites her. The joy one woman experiences while cooking cannot be disassociated from the impact upon her essential creative nature. Without excitement, there is no reason to pursue the struggle of the creative process. Without inspiration and passion, there can be no resolution to the creative process. Productive self-expression can only flourish if you engage the world in some personal fashion. Without leisure-time activities that stimulate and please, the fire of the realm of the hearth does not burn as intensely.

## MENTORSHIP: A TOOL FOR BUILDING THE INTERNAL STRUCTURE

Self-expression is not a guarantee of creative behavior, but it is a result of creative behavior. It reflects the intrinsic motivation behind creative behavior. In order to pursue self-expression, a woman needs to identify what her passion and her vision may be. Learning positive, productive self-expression generally requires guidance and/or a role model. Mentorship, like environment and leisure-time activities, affects the center of a woman's world and therefore must be housed within the realm of the hearth.

In many cases, the struggle and/or the inability to identify and express creativity can be connected to issues around mentoring, tutoring, or guidance. The majority of women in this country have not had the benefit of working with someone who inspires them, someone who teaches them, someone who helps to develop their craft, their passion, and their understanding of process. A majority of women have not had the special experience of a mentor who cares about and pays attention to their development. They have not experienced someone who challenges their development, bolsters their self-esteem, and helps to ensure a solid sense of self-worth. At all levels of schooling, social expectations threaten to hinder a young woman's essential creative nature. The antidote is simple but too often unavailable: the presence of mentors for girls. Teenage years are tenuous times for both girls and boys. Because the impact of societal expectation upon girls is so great and the demand for conformity so intense, a young girl, as young as junior high school, may willingly sacrifice herself and her talents to conform. Issues relating to relationships and affiliations bear down heavily upon a young woman's mind and emotional well-being. "Being too smart" or pursuing one's vision becomes a dangerous thing. The example of the talented female college students in Chapter Two who did not consider making their art to be as valuable as their looks, clearly illustrates the problem of image, place, and productivity. However, those young women were lucky. Jossey, the artist who struggles against her "family curse" and the young female students' art instructor cared enough about them to challenge their choices. Had they had mentors earlier in their lives, their paths may have looked quite different. They may have viewed their talent as a valid barometer of their worth in the world, one which was more significant than their looks.

Opportunities for young women to participate in a mentor-student relationship is vital for their development. E. Paul Torrance, an educator and a creativity researcher, wrote in his book *Mentor Relationships* that career problems are different for men and women who have not had the opportunity to work with mentors and those who have. Some of the problems faced by those without the benefit of a mentor relationship were: lack of career goal or focus, lack of enthusiasm or love for anything, missed opportunities, fear of pressure to conform, frustrated creativity, and noncreative jobs that drain creative energy. The role model or the mentor can be crucial for anyone wishing to develop her creative expression. A woman can develop as a creative being without a mentor, but a personal sense of worth and talent may be harder to grasp, and the road to her development may be more arduous. There is evidence that people who work with good mentors develop a secure and solid sense of themselves, of their talents and their worth. A strong inner structure promotes personal and creative growth and helps combat self-destructive behavior.

A sense of worth and the ability to take risks, maintain focus, and motivation were discussed earlier in Chapter Two as personality traits of creative people. Researchers have found that the traits just mentioned are enhanced and developed by working with a mentor. Only a few of the women I spoke with were privileged enough to have worked with a mentor. To fill that deeply felt void, several women found a public figure and used the image of that person as a role model. Copying the life or work of the model helped these women develop their own sense of self and their work. Overcoming the fears, obstacles, and challenges to self-growth in isolation and without help can be difficult. The mentor provides the challenge and the demand to develop, while simultaneously encouraging and supporting the emotional growth of the student as a creative, productive individual.

On those occasions when the women of this study were afforded the opportunity to work with a mentor, the mentor was male. Consistently, sexual attraction shifted the relationship from mentor-student to one of lover. When such a shift in the mentor-student relationship occurs, the relationship becomes potentially dangerous and destructive for the developing young woman. A trusting, secure relationship suddenly becomes tenuous. Pleasing, which is part of the mentor-student dynamic, takes on sexual overtones. It is not productive; the focus is no longer about developing an independent, creative woman. Sexual issues may cause the student to leave the mentor, or the mentor to leave the student. In a healthy mentor-student relationship, the mentor and the student part ways because the student has outgrown the relationship. Despite the potentially negative influences that existed, these women spoke fondly of their male mentors. The intensity and intimacy of such a relationship can lead to the sexual component, but it is the mentor's responsibility to control the dynamic, to preserve and protect everyone's integrity. It is a subject for reflection for any woman working with a male mentor, or in any situation where a mentor-student relationship is verging on something more physically intimate.

Except for those women who are teachers and who, by extension of their teaching role, have naturally become mentors, none of the more successful women in this study have been formal mentors for younger women. This is a sad reality. Research indicates that the mentor-student relationship has a profound impact upon the student. Younger women will be privy to this special experience only when older women offer themselves in that role. Many women expressed a sadness and a sense of loss at never having had the opportunity to work with a mentor. Indeed, the mentor role provides an opportunity for growth for the woman who chooses to share her talent, knowledge, and passion in such a capacity.

In "A Developmental Investigation of the Lives of Gifted Women," a 1992 study published in the *Gifted Child Quarterly*, Betty Walker, Sally M. Reis, and Janet S. Lenoard included a section labeled "Putting the Research to Use." In that section, the authors concluded that "[t]he most common concerns of the gifted women in this study related to personal, educational, and vocational growth. These women specifically cited concerns that can be addressed in schools. . . . These concerns include: the lack of role models for gifted females, denial of giftedness by gifted females, little organized mentoring and few networking skills, and 'unhelpful, unchallenging, and perfunctory guidance and counseling.'"

The context behind "giftedness" is intellectual, but all young women could benefit from positive role models, helpful counseling, mentorship, and networking skills, regardless of the form or manifestation of their creative expression. The mentor can help a woman to develop and expand her gift. In *The Social Psychology of Creativity*, Teresa M. Amabile wrote that young people working with mentors who had received public acknowledgments, in this case Nobel laureates, tended to go on to become Nobel laureates themselves. That is powerful evidence of the impact upon the student in the mentor-student relationship.

If some of you think that age is a barrier and all is lost, know that it is never too late to start working with someone you respect and admire. It is never too late to work with someone who can help you develop your creative expression. Research also indicates that creativity does not wane with age. In fact, many women begin to feel liberated once they become seniors. At any point in time, a woman can follow her passion. Kathy Goff writes in her article "Enhancing Creativity in Older Adults," "[S]tudies have shown that creative attitudes and interests do not necessarily decline with age . . . and even appear to change with intervening programs. . . . [O]lder adults who participated in creative programs or who were creatively productive perceived an increase or stability in creativeness with age, not decline."

Go ahead: find a class you have always wanted to take; learn about a discipline that has always inspired you; become a mentor and allow yourself to fulfill your passion. Pay attention to Hestia, and build the flame of inspiration that burns in the realm of the hearth.

## BIOLOGICAL CHANGES THAT CAN ALTER THE FLOW OF A WOMAN'S CREATIVE EXPRESSION

The discussion must now turn inward. We move from those elements that connect to the realm of the hearth through the outer world to those aspects that influence the realm of the hearth from within. A variety of changes occur within a woman's body throughout her lifetime. Some of the changes are cyclical, like menstruation; some are temporary, like pregnancy. Some changes are dramatic and signal life transformations, as with menopause. Do these different and distinct changes in the body affect a woman's creative impulses, behavior, and output? Little research exists on the relationship between a woman's inner body rhythms and creativity. It is a complex area worthy of investigation. The relationship, if there is one, between a woman's biological life rhythms and creativity is a provocative subject, ripe for self-exploration and scientific review.

I did not conduct a full study of this issue, one dedicated to this question, so while certain specific patterns may exist, I did not find them. What I did find was confirmation that, in general, shifts in behavior and attitude do exist. I asked each woman about her work, her work process, her behavior, and her attitude during premenstrual and menstrual cycle, pregnancy, early infant care, and menopause. I also asked, though it is not directly related to a biological rhythms, whether the presence of children in her life had altered her perceptions, creative process, or creative product.

## Premenstruation

I came upon three studies, two on premenstruation experiences and one on the experience of menstruation. These studies examined attitudes about the two monthly phases but did not relate the experience of a woman's monthly cycle to creative behavior. These three studies found, at least as it pertains to women in this culture, that premenstrual and menstrual symptoms were dependent upon a woman's expectation of her experience. In other words, if a woman expected her premenstrual phase to be difficult, it was. The study "Placing Premenstrual Syndrome in Perspective," published in *Psychology of Women Quarterly*, found that PMS was mistakenly attributed to a "down period" when the symptoms were not properly indicated. The researchers felt "[s]ome of these women had a terrific other phase of their menstrual cycle which, in contrast to their neutral premenstrual phase, might make the premenstrual phase seem down. It seems likely that some of these women said they had PMS because they knew they experienced cyclicity over their menstrual cycle, and their North American culture has told them that most women experience the same pattern of menstrual cyclicity, that is PMS."

If women experience this "neutral time" as a "down period," in contrast to some other phase in the menstrual cycle, then their creative behavior, inspiration, and output would likewise be negatively affected. Because the researchers spoke of a "terrific other phase" that occurred within the women's cycle, it would seem logical that creative output would be greater during those terrific other phases rather than during the "neutral phases."

The women's comments to me reflected how they experienced these two phases of their menstrual cycle with regard to attitude, behavior, and creativity. In general, they supported the notion that women experience a "down period" or a "neutral period" during the premenstrual phase. Most women, not all of whom suffered pain and anxiety, possessed a clear and precise understanding of how these monthly changes affected their attitude and their work. Generally women worked despite any physical discomfort they may have been experiencing. But their view of themselves and the world was greatly influenced by the bodily changes. Many women expressed the following sentiments. "I am short-tempered and easily frustrated; it is harder for me to concentrate; I fight with people." Sometimes the women experienced major shifts in the symptoms of their cycle over the years. Where once they experienced no discomfort, now they did. "I get bloated; I cry a lot; I take vitamins and exercise to control my mood swings." The reverse was true for several women. There were only a handful of women who experienced little or no alteration in their physical or emotional well-being during the premenstrual phase of their cycle.

As these few comments reflect, the overall emotional tenor of the premenstrual phase was negative, and the physical discomfort noticeable. For many of these women, life perspectives and the ability to make connections are temporarily hindered. Some women were able to understand and control the negativity, knowing it would last only a few days. Other women were overwhelmed by the turmoil they felt within and barely managed to function during the day. I cannot attest with any certainty that creative behavior was not at its optimum, but I am willing to make an assumption that creative output and creative impulses were diminished during this phase. But while creative impulses may be diminished, creative behavior may really occur in an effort to maintain a "normal" level of performance. As I stated earlier in the book, creative energies can be used as a means of surviving. Just getting through the day sometimes takes enormous amounts of creative output.

Menstruation

The other phase of the menstrual cycle concerned changes occurring with the onset of the menses. Fewer women were as burdened during this phase as during the premenstrual phase. While some women still experienced discomfort, the negativity that accompanied the discomfort in the earlier stage was not as keenly felt. Many women described a real and tangible shift emotionally and physically during this phase. There was no tendency toward a common experience of this phase, as there was in the premenstrual phase. The women's comments were distinctly varied and at times at odds: "There is a weight that gets lifted; I feel open and optimistic and happy," compared to "I get headaches and cramps; I have mood swings. When I get cramps, I just want to curl up, but I can't."

Despite the variety of responses to this phase of the cycle, no one indicated that there was an increase in creative behavior. While many women felt a release, their focus remained directed toward the experience of their menstrual cycle rather than being stimulated toward new creative behavior. One specific comment encapsulates an image of a woman working hard to be focused and to do what is expected of her: "A deadline can make you forget your cramps."

Some women suffer greatly before the onset of the menses and seem to experience a heightened sensitivity to negative feelings and depression. Some women experience this negativity throughout their premenstrual and menstrual cycle, while a few women expressed relief once their menses began. To analyze its true effect upon creative output, researchers would have to follow these women for several months charting their creative output as well as the hormonal, chemical, and emotional shifts occurring during their cycle. They would have to identify when creative inspiration occurred, whether there was a relationship to the menstrual cycle, and finally whether any distinct patterns within each woman could be identified.

The most profound awareness and effort that all women expressed was negotiating depression and negativity. This change in attitude should not be taken lightly. The next time you are being critical about yourself, you might take a moment to reflect on where you are in your monthly cycle. Take stock of how mood swings affect your physical and emotional well-being. Perhaps you need to be slightly less critical. Perhaps your expectation of performance during this time is unrealistic, especially if you suffer from serious mood swings and physical discomfort. If you are in the midst of a deadline and a creative product is due, remember to be gentle with yourself. Take a moment or two to meditate or take a walk. Do something that is based in pleasure, something that is life-affirming. Engage in an activity that soothes your innermost being or stimulates your vision. Creative energy can be renewed at such a time with self-nurturing and self-affirmation, and with the warmth from the realm of the hearth.

Pregnancy

While I was in the library researching the subject of women and creativity and while I was conducting interviews for this book, I was pregnant and then nursing my second child. Generally I was tired, uncomfortable, and emotional. During several interviews I had to nurse my baby. I was grateful that none of the women objected. But I wondered whether women felt that their creative expression was altered during pregnancy, early infant care, and by the ongoing presence of children in a woman's life on a daily basis. Most women held a personal perspective of pregnancy; they spoke of their pregnancies in the context of their lives. It was based upon two realities, the physical and intellectual changes occurring within the body and any other significant experiences coloring their lives at the time. For example, Patricia, a thirty-eight-year-old woman who now works as the director of admissions for a performing arts school, recalls that when she was six months pregnant she left her job. She says, "My attitude was starting to shift to my own life and away from work." Jill, a forty-two-year-old woman who has a master's degree from Harvard University in city and regional planning, and who has worked as a planner for women's economic development programs, recalls, "I had a difficult time conceiving. Then I found out I was pregnant and my mother died. I decided to stop traveling for work. I had to lie down during the day and rest. I had been at work long enough to be given some leeway. I worked until one week before the birth of my child." I found that women move through their lives doing what is demanded or expected of them. Despite discomfort, fatigue, fear, joy, or other emotions, they do their work. Since creativity is inherently tied to our emotional and physical states, one impacts the other. Victoria, the eldest painter from Chapter Two, recalls, "I was very sick during my last pregnancy. I could not paint. I was hospitalized. It took me a full year to recover."

I found no pattern to indicate that creative behavior was at its height in the second trimester, nor were there any indications that it waned in the first or third trimesters. But I think it fair to assume that creative output would not be at its peak at the end of pregnancy. A woman's creative energies are preparing her for the experience of labor and birth. With the hormonal changes that make the actual birth possible, muscle tone changes, bones shift, and it becomes harder to concentrate. A woman may attempt to ignore these changes, but they do occur. Energy for creative output is funneled into preparing her body for the birth.

## Effect of Early Infant Care upon Creativity, Work, and Attitude

Most women who have taken care of a newborn child know that those first few months can place a great strain upon her emotional and physical existence. It is the start of an adjustment period. The woman is changing her identity. There is a new dimension: she is now a mother. While this adjustment is occurring, the demands of a newborn baby are continuous. Most women in this study did not view this time as one characterized by high creative output, at least not in the traditional sense. Creative behavior occurred through the exploration of the mother/child relationship. I think the process of redefining and understanding oneself and one's place in the world as a mother is a significant process. Some form of this redefining occurs with each birth. Though the process begins at birth, it is ongoing. As a result, a woman's identity and her priorities may begin to shift. Some women cope with the shift better than others. They are able to stay open to the change. Nevertheless, issues of how one defines oneself are ripe. For some women, leaving their baby to return to work was painful; for others, giving up their work and staying at home with the baby was painful. Women who nursed had an added physical demand to negotiate. Sonia, the photographic research consultant and mother of two daughters, reflects, "After three months off, I went back to work. It was hard bringing my daughter to day care. With my first child, I felt like she was being torn away from me. Initially I went back to work part-time. I had a lot of women around me who were sympathetic, and that helped me." The women's comments reflected the depth of their experience during this transition. They also revealed that creative expression is blurred during this time because a woman's sense of place, her sense of her role, her expectations of herself as a mother and as an independent creative being are still being formed. Ashley, a thirty-nine-year-old painter, who was in her first trimester of pregnancy with her second child at the time of our interview, recalls, "I have this hierarchy in my head. First, I am a mother. When I go back to my studio to paint, my mind is back at home. It took me a long time to be able to go straight to my studio and work instead of running errands and wandering in and out of stores."

For many women it was a confusing, painful time, despite the joy of being a mother. Patricia, the director of admissions for a performing arts school, states, "I took nine months off from work. It was a difficult transition. I needed to earn money. I was not feeling positive about myself and my contribution. I lost confidence in myself. I began to work part-time. I was very conflicted. I felt like my insides were being torn out when I had to leave my daughter. I found a woman at work who was incredibly positive. Slowly my confidence began to come back."

But the conflicts can cause women to choose not to work as well. Debra, a forty-one-year-old mother of two daughters who works as a free-lance reporter, explains, "Initially, there was no issue about leaving my oldest daughter. She was so young. But as she developed and started doing things, I got jealous of the babysitter. When I became pregnant with my second child, I thought, I do not even know the first baby. Why am I going to work? Why am I having another baby? I felt I would stay home with my children if I could. Then I got fired." Since then, Debra has had another child and tries to manage free-lance writing and parenting by doing her own work in the middle of the night.

## Influence of Children on a Woman's Creative Expression and Work

Being a mother and working on ourselves as creative human beings requires time, discipline, energy, insight, and patience. In "Creative Tension: Being a Writer and a Mother," Judith Pierce Rosenberg states, "[W]ithout sufficient time alone and a quiet place to work, 'the circumstances for sustained creation are almost impossible.' ... Constant interruption interferes with a mother's ability to concentrate and thus 'it is distraction not meditation that becomes habitual.'" While the focus of the article is on writing, any form of creative expression requires time to develop without distraction. Mothers tend not to have an abundance of quiet time. How then did women see the influence of children upon their work and their creative expression? All the women of this study who had experienced negotiating the needs of a child felt the experience had a positive effect upon their creative expression, even if that expression seemed to be placed "on the back burner" for a time. Jill, the mother of one child who is an economic development planner for women's projects states, "At five P.M. I felt that I had to walk out the door of my office to be a mommy. There was a combination of wanting to and feeling guilty. I was still nursing my son; I had to take time in the morning and the afternoon from work to pump my breasts for milk. It put my work in perspective. Also my mother's death put things in perspective. Now I have no conflict about taking care of myself and my child." But all experiences feed the flame of creative inspiration. Mercedes, an activist for women from Chapter

Five and a mother of two children, believes, "Children altered my world view. I shifted and strengthened my priorities. My activism was enhanced. I deepened my process. Children give you an understanding of the complexity of life in a whole new way—how complex and how simple everything is."

As a woman moves through the transition periods of childhood from early infant care to adolescent and teenager, her creative process may initially suffer, along with her ability to produce a product. The experience is not lost. A new dimension has been added to the elements of the realm of the hearth and to the expression of her vision. The problem appears to be managing time and feelings of conflict. That is countered by the influence children have on a woman's perception of her world. Patricia, the director of admissions for a performing arts school, says, "I do not work the same way now. My approach to work is on a human level. Working with children, I see them now as a parent. I have more empathy, something I did not have before."

Process and product may be altered. While it may be trying initially, the woman who is open to experiencing her essential creative nature absorbs the change and incorporates it into her life. It is not a simple transition. In her article "Creativity, Gender and the Family: A Study of Creative Writers," Livia Pohlman writes, "[I]n their struggle to form a sense of self as writers, women confronted a peculiar dilemma. Their identities were often divided three ways—as a wife, a mother, and a writer— with their sense of self as a writer being in conflict with the gender expectations of being a good wife and mother. . . . For women, the institution of marriage and family often conflict with their career path as writers." She found that men benefitted psychologically by the presence of a wife and children; the family supported the men's work. Their role as "provider" (the majority of the primary income producers were the men) was used as a mechanism to produce more. Because of their families, men felt more connected to the world. Women writers experienced a sense of isolation because of the demands upon them to take care of home and family first.

The women I spoke with were at varying stages of seeking a solution to the "creating a room of one's own" or time for developing personal creative expression while attending to the needs of their children. Unfortunately, many women do not allow time for themselves or for their creative expression. What they offer themselves and their children is less than it could be. Looking inward, the woman who is not attending to her essential creative nature, who neglects the realm of the hearth, is generally dissatisfied with her experience and her abilities. The irony is that in taking care of herself, a woman can offer her children more of herself.

## Menopause: A Physical and Spiritual Creative Transformation

Maturing transitions occur both physically and emotionally in a woman between her twenties and her late forties, but the major transition after menstruation and childbearing is menopause. The hormonal shift that marks menopause has an average age of onset of between forty-five and fifty. Menopause signifies the end of a woman's childbearing capacities and the disappearance of her menses. It can be a time of physical discomfort and emotional upheaval, or a time of renewed energy and a newfound sense of self. Just as the transition that occurs in the early infant care stage alters a woman's sense of identity, so too can the experience of menopause. For some women, it is the first time in their lives that they are able to stop and look at themselves as separate individuals. In the past, most women entered menopause with their children grown. While that may still be the norm, a growing segment of the population is reaching menopause childless, or reaching menopause with young children. The women who had passed through this phase or were in the process of passing through this phase were diverse. They were married with grown children, single with teenagers, married with teenagers, single and childless, married and childless. Some of the women in the midst of the transition were taking hormone treatment to control their emotional swings and lift the bottom of their anxiety. Those who had moved through the transition experienced a release at the end of the process. Regardless of whether they had experienced discomfort or not during the transition, all of them felt a release at the end. Teresa, a fifty-three-year-old single women who is a social worker, believes, "Menopause was a rediscovery of my own self-worth, of energy and ideals. I felt like I was losing something by not having my period, but I am more relaxed, more positive. I am not as emotional now." How specifically these hormonal changes impact the creative spirit is difficult to determine, but these women generally indicate that there is a renewed vigor for life and a new commitment to self. Suzanne, from Chapter Three, says, "I had an easy time. I was feeling terrific about myself. My late forties until around sixty I thought were terrific years. I was strong and vigorous." In some cases this commitment to self meant going to work for the first time. In some cases it meant experimenting in their work without fear; in others, it meant exploring their passion for the first time. For some women, there was a sense of vigor and well-being that enabled them to become more active and productive. Eileen, the retired supervisor of guidance counselors, recalls, "It was easy. I never got hot flashes. It was a wonderful time. I stopped worrying about getting pregnant. I felt good. I was being challenged by my work." These women were willing to try new things and began to look at the world and themselves differently. For most women, the passage through menopause became a positive creative process.

The reward of this crucial, life-transforming stage for women seems to be in a renewed commitment to self. You have read several stories of women who have willingly engaged in creative behavior after this transformation occurred. Though the transition may not always be calm, the potential for new paths of self-expression or a deeper commitment to one's passion is present. A woman's creative expression can begin to crystallize if she stays open and available to it throughout this intimate process.

## SEX: MAKING CONNECTIONS, EMOTIONALLY, SPIRITUALLY, PHYSICALLY, CREATIVELY

The realm of the hearth would not be complete without mentioning the topics of sex and sexuality and their impact on creativity. What do women think about sex, sexuality, and creativity? Do they see a connection by which one aspect of expression influences another? This subject, like the others in the realm of the hearth, is complex and worthy of more in-depth exploration.

This study did not look at the specifics of sexual behavior. I was not interested in the mechanics of sexual experience, or in gender preference for sexual encounters. Rather I focused on whether women had a conceptual and emotional connection to the subject and how they articulated their understanding. Most of the women agreed that everything is an expression of creativity. Most women felt that the relational aspect of sex was a creative expression, not the physical act or the specific activities engaged in. I was surprised to hear women describe their thoughts about sex and sexuality in terms that recall the three definitions of creativity: creativity is a personal expression; creativity is the ability to take risks, an openness to life; creativity is transformations and making something new. Rose, the director of education for nurses from

Chapter One, explains, "Intercourse is a small piece. Sex is more about touching. How and what you can do to make an individual feel good besides the act of having intercourse. It requires an openness, a willingness to explore new things. There can be no boundaries. It requires taking a risk." Merle, a forty-six-year-old bookkeeper who is single, believes, "Sex is a creative expression. I am a good lover. That is a late realization. There is something magical in meshing two energies. It opens you up. It takes you out of your body and gives you another perspective." Some women believed that the suppression of one form of expression fed another. Eileen, the retired supervisor of guidance counselors, articulates this concept succinctly when she says, "The most productive time in my life was when my husband was in the army and I had all this energy. It was sublimated."

What are your thoughts about the relationship between sex, sexuality, and creativity? Are you able to express yourself as a creative woman through your sexuality? Do you think that sexual energy feeds creative energy, or that the expression of creativity feeds your sexuality? Teresa, the social worker, states, "Sex identifies you with your gender. The drive and the need is part of your sexuality. Clearly there are times when I am aware that without my sexuality I am not creative. I need to express that part of myself as well." These were not easy questions for some of the women to answer. They may not be for you either. But most women felt the process of exploring what they believed to be a valuable experience. For some, it was the first time they had articulated their thoughts. Self-expression, supported by the innermost things or the realm of the hearth, is the concept that most easily characterized the responses women offered about the relationship between sex, sexuality, and creativity.

If you do not recognize what your realm of the hearth comprises, or if you are unaware of the influences that can be exerted by the realm of the hearth, you may be depriving your essential creative nature of the nourishment it needs. Take time to attend to bodily transitions, to stimulate and excite the innermost things within you, to learn what is necessary to pursue your passion and to enlarge and strengthen your self-esteem and your self-worth. The deeper your sense of well-being, the deeper will be your commitment to your essential creative nature. Hestia's vigil over the realm of the hearth offers a powerful image to women who care about themselves as creative beings. The fires of the hearth must be kept burning or the warmth and light will not reach the innermost things of your being. Responsibility for the warmth and the light, for the flame of inspiration, will always be in your hands. You are, like Hestia, the guardian of the center of your world.

## EXPANDING THE FLAMES OF INSPIRATION

Most of the exercises and suggestions offered throughout this book directly impact upon the realm of the hearth—if you commit yourself to experiencing them. For example, if you take a class, any class, whether it is an exercise class or a drawing class, you are attending to leisure time. The class may heighten your sense of yourself as a woman and bring forth issues of gender perceptions and expressions that you were unaware of before. Perhaps the way you see an object or the manner in which you place it in relationship to other things will raise a connection to gender for you. Perhaps your body moving through space stimulates you and you become aware for the first time, or in a new way, of the energy that pulses through your groin, your abdomen, and your chest. These shifts in perception and experience can awaken or heighten your sense of your sexuality.

If your teacher inspires you to challenge yourself, you are attending to building the internal structure of the realm of the hearth through a mentor. Taking one class may lead you in a different direction. You may find your passion changing; you may be drawn toward a new direction or a new form of expression. Maybe the shift is related to a physiological shift occurring within your body. Perhaps the class you take will provide a key to structuring your outer environment. That knowledge can then be used to center yourself. The act, whether jogging, rollerblading, gardening, or working with clay on a wheel, may lead you into a new internal environment. You can begin to channel your energies creatively because your sense of external and internal environments is growing. The effects of taking one action, such as a class, can be linked to a multitude of aspects that feed your essential creative nature. Because the realm of the hearth is the center of your household and the place were the innermost things reside, any action you take that gives you pleasure and challenges your senses and abilities keeps the realm of the hearth in order.

If you wish to track your responses, carry a small note pad with you and jot down key words or phrases about your new feelings, thoughts, and sensations. After a few months, review your path. How have you changed? Has your perspective of yourself as a woman in the world altered? Do you honor the changes that have occurred?

CHAPTER EIGHT

# THE POWER WITHIN:
## AWAKENING THE GODDESS

❧

She is called Sophia. She is a complex figure who is written of in Jewish theology, Greek philosophy, and early Gnostic Christian writings. She has ties to Mother Goddesses of the Middle East. She is referred to as queen of the heavens and Lady of Wisdom. She is beyond form, yet she is within everything. She is the feminine force, the wisdom within.

> ". . . Sophia speaks with the full authority of the former goddess [those of the Middle East, Inanna, Isis, Maat]. Elsewhere, she personifies an attitude of the deity, as the wisdom and creativity out of which emerges the active power that gives form to life. . . ." (*The Myth of the Goddess*)

Sophia is linked to other Greek and Egyptian goddesses. She

> "insists on a struggle for insight and understanding. [She is] the implacable nature of wisdom as the Law of Life, a com-

posite blend of love and knowledge, whose workings are inscrutable to humanity and bring suffering as well as joy. . . ." (*The Myth of the Goddess*)

Sophia offers women the image of a feminine concept beyond her physical limitations. She is a combination of the feminine deities and their dedication to their domain. Her essence demands the seeking of truth, knowledge, and understanding. Dedication to seeking brings you into the place of creative behavior. Without seeking, without the passion to understand and the need to solve a problem, there is no creative activity.

The Goddesses, personified in the image of Sophia, honor their essential creative natures. They understand and accept their personal form of creative expression. Compelled by their nature and those who believe in them, they express their essential creative natures in their own style. They do not hesitate to move through time cloaked in their uniqueness. The Goddesses do not question their value or their existence, though they relentlessly seek their essence. Theirs is a realm of certainty, decisive action, and immense power. Theirs is a world of constant creation and destruction. They demand attention, offer guidance, and provide a way of interpreting life, death, joy, and sorrow. The manifestation of each Goddess's unique creative ability is different, shaped by her perceptions of the world and the pursuit of her essence. The power and the ability of each Goddess to express that which is within her domain parallels the reality of a woman negotiating her world on a daily basis. She finds a way to express her beliefs, be they positive or negative, productive or destructive.

Sophia engages life and makes reliance upon intellect and intuition necessary. It is so with a woman seeking her essential creative nature. Her intellect, intuition, passion, and desire for knowledge and understanding are the tools she uses to give form to who she is in the world. Are you like the Goddess attuned to her essential creative nature? Do you seek to understand and learn how to express your personal style? Do you move through your life invisible to yourself and to the world around you? The energy you create just by being alive is either negative or positive. It issues forth from within you out into the universe. The space that your energy fills extends beyond your body in every direction. Your influence in the world is already greater than you think. Like the Goddesses, your domain extends beyond your physical limits when you choose to release your creativity. Unlike the Goddesses, your dominion is expansive and ever-broadening. Within your one being, you contain all that the Goddesses possessed in all their numbers. Your capacity for growth is limitless, your potential continually unfolding. Think of it. One woman possessing all the power of all the Goddesses combined! But to get to that power you must learn. You must seek out that which Sophia demands: truth, understanding, and knowledge. It is that power that will lead you beyond your wildest dreams and will never fail to protect you through your journey of becoming. As Merlin, the Arch Druid, told Arthur, the young knight: "You may grow old and trembling in your anatomies, you may lie awake at night listening to the disorder of your veins, you may miss your only love, you may see the world about you devastated by evil lunatics, or know your honour trampled in the sewers of baser minds. There is only one thing for them—to learn. Learn why the world wags and what wags it. That is the only thing which the mind can never exhaust, never alienate, never be tortured by, never fear or distrust, and never dream of regretting." The ability to learn protects you, nurtures you, and inspires you. It will, however, challenge you to become, through creative behavior, that which is your potential. Learning and creativity are entwined. You can invent your universe and give form to your domain only when you open yourself to learn the lessons that creativity can bring to you.

In this book, I have shared with you the stories, feelings, and creative expressions of a number of women. Reflecting upon the life experiences of those women reveals how the essential creative nature is experienced and expressed in our daily lives. In every aspect of one's life, opportunities are afforded to a woman to learn about and honor her essential creative nature. You have seen how, in the midst of intensely private moments like the death of a child or the depths of addiction, creative choices offer women a way to cope with their anger, sadness, sickness, or depression. Allowing the power found in creativity to flow through her body, a woman moves forward out of despair and into the light. A woman's path is grounded in seeking, in learning who she is and what she has to share with the world.

The creative paths of the women in this book have not necessarily been easy, but in the final analysis they have been the least painful and the most liberating possible for that particular woman. They have had to work to recognize their essential creative natures and to develop their personal visions. In their searching for understanding and a personal path, they have awakened the concepts contained within Sophia, Minerva, and their sister Goddesses. The quest for knowledge and understanding, like the nature of creativity itself, challenges everything. Once a woman chooses to honor her essential creative nature, she, in the spirit of that commitment, also chooses to recognize and accept her own creative voice. The process of being engaged in creating her life strengthens her core spirit and determination for creative expression. That commitment and the reawakening of her potential can be reached by a woman regardless of age, education, and ethnic and economic background. The opportunity for seeking and becoming a creative being remains the same whether a woman has spent her life working as an artist, nurse, executive, teacher, volunteer, professional, or homemaker. Whether a beginner or long-time student of creativity, public or private in her expression, amateur or professional, there is always more to be sought and revealed from the woman/Goddess within. In Frank Barron's article "Putting creativity to work," he writes, "one's life itself is there to create. Family, friends, and associates, personal style, inner experience, general behavior, dress, character—these are creations in the opportunity available to us all as human beings."

The effective force of a woman's essential creative nature is expansive. Without paying homage to the source of this power, it withers and grows sickly. Shifting destructive behaviors, altering negative views, learning self-sufficiency, revelling in the process of seeking the wisdom contained within leads a woman toward that which she is meant to be. That path may mean achieving where others dear to her have failed. It may require facing disapproval or shedding guilt and a sense of being undeserving. A woman must grasp on to her creativity and cherish it. She must believe that she deserves success, love, and fulfillment. She must trust that she can give something of value back to the world.

The women in this book are not the exceptions. The positive results and the potential for becoming that these women have experienced are the results of approaching self with an openness and a willingness to learn. They have honored the image of Sophia and Minerva in seeking wisdom, and have used the powers of the other Goddesses to step into their time of emergence. The opposite of choosing the time of emergence is obvious. You need only recall the life experiences of the young women artists Lucy and Cathy in Chapter Two, the destructive behavior of Lilly, the young woman completing her divinity training in Chapter Three, the torments of overeating and depression of Nancy, the Episcopalian minister in Chapter Three, and the perfectionism of Phyllis, the retired business school teacher in Chapter One. Part of their lives were characterized by fear and tenuousness, despite the enormous possibilities of their talents. Choosing creative behavior energizes a woman's life and sensitizes her to seeking and seeing the world around her and in her. Creative behavior, in a personal sense, offers every woman the same opportunities to find meaning and significance in life.

There is a direct relationship between the way a woman defines the act of creating and the path she takes to personally express her essential creative nature. The definitions held by a woman and the style by which she lives her life are complementary. Of the women interviewed for this book, if creativity was understood in the context of personal expression, those women also saw their lives through the need to express themselves in everything they did. If creativity was defined as the ability to take risks and maintain an openness to life, those women demonstrated the need to take risks and to push themselves on into the unknown. If creativity was defined as transformation and the act of making something new, the women who defined it as such had an approach to the world with that same focus. These transformations would occur in a variety of areas: personal relationships, work, or emotional responses. It did not matter if the transformation was a change in lifestyle or a shift in the products produced. The act of engaging the process of transformation always led these women to experience something new. The positive alteration of personal vision and inner knowledge, regardless of the definitions you hold, results in the strengthening of personal expression, the ability to take risks, and the desire to create. These definitions are not just the reflections of an intellectual exercise. They are paramount to a woman's ability to define her vision.

In general, women do not sit down and articulate their need to negotiate the world from one or another philosophical stance. They are more apt to feel compelled to change, or to challenge themselves physically, intellectually, emotionally, or spiritually. The impetus that necessitates their response comes from the environment around them and within them. If you have always envisioned creativity as something unobtainable or as something possessed by others more fortunate than you, the examples set by the women in this book should give you pause to rethink that position. I hope they have urged some of you to look at yourself and your essential creative nature differently. Definitions are a starting point, a place to anchor your journey of becoming—and the movement toward awakening the Goddess within.

The decision to explore creativity becomes an adventure in process. One step leads to the next. Like a child learning to walk, there is one way to accomplish the goal, one step at a time. We meet the challenge to release the creative force within by embracing it. Every action sets off a reaction and brings forth the need to make another choice. Every step voluntarily taken propels a woman forward. Every step not taken either stops the process or sends the woman retreating to something old, something known. Do you continue to explore, or do you stay in one place? Whether a woman chooses to find her essential creative nature and its associative powers or is stopped by fear of the process, she is making a choice. If she allows her imagination to soar, if she allows the sensation of the excitement that accompanies the journey to feed her, the choice to continue is easily made. It might even be lustfully made, because the energy connected with creative behavior is stimulating, enthralling, and vital.

In Mel Rhode's article "An Analysis of Creativity," he addresses the importance of attitude and habits. To describe the posture most conducive for creative behavior, he writes, "If you would invent, acquire the good habit of observing. Observe and question! Ask yourself questions: Why did that happen? Why did not something else happen? What started that? What stopped that? For example, why can a spider walk on its web without getting tangled? . . . In brief, day dream with a purpose." Without the nudge caused by seeking to learn, there can be no reason for creative behavior.

Any woman, choosing of her own free will, can structure her internal environment so that she experiences the expansive force of her essential creative nature. A woman faced with a horrific domestic situation can find her way out to a better life when she begins to believe there are other possibilities. Then she must open herself up to exploring those possibilities. That is the function that day dreaming, imaging, questioning, and learning serve. The imagination takes you beyond your present reality. It is the inspiration for action. Learning explores the possibilities of the imagined conditions. These two functions are basic to all manifestations of creative behavior. It does not matter if you are exploring science, teaching, health care, or parenting. Imagination helps shape your vision. Learning gives your imagination a context through which it can be translated into reality. One without the other brings a woman half the possibilities. Kerry S. Walters in her article "Critical Thinking, Logicism, and the Eclipse of Imagining," discussed the life work of Lewis Carroll to illustrate the need for using and valuing both rational thinking and the imagination in creativity. Not only was Lewis Carroll the author of many works, among them *Alice's Adventures in Wonderland* and *Through the Looking Glass*, but his expertise spanned storytelling, mathematics, and symbolic logic. Walters writes, "[T]he degree to which an individual fulfills her potential as a thinking being is directly proportionate to the extent to which she nurtures both logical and imaginative abilities."

A woman in the process of creating her life must see all that is within her domain. Her mind and her spirit contain the potential for great invention, if she learns to exercise the imagination, the intellect, the emotions, and the spiritual realm together. If she allows herself to be open to the possibilities and to imagine herself as creator of her own life and personal expression, the potential is astounding. Indeed, the process of creating demands that a woman learn to function as both the inventor and the critic. That is how the end product, be it a tangible thing or a thought, comes into being.

There are, as I have tried to emphasize throughout this work, different modes of creative behavior and different kinds of creative products. This perspective is grand enough to incorporate both "big C" creativity and "little c" creativity. It encompasses both public and private acts of creating and both creating art and creating life. The women whose stories you have been introduced to in this work provide a glimpse of that reality. Value must be placed on those creative efforts that are special and unique, whether that is in the context of "big C" or "little c" creativity. Are you in a place that fully expresses the expansive and effective force of your essential creative nature?

The Goddesses accepted nothing by default. They made their choices and responded to the world from a place of knowledge and responsibility to their Goddess domain. Awakening the woman/Goddess within allows the power of your essential creative nature to lead you to lands beyond your wildest imaginings. Perhaps those lands are public, perhaps they are private. It is your responsibility to learn what it is you have to say in this world and to whom.

A woman assertively grasping on to that creative staff of life can experience her power in many self-enhancing ways. Sometimes she is compelled to express her vision in more than one discipline. If she retreats from herself, she buries the Goddess within and limits her own ability to learn, to see, to make her presence felt in this universe. In such cases, not only does a woman deny herself the possibility of publicly proclaiming herself, but more than likely she will deny herself the possibility of privately proclaiming herself as well. Instead of a celebration of self through her essential creative nature, instead of feeling the pulsing power expressed through creative behavior, a woman is left with a deadly sense of uneasiness and loss. In such a state, the woman/Goddess cannot resist the slow seeping from her being of her creative energy and lust for life.

The women in this book, in most cases, are on the path to deepening their understanding of their essential creative natures. They are at varying points in their development, awareness, and ability to give form to their personal creative expression. Their essential creative natures have taken them in many directions in business, the arts, everyday life, relationships, and into the land of imagination and the realm of endless possibilities. Creativity for them, as for everyone, can only be understood as a personal experience. The literature on creativity can give you a glimpse of what is thought to be the nature of creativity. The literature can offer you steps that may lead you to deepen your connection to your personal form of creative expression. It may offer you a way to open and exercise your imagination. These works may stimulate your impulses, increase your tolerance for the unknown, or help you see anew the environment in which you exist. What you do with the information is your responsibility. Only you can take the words and make them into personal experiences.

The Goddesses stood squarely on this earth. They did not shy away from their personal responsibility. Nor can you. Whether public or private, the world will benefit when a woman fulfills her creative potential by bringing to her life and the lives she touches daily that which is uniquely hers. Her vision expands her domain. Grasping the reigns and feeling the effective force of the essential creative nature emboldens a woman. Creativity challenges the parameters of what a woman believes possible for herself. Nothing is lost by engaging the creative process. Without the engagement there are no failures, no successes, no knowledge or understanding of one's self or one's life, no place for possibility. A woman can always choose to live a life of sameness and numbness, and can slowly, painfully, continue to repress her creative spirit and the power within. Which do you choose?

---

# REFERENCES

❧

PREFACE

1. Carl Olson, introduction, *The Book of the Goddess, Past and Present: An Introduction to Her Religion*, Carl Olson, ed., (New York: Crossroad Publishing Company, 1992) 1.

2. Joseph Campbell, interview, *Joseph Campbell: The Power of Myth with Bill Moyers*, Betty Sue Flowers, ed., (New York: Doubleday, 1988) 170.

3. Clarissa Pinkola Estés, Ph.D., *Women Who Run with the Wolves: Myths and Stories of the Wild Woman Archetype* (New York: Ballantine Books, 1992) 299.

INTRODUCTION

1. Frank Barron and David M. Harrington, "Creativity, Intelligence, and Personality," *Annual Review of Psychology*, 32 (1981) 439–476.

2. Rowena Helson, "Inner Reality of Women," *Arts in Society*, 11 (1974) 25–36.

3. Frank Barron and David M. Harrington, "Creativity, Intelligence, and Personality," 439–476.

4. Jerry A. Stanford, book review, "Revolving Doors: Sex Segregation and Women's Careers," *Gender and Society*, 5.2 (1991) 262.

5. William J. J. Gordon, "Metaphor and Invention," *The Creativity Question*, Albert Rothenberg and Carl R. Hausman, eds. (Durham, N.C.: Duke University, 1976) 251–253.

6. Howard Gardner, *To Open Minds*, (New York: Basic Books, 1991) 111.

7. Albert Rothenberg and Carl R. Hausman, introduction, *The Creativity Question*, 6.

## CHAPTER ONE

1. Barbara G. Walker, *The Woman's Encyclopedia of Myths and Secrets*, (San Francisco: HarperCollins Publishers, 1983) 69–70.

2. Anne Barjing and Jules Cashford, *The Myth of the Goddess: Evolution of an Image*, (London: Arkana, Penguin Books, 1991) 458–460.

3. Howard Gardener, *To Open Minds*, (New York: Basic Books, 1991) 72.

4. Susan K. Deri, *Symbolization and Creativity*, (New York: International Universities Press, Inc., 1984) 3–4.

5. Morris I. Stein, "Creativity Research at a Crossroads: A 1985 Perspective," *Frontiers of Creative Research: Beyond The Basics*, Scott G. Isaksen, ed. (Buffalo: Bearly Limited, 1987) 417.

6. Donna Y. Ford and J. John Harris, III, "The Elusive Definition of Creativity," *The Journal of Creative Behavior*, 26.3 (1992) 186–198.

7. Silvano Arieti, *Creativity: The Magic Synthesis*, (New York: Basic Books, Inc., 1976) 29.

8. Maija Blubergs, Ph.D. "Personality Studies of Gifted Females: An Overview and Commentary," *Gifted Child Quarterly*, 22.4 Winter (1978) 539–547.

9. Betty A. Walker, Sally M. Reis, Janet S. Lenoard, "A Developmental Investigation of the Lives of Gifted Women," *Gifted Child Quarterly*, 36.4 Fall (1992) 201–206.

## CHAPTER TWO

1. Barbara G. Walker, *The Woman's Encyclopedia of Myths and Secrets*, 232.
2. Teresa M. Amabile, Ph.D., *Growing Up Creative: Nurturing a Lifetime of Creativity*, (New York: Crown Publisher, Inc., 1989) 32.
3. ———, *Growing Up Creative: Nurturing a Lifetime of Creativity*, 49.
4. Silvano Arieti, *Creativity: The Magic Synthesis*, 359.
5. Louise M. Bachtold and Emmy E. Werner, "Personality Characteristics of Creative Women," *Perceptual and Motor Skills*, 36 (1973), 311–319.
6. E. Paul Torrance, "The nature of creativity as manifest in its testing," *The nature of Creativity: Contemporary psychological perspectives*, Robert J. Sternberg, ed. (Cambridge: Cambridge University Press, 1988) 68.
7. Howard E. Gruber and Sara N. Davis, "Inching our way up Mount Olympus; the evolving systems approach to creative thinking," *The nature of Creativity: Contemporary psychological perspective*, 265.
8. Beth A. Hennessey and Teresa M. Amabile, "The conditions of creativity," *The nature of Creativity: Contemporary psychological perspective*, 11-38.
9. Michael F. Shaughnessy, "Creativity Counseling the Unemployed, Undercreative and under the weather," *The Creative Child and Adult Quarterly*, XIII. 2 (1988) 104–107.
10. Livia Pohlman, "Creativity, Gender and the Family: A Study of Creative Writers," *The Journal of Creative Behavior*, 30.1 (1996) 10–24.

11. Donald W. MacKinnon, "The Study of Creative Persons," *Creativity and Learning,* Jerome Kagan, ed. (Houghton Mifflin Company, 1967) 34.

CHAPTER THREE

1. Christine R. Downing, "The Mother Goddess among the Greeks," *The Book of the Goddess Past and Present: An Introduction to Her Religion,* 50–53.
2. Edward S. Ebert, II, "The Cognitive Spiral: Creative Thinking and Cognitive Processing," *The Journal of Creative Behavior,* 28.4 (1994) 275–290.
3. Joseph S. Renzulli, "A General Theory for the Development of Creative Productivity Through the Pursuit of Ideal Acts of Learning," *Gifted Child Quarterly,* 36.4 Fall (1992) 170–182.
4. "Regret and the Road Not Taken," *New Woman,* April (1995) 60.
5. Clarissa Pinkola Estés, Ph.D., *Women Who Run with the Wolves,* 300.
6. Anne Roe, "Painters and Painting," in *Perspectives on Creativity,* Irving A. Taylor and J. W. Getzels, eds. (Chicago: Aldine Publishing Co., 1975) 161–166.

CHAPTER FOUR

1. Barbara G. Walker, *The Woman's Encyclopedia of Myths and Secrets,* 218.
2. Jean Shinoda Bolen, M.D., *Goddesses in Everywoman: A New Psychology of Women,* (New York: Harper Perennial, 1984) 171.
3. Mary Field Belenky, Blythe McVicker Clinchy, Nancy Rule Goldberger, Jill Mattuck Tarule, *Women's Ways of Knowing: The Development of Self, Voice and Mind,* (New York: Basic Books, 1986) 72.
4. Carolyn G Heilbrun, *Writing a Woman's Life,* (New York: Ballantine Books, 1988).

5. Elizabeth V. Spelman, *Inessential Woman: Problems of Exclusion in Feminist Thought*, (Boston: Beacon Press, 1988) 136.

6. Kathleen D. Noble, "The Dilemma of the Gifted Woman," *Psychology of Women Quarterly*, 11 Spring (1987) 367–378.

7. Lois Wladis Hoffman, "Early Achievement Motives," *Journal of Social Issues*, 28.2 (1972) 129–155.

8. Constance L. Hollinger, Elyse S. Flemming, "A Longitudinal Examination of Life Choices of Gifted and Talented Young Women," *Gifted Child Quarterly*, 36.4 Fall (1992) 207–212.

## CHAPTER FIVE

1. Anne Barjing and Jules Cashford, *The Myth of the Goddess: Evolution of an Image*, 176.

2. Merlin Stone, *Ancient Mirrors of Womanhood*, 105.

3. ———, *The Myths of the Goddess: Evolution of an Image*, 193.

4. Merlin Stone, *Ancient Mirrors of Womanhood: Our Goddess and Heroine Heritage*, Volume 1, (New York: New Sibyline Books, 1979) 107.

## CHAPTER SIX

1. Anne Barjing and Jules Cashford, *The Myth of the Goddess: Evolution of an Image*, 358.

2. ———, *The Myth of the Goddess: Evolution of an Image*, 356.

3. Jean Shinoda Bolen, M.D., *Goddess in Everywoman: A New Psychology of Women*, 241.

4. Irving A. Taylor, "A Retrospective View of Creativity Investigation," *Perspectives in Creativity*, 5–11.

5. Irving A. Taylor, "A Retrospective View of Creativity Investigation," 20.

6. Donna Y. Ford and J. John Harris, III, "The Elusive Definition of Creativity," 186–198.

7. Mel Rhodes, "An Analysis of Creativity," *Frontiers of Creativity Research: Beyond the Basics*, 219–220.

8. Rollo May, *The Courage to Create*, (New York: Bantam Books, 1975) 40.

9. ————, *The Courage to Create*, 46.

10. ————, *The Courage to Create*, 49.

11. ————, *The Courage to Create*, 40.

12. Robert Grudin, *The Grace of Great Things*, (New York: Ticknor and Fields, 1990) 91.

CHAPTER SEVEN

1. Barbara G. Walker, *The Woman's Encyclopedia of Myths and Secrets*, 400.

2. Beth A. Hennessey and Teresa M. Amabile, "The conditions of creativity," *The nature of Creativity: Contemporary psychological perspectives*, 11.

3. Beth A. Hennessey and Teresa M. Amabile, "The conditions of creativity," 29.

4. E. Paul Torrance, *Mentor Relationships: How They Aid Creative Achievement, Endure, Change and Die*, (Buffalo: Bearly Limited, 1984) 46–52.

5. Betty A. Walker, Sally M. Reis, Janet S. Lenoard, "A Developmental Investigation of the Lives of Gifted Women," 201–206.

6. Teresa M. Amabile, *The Social Psychology of Creativity*, (New York: Springer-Verlag, 1983) 33.

7. Kathy Goff, "Enhancing Creativity in Older Adults," *The Journal of Creative Behavior*, 26.1 (1992) 40–48.

8. Jesseca Motherwell McFarlane and Tannis MacBeth Williams, "Placing Premenstrual Syndrome in Perspective," *Psychology of Women Quarterly*, 18 (1994) 339–373.

9. Judith Pierce Rosenberg, "Creative Tension: Being a Writer and a Mother," *Ms. Magazine*, January/February (1994) 64–70.

10. Livia Pohlman, "Creativity, Gender and the Family: A Study of Creative Writers," *The Journal of Creative Behavior*, 10–24.

CHAPTER EIGHT

1. Anne Baring and Jules Cashford, *The Myth of the Goddess: Evolution of an Image*, 470.
2. ———, *The Myth of the Goddess: Evolution of an Image*, 475.
3. E. B. White, *The Once and Future King* (New York: Berkley Medillion Books, 1969) eleventh printing, 183.
4. Frank Barron, "Putting creativity to work," *The nature of Creativity: Contemporary psychological perspective*, 95.
5. Mel Rhodes, "An Analysis of Creativity," *Frontiers of Creativity Research: Beyond the Basics*, 219.
6. Kerry S. Walters, "Critical Thinking, Logicism, and the Eclipse of Imagining," *The Journal of Creative Behavior*, 26.2 (1992) 130–144.

## SELECTED SOURCES CONSULTED

1. Saroj Agarwal, "A Correlational Study of Risk-taking and Creativity with Special Reference to Sex Differences," *Indian Educational Review*, (New Delhi: National Council of Educational Research and Training) 17.3 (1982) 104–110.
2. Jennifer A. Sasser-Coen, "Qualitative Changes in Creativity in Second Half of Life: A Life-Span Development Perspective," *Journal of Creative Behavior*, 27.1 (1993) 18–27.
3. Edward S. Ebert, III, "The Creative Spiral: Creative Thinking and Cognitive Processing," *The Journal of Creative Behavior*, 28.4 (1994) 275–288.
4. (Kum.) Madhu Deb, "Relationship Between Creative Thinking and Field Dependence-Independence Cognitive Styles of Rural and Urban Female Students," *Indian Educational Review*, (New Delhi: National Council of Educational Research and Training), 22.1 (1987) 97–103.
5. Elizabeth Douvan, "The Role of Models in Women's Professional Development," *Psychology of Women's Quarterly*, 1 Fall (1976) 5-20.

6. Barbara L. Forisha, "Creativity and Imagery in Men and Women," *Perceptual and Motor Skills*, 47 (1978) 1255–1264.

7. Brewster Ghislen, ed. *The Creative Process: A Symposium*, (Ontario: Mentor Book, 1952).

8. Carol Gilligan, *In a Different Voice: Psychological Theory and Women's Development*, (Cambridge, Mass.: Harvard University Press, 1982).

9. Rowena Helson, "Creativity in Women: Outer and Inner Views Over Time," *Theories of Creativity*, Mark A. Runco and Robert S. Albert, eds. (Newbury Park: Sage Publications, 1990) 46–58.

10. Constance L. Hollinger and Elyse S. Flemming, "Internal Barriers to the Realization of Potential: Correlates and Interrelationships Among Gifted and Talented Female Adolescents," *Gifted Child Quarterly*, 28 Summer (1984) 135–139.

11. Constance L. Hollinger, "Female Adolescent: The Relationship Between Social Self-Esteem and Traits of Instrumentality and Expressiveness," *Gifted Child Quarterly*, 27.4 (1983) 157–161.

12. P. C. Katiyar, "The Role of Sex in the Enhancement of Creativity among Adolescents through Process-oriented Training Programme," *Indian Educational Review* (New Delhi: National Council of Educational Research and Training), 18.1 (1983) 40–46.

13. Pamela Kato Klebanov and John B. Jemmott, III, "Effects of Expectations and Bodily Sensations on Self-Reports of Premenstrual Symptoms," *Psychology of Women Quarterly*, 16 (1992) 289–310.

14. Carolyne Larrington, ed., *The Feminist Companion to Mythology*, (Kent, England: Pandora Press, 1992).

15. Alice Miller, *The Untouched Key: Tracing Childhood Trauma in Creativity and Destructiveness*, (New York: Anchor Books, 1990).

16. Samuel Mudd, "Suggestive Parallels Between Kirton's A-I Theory of Creative Style and Koestler's Bisociative Theory of

the Creative Act," *The Journal of Creative Behavior*, 29.4 (1995) 240–254.

17. Gloria Feman Orenstein, *The Reflowering of the Goddess*, The Athene Series, (New York: Pergamon Press, Inc., 1990).

18. Sidney J. Parnes, ed., *Source Book for Creative Problem Solving*, (Buffalo: Creative Education Foundation Press, 1992).

19. Mary Clare-Powell, "On Creativity and Social Change," *The Journal of Creative Behavior*, 28.1 (1994) 21-32.

20. Robin Robertson, *Beginner's Guide to Jungian Psychology*, (York Beach, Maine: Nicholas-Hays, Inc., 1992).

21. Robyn Rowland, *Women Herself: A Transdisciplinary Perspective on Women's Identity*, (Oxford: Oxford University Press, 1988).

22. Robert Sternberg, "Mental Self-Government: A Theory of Intellectual Styles and Their Development," *Human Development*, 31 (1988) 197–224.

23. Janet Sternburg, ed., *The Writer on Her Work*, (New York: W. W. Norton, 1980).